A Transnational Critique of Japaneseness

New Studies in Modern Japan

Series Editors: Doug Slaymaker and William M. Tsutsui

New Studies in Modern Japan is a multidisciplinary series that consists primarily of original studies on a broad spectrum of topics dealing with Japan since the mid-nineteenth century. Additionally, the series aims to bring back into print classic works that shed new light on contemporary Japan. The series speaks to cultural studies (literature, translations, film), history, and social sciences audiences. We publish compelling works of scholarship, by both established and rising scholars in the field, on a broad arena of topics, in order to nuance our understandings of Japan and the Japanese.

Advisory Board

Recent Titles in the Series

Living Transnationally between Japan and Brazil: Routes beyond Roots, by Sarah A. LeBaron von Baeyer

Tawada Yōko: On Writing and Rewriting, edited by Doug Slaymaker

Imagining Prostitution in Modern Japan, 1850–1913, by Ann Marie Davis

Japan Viewed from Interdisciplinary Perspectives: History and Prospects, edited by Yoneyuki Sugita

Single Mothers in Contemporary Japan: Motherhood, Class, and Reproductive Practice, by Aya Ezawa

Creating Japan's Ground Self-Defense Force, 1945–2015: A Sword Well Made, by David Hunter-Chester

Rethinking Japan: The Politics of Contested Nationalism, by Arthur Stockwin and Kweku Ampiah

The Politics and Literature Debate in Postwar Japanese Criticism: 1945–52, edited by Atsuko Ueda, Michael K. Bourdaghs, Richi Sakakibara, and Hirokazu Toeda

Yokohama and the Silk Trade: How Eastern Japan Became the Primary Economic Region of Japan, 1843–1893, by Yasuhiro Makimura

The Unfinished Atomic Bomb: Shadows and Reflections, edited by David Lowe, Cassandra Atherton, and Alyson Miller

Literature among the Ruins, 1945–1955: Postwar Japanese Literary Criticism, edited by Atsuko Ueda, Richi Sakakibara, Michael K. Bourdaghs, and Hirokazu Toeda

A Transnational Critique of Japaneseness: Cultural Nationalism, Racism, and Multiculturalism in Japan, by Yuko Kawai

A Transnational Critique of Japaneseness

Cultural Nationalism, Racism, and Multiculturalism in Japan

Yuko Kawai

LEXINGTON BOOKS
Lanham • Boulder • New York • London

Published by Lexington Books
An imprint of The Rowman & Littlefield Publishing Group, Inc.
4501 Forbes Boulevard, Suite 200, Lanham, Maryland 20706
www.rowman.com

6 Tinworth Street, London SE11 5AL, United Kingdom

Chapter 1 was originally published with the title "Deracialised Race, Obscured Racism: Japaneseness, Western and Japanese Concepts of Race, and Modalities of Racism" in *Japanese Studies* (volume 35, issue 1) in 2015.

An earlier version of chapter 2 was published with the title "Neoliberalism, Nationalism, and Intercultural Communication: A Critical Analysis of a Japan's Neoliberal Nationalism Discourse under Globalization" in *Journal of International and Intercultural Communication* (volume 2, issue 1) in 2009.

British Library Cataloguing in Publication Information Available

Library of Congress Control Number: 2020945946
ISBN 978-1-4985-9900-9 (cloth)
ISBN 978-1-4985-9902-3 (pbk)
ISBN 978-1-4985-9901-6 (electronic)

Contents

A Note on Personal Names

Chinese, Korean, and Japanese names are written in their conventional order, with the family name preceding the given name, except for the names of authors whose books or articles are written in English.

Acknowledgments

I owe a great debt to many scholars, colleagues, and friends, some whom I know personally and others whom I "know" from their scholarly works for writing this book. I have learned so much from all of them and I am deeply grateful.

I would like to thank Taylor & Francis for granting permission to make use of the following two papers published in their journals. Chapter 1 was originally published with the title "Deracialised Race, Obscured Racism: Japaneseness, Western and Japanese Concepts of Race, and Modalities of Racism" in *Japanese Studies* (volume 35, issue 1) in 2015. I have updated the discussion on the contemporary situation of racism in Japan. This study was supported by Grant-in-Aid for Scientific Research (S): "A Japan-Based Global Study of Racial Representations" (No. 22222003; Principal Investigator, Yasuko Takezawa). An earlier version of chapter 2 was published with the title "Neoliberalism, Nationalism, and Intercultural Communication: A Critical Analysis of a Japan's Neoliberal Nationalism Discourse under Globalization" in *Journal of International and Intercultural Communication* (volume 2, issue 1) in 2009. I made changes in the discussion of neoliberalism, incorporating more recent theoretical debates. In addition, I updated the conclusion section by taking into account Japan's political, social, and cultural changes after its original publication.

Lastly, I would like to express my gratitude to the anonymous reviewer who offered important comments and the editors who helped me with the publication of this book.

Introduction

A Transnational Critique for a Multiculturalist Japan

The ideological notion of Japan as a single race/ethnic nation (*tan'itsu minzoku*) has influenced what it means to be Japanese in post-war Japan until today, despite scholarly criticisms that started in the 1980s and the counter-narrative of "multicultural Japan" that emerged in the 1990s. A most recent example is Deputy Prime Minister and Finance Minister Aso Taro's remark made in January 2020: "there is no other nation but (Japan) where a single race has spoken a single language at a single location and maintained a single dynasty with a single emperor for over two thousand years" (Kakihana 2020). This conception of racial/ethnic uniformity, which intersects with Japanese nationalism and racism, has marginalized ethnic minorities in Japanese society. However, the meaning of Japaneseness is not fixed, as it is constructed in relation to multiple Others and through communication—the process of making meaning in which context plays a crucial role (e.g., Martin and Nakayama 2013, 115–16). In other words, the meaning can change depending on the discursive Other and the context in which it is created.

In the first two decades of the twenty-first century, exclusionist discursive practices have become conspicuous as Japan struggles with its "lost two decades" of economic recession after the collapse of the bubble economy, globalization, neoliberalization, and the massive earthquake and nuclear disaster of 2011. These practices are exemplified by the rise of racist demonstrations and the prevalence of "hate books" and magazine articles denigrating Korea/Koreans and China/Chinese in particular. Meanwhile, the migrant population in Japan has continued to increase largely due to the Japanese government's "side-door" immigration policy of recruiting trainees and international students from other parts of Asia to mitigate labor shortages in agricultural, food production, manufacturing, construction, nursing, and other service industries. The number of foreign nationals in

Japan rose from 1,686,444 in 2000 to 2,933,137 in 2019 (Ministry of Justice 2001, 2020).

Under these circumstances, the construction of Japaneseness, which is inextricably tied to nationalism, racism, and multiculturalism, is a very important topic to be explored. Academic books in English critically examining Japaneseness based on the influential ideology of Japan as a single race/ethnic nation once concentrated on those investigating *nihonjinron* (e.g., Befu 2001; Dale 1986; Mouer and Yoshimoto 1986; Yoshino 1992). Literally meaning "discussions of the Japanese," *nihonjinron* (日本人論)—a body of academic, journalistic, popular texts that insisted upon the "uniqueness" of Japanese culture, society and national character—popularized the idea of Japan as a single race/ethnic nation in the 1970s and 1980s. More recently, the focus and methods used to discuss this topic have been diversified: overviewing influential academic and journalistic writings between the late nineteenth and the twentieth centuries (Oguma 2002 [1995], 2014 [1998], 2017 [1998]); attending to key concepts of Japanese nationhood such as nature, culture, race, and gender and their shifting meanings until the 1990s (Morris-Suzuki 1998); highlighting ethnic minorities through examining interviews, documents, and ethnographic data (Lie 2001), historical and contemporary identity and cultural practices (Graburn et al. 2008; Weiner 2009; Willis and Murphy-Shigematsu 2008), cinema (Ko 2010), and racism against visible minorities (Arudou 2015); attending to transnational media and cultural connections (Iwabuchi 2015); investigating communication concerning gender, sexuality, ethnicity, social movements, and education (Toyosaki and Eguchi 2017).

This book hopes to connect the "older" studies that focused on examining the construction of Japaneseness itself, with the "newer" ones that illuminated it through studying related issues and wider discursive practices. In this book, I critically investigate the construction of Japaneseness in a variety of communication during the first two decades of the twenty-first century while situating it in its longer historical transformation since the late nineteenth century. Closely reading a political document, television drama series, "hate books," and interviews, I examine governmental and popular ideas of Japaneseness in light of local, global, historical, and contemporary contexts as well as in relation to diverse Others: the West, Asia, the English language, Japanese Americans, Japanese Brazilians, white America/Americans, China/Chinese, and Korea/Koreans.

TRANSNATIONAL CRITIQUE

The central analytical principle of this book is transnational critique informed by critical studies' perspectives. The term "critical" has been attached to various academic fields to distinguish them from the mainstream counterparts, for example, critical pedagogy (e.g., Darder et al. 2009), critical psychology (e.g., Fox and Prilleltensky 1997), critical discourse analysis (e.g., Fairclough 1995), critical intercultural communication (e.g., Nakayama and Halualani 2011), and many others. Explicitly or implicitly drawing upon the critical theory tradition of the Frankfurt School (Horkheimer 2002, 188–243) and cultural studies that challenged the mainstream study of culture by receiving heavy influences from this tradition, these critical studies commonly criticize positivism, decontextualization, and the idea of value neutrality often stressed in social sciences. Instead, they propose to look into more than the immediate surface of things by taking into account historical contexts, power relations, and other structural forces and also by connecting these macro aspects with personal or micro practices. Questioning "value free" or "neutral" research, they are concerned "not merely with how things [are] but how they might be and should be" for social transformation (Bronner 2011, 1–2). In his discussion of critical cosmopolitanism, Gerard Delanty (2012) suggests that "critique" in the Frankfurt School's critical theory tradition is based on the dialectical view of society, or the idea that society is marked by contradictions and thus contains both tensions and possibilities, and also on the idea of immanent transcendence, which refers to "the notion that society can transcend the given through a re-working and re-appropriation of its own self-understanding" (39). Put simply, critique is "forward-looking and concerned with shifts in self-understanding" (40).

Transnational critique thus means examining and understanding nationhood by attending to the role of non-national discursive Others and by linking the past with the present, the discursive with the material, the cultural with the political and economic, the local with the global, the self with the other, and a practice with structural forces to denaturalize the national or the given ultimately in search for an alternative. In order to re-work and re-appropriate a nation's self-understanding, it is crucial to dig into the process of constructing the national so as to illuminate where in the process an intervention for transformation is possible. This should be necessarily transnational, considering that constructing nationhood involves imagining non-national groups (Billig 1995, 79).

MULTICULTURALIST JAPAN

Critiquing Japaneseness is intended to create a multiculturalist Japanese society. Japan, with multiple ethnic groups living together, has always been multicultural in a descriptive sense. However, it is not in a normative sense or not multiculturalist in the sense that ethnic minorities' cultural practices are encouraged and not used as the Other for the majority group's identity construction, while their pursuit of socio-political and economic equality is treated as an important national agenda.

Multiculturalism and Interculturalism

Despite the prevalence of "the end of multiculturalism" discourses in Western countries, I believe multiculturalism has not lost its relevance when thinking about racial/ethnic relations in Japanese society. Multiculturalism emerged as a major political and philosophical agenda in the 1960s and 1970s in historically immigrant-populated countries, namely Canada, Australia, and the United States, and in the following decades in Western European countries, such as Britain, the Netherlands, and Sweden, in response to the increase of non-Western migrants and the intensification of minority voices seeking for recognition and equality (e.g., Meer and Modood 2016; Parekh 2016; Rattansi 2011). Initially multiculturalism was discussed in Canada and Australia primarily in relation to state policy, whereas in the United States, the focus was on cultural representation and educational curriculum (Meer and Modood 2016, 31).

Multiculturalism has been conceptualized in various manners since then. For example, Peter McLaren (1994) identifies four positions of multiculturalism: conservative, liberal, left-liberal, and critical. The conservative position, overlapping with what Tessa Morris-Suzuki (2002) calls "cosmetic multiculturalism" (154) or what Angela Davis (1997) names "corporate multiculturalism" (41), celebrates and utilizes minorities' cultural difference as long as they do not threaten the status quo of a majoritarian and capitalist society (McLaren 1994, 47–51). The liberal position, a universalism, stresses similarity, considering that all cultural groups are equal and equivalent (51). The left-liberal position is a particularism, emphasizing difference and paying attention to inequitable power relations between majority and minorities that bar them from being equal (51–52). These three positions apparently differ in their understanding of multiculturalism but converge in viewing cultural boundaries as given. The last position, critical multiculturalism, sees cultural boundaries as constructed and cultural identities as intersecting with multiple categories, and regards similarity and difference dialectically operating in making those boundaries that distinguish between majority and minorities (53–55).

Anti-multiculturalist discourses spread rapidly in the West in the twenty-first century after a series of cases that involved Muslim suspects, such as the 9/11 attacks of 2001 in the United States, the March 2004 bombings of commuter trains in Madrid, and the 7/7 London bombings of 2005. It drew an international attention especially when British, French, and German conservative political leaders' negative comments on multiculturalism in 2010 and 2011.

Prior to these leaders' attacks on multiculturalism, the Council of Europe's 2008 report "Living Together as Equals in Dignity" and the UNESCO's report "Investing in Cultural Diversity and Intercultural Dialogue" published in 2009 advocated replacing multiculturalism with interculturalism (or intercultural dialogue). The former report attacked multiculturalism of "having fostered communal segregation and mutual incomprehension, as well as having contributed to the undermining of the rights of individuals—and, in particular, women—within minority communities, perceived as if these were single collective actors" (Council of Europe 2008, 19). The report posited that what is needed is intercultural dialogue, "a process that comprises an open and respectful exchange of views between individuals and groups with different ethnic, cultural, religious and linguistic backgrounds and heritage, on the basis of mutual understanding and respect" (17). The latter report raised as the central shortcoming of multiculturalism "encouraging a drift towards cultural isolationism" (UNESCO 2009, 29). It argued that it is necessary "to go beyond assimilation and multiculturalism conceived in terms of separateness, in order to highlight multiple interactions and allegiances and facilitate access to other cultures, particularly through the development of networks and new forms of sociability" (29).

Thus interculturalism started to be discussed as an alternative to multiculturalism. Interculturalists criticized multiculturalism for neglecting interpersonal contacts among different cultural groups with its cultural rights-based approach and for not being mindful of gender and other differences with its focus on racial/ethnic/national difference. One central idea of interculturalism is the importance of interaction among people with different cultural backgrounds to create commonality and social cohesion (Zapata-Barrero 2016). Interaction means "acting together, sharing a public sphere and working for some common purpose" (55). Interculturalism also emphasizes plural identities based on the view of society as "superdiverse" (62)[1] as well as the assumption that "the powers of the state have been substantially eroded, along with a simple national identity" and thus "'difference' now crosses national boundaries and also reflects the heterogeneity of national, ethnic and faith groups" (Cantle 2016, 134).

Apparently, interculturalists' criticisms neglect critical multiculturalism, which attends to the complexity and intersectionality of identities and the dialectical relationship or interconnection between majority and minorities. Although scholars with this position certainly have stressed racial/ethnic/national identity and macro-level issues, their emphasis is derived from the fact that multiculturalism emerged in the 1960s and 1970s in opposition to the idea of the monocultural nation-state, which was dominant between the late nineteenth century and the first half of the twentieth century (Goldberg 1994, 3–6). Problematizing homogeneity and assimilationism emphasized in monoculturalism was the starting point of multiculturalism (7–12). This explains why nationalism and racism, which are closely associated with monoculturalism, have been major issues for attack among multiculturalists.

Multiculturalism is more sensitive about issues confronted by minority groups, while interculturalism is more responsive to concerns posed by majority groups. Contrasting the predominant use of the term "multiculturalism" in Canada outside Quebec to the use of the term "interculturalism" in Quebec, Charles Taylor (2012) argues that differences between them "lie less in the concrete policies than in the stories" (416). The story of Canadian multiculturalism decenters the normative position of people of British origin and include people of other origins as equal members of the Canadian nation. However, Taylor contends that a similar storyline does not suit for Quebec and many European countries where the great majority of their citizens share "a long-standing historic identity" and a language plays a key role in such a national identity (420). Put differently, the "multiculturalism" story does not work there because people of the majority group feel more strongly entitled to their nation. Taylor suggests that interculturalism is useful in these nations because the "interculturalism" story starts from the majority's identity even though they will need to modify it through intercultural dialogue (418).

What tends to be forgotten in interculturalism is the role of structural and historical forces and the problem of nationhood that marginalize minorities. Will Kymlicka (2016) contends that interculturalism "offers rather tepid and apolitical diagnosis of the problem facing minorities," whereas multiculturalism "highlights the problem in the state-sponsored privileging of nationhood, and in the exclusions this has entailed" (172–73). It is undeniable that the world under globalization is becoming more diverse as the escalation of the movement of people, ideas, and commodities makes people's identities and local societies more complex and fluid. Yet, such a globalizing world simultaneously intensifies essentialist and exclusionist identity constructions based on nation, race, ethnicity, and others (e.g., Tomlinson 2003, 2007). In addition, interculturalism's stress on commonality and inclination of prioritizing the majority's concerns can be easily appropriated by parochial nationalist discourses. Kymlicka continues to argue that "I'm sceptical that we can make enduring progress on diversity unless or until we explicitly tackle ideas of nationhood and show how multiculturalism (or interculturalism) can be a constitutive feature of nationhood" (173).

I concur with the idea that interculturalism is "less an alternative, more a modification of multiculturalism" (Modood 2016, 247). Although interculturalists tend to criticize multiculturalism without considering different positions of multiculturalism, their criticism against multiculturalists' primary focus on the macro and insufficient attention to difference within a cultural group is relevant. At the same time, the starting point of multiculturalism—its stronger attentiveness to minorities' concerns and the problem of nationhood—should not be forgotten. What is needed is further efforts to view macro and micro issues as well as the self and the other as interconnected, for which transnational critique provides a useful perspective.

Multiculturalism in Japan

"The end of multiculturalism" discourses and the multiculturalism and interculturalism debate are not very popular in Japan. Multiculturalism cannot "end" because it has not been an important national-level agenda and thus has not started yet in a substantial sense. This indicates that criticisms against the monocultural nation-state, the starting point of multiculturalism, have not been strong enough, or conversely, the ideology of Japan as a single race/ethnic nation has been very strong. However, activists, academics, NGOs, and municipal governments have engaged in multiculturalism issues, and the different positions of multiculturalism are also observable in their discussions although very few activists and organizations adopt the critical multiculturalism position (Tai 2003, 50–51).

The most common Japanese term for multiculturalism is *tabunka kyōsei*, literally meaning multicultural (*ta-bunka* 多文化) co-living (*kyōsei* 共生). The word "multi" (*ta* 多) signifies diversity, while connoting equality, the notion of "co-living" (*kyōsei* or *tomoni ikiru*) first started to be used in the late 1970s by ethnic Korean activists in their demand for a more equitable Japanese society (Tai 2003, 45). The term *tabunka kyōsei* was popularized after the Center for Multicultural Co-living was established by a local NGO and provided aides to non-Japanese victims of the 1995 earthquake in Kobe. Municipal governments also started to use it when referring to policies for non-Japanese residents, whose number began to rise in the late 1980s against the backdrop of a rapid appreciation of the yen and the emergence of the bubble economy.

The discourse of multicultural co-living is tinged with the Japanese-foreigner dichotomy stressed in the dominant internationalization discourse (Kashiwazaki 2010). The Japanese government promoted *kokusaika* or internationalization policies in the 1980s in response to trade frictions with the United States and Western European countries, which were accusing Japanese markets of being unfairly closed to them. The dominant discourse of internationalization stressed the necessity of nurturing open-mindedness to foreign peoples and cultures, which was based on and reinforced the Japanese-foreigner distinction emphasized in *nihonjinron*. At the same time, it also stimulated the discourse of "internationalization within" (*uchinaru kokusaika*), which advocated respecting difference not only outside but also inside Japan and rectifying the marginalization of ethnic minorities, such as the Ainu, an indigenous group, and ethnic Koreans, who had been part of Japanese society for generations. Although (and because) the "internationalization within" discourse was an appropriation of the government-led internationalization, it was not completely detached from the dichotomy between Japanese and non-Japanese, leaving the issue of Japanese nationhood to be further questioned.

In 2006, the Ministry of Internal Affairs published the first national-level policy paper concerning multiculturalism, "*Chiiki ni okeru tabunka kyōsei suishin puran*" (Multicultural co-living promotion plan in municipalities). The plan defined multicultural co-living as a condition in which "people with different nationality and ethnic backgrounds respect each other's cultural difference, build equal relationships, and live together as members of a local community" (Ministry of Internal Affairs 2006, 1). The plan was a part of strategies to increase Japan's competitiveness under globalization in the report "*Gurōbaru senryaku*" (Strategies for globalization) published by the Council on Economic and Fiscal Policy (2006), the Japanese government's top economy advisory board (6). This suggests that the multicultural co-living defined in the plan is closer to the conservative position of multiculturalism. It pays scant attention to the issue of reimagining nationhood and grasps cultural difference only in terms of nationality and ethnic backgrounds, neglecting other factors such as gender, sexuality, and class.

A multiculturalist Japan, the ultimate purpose of a transnational critique of Japaneseness, does not refer to conservative multiculturalism exemplified by the Ministry of Internal Affair's policy paper. It entails perspectives based on critical multiculturalism, which challenge the majoritarian logic while acknowledging heterogeneity within a cultural group and the importance of intercultural interactions. In this book, I elucidate problematic processes in which Japaneseness is constructed in relation to diverse discursive Others, searching for clues to make Japanese nationhood more inclusive.

CHAPTER OUTLINES

Chapter 1 approaches the construction of Japaneseness conceptually, historically, and transnationally, focusing on the concept of race. I examine the interrelationships among Japaneseness, the Western and Japanese concepts of race, and the obfuscation of racism in contemporary Japanese society. The concept of race, which was conceived in the West in the modern era, has influenced the Japanese concepts of race, *jinshu* and *minzoku*. These two concepts played a key role in constructing modern Japan's identity by distinguishing it from its significant discursive Others: Asia and the West (Yamamuro 2000). Today Japanese people rarely use the terms *jinshu* and *minzoku* for self-reference, and racism has not been generally viewed as an important domestic issue. In this chapter, I explicate how the Japanese concepts of race, *jinshu* and *minzoku* were constructed transnationally by intertwining with Western notions of race, nation, *Volk*, and ethnicity, and have shaped the dominant meaning of the Japanese during the twentieth century. Following this discussion, I argue that the conceptual presence and nominal absence of *jinshu* and *minzoku* in defining Japaneseness is responsible for obscuring racism in contemporary Japan. Then, I explore how the contemporary modality of racism in Japan overlaps with and differs from racisms in the West.

The following four chapters are case studies in which I investigate the construction of Japaneseness. The first three chapters analyze three kinds of texts that appeared between the 2000s and 2010s: a political document (the year of 2000; chapter 2), television drama series (2005 and 2010; chapter 3), and "hate books" (2017 and 2018; chapter 4). Each chapter can be seen as a "snapshot" that captures a moment of the process of constructing Japaneseness. People take a photograph of a certain object or scene because they find it worth recording. Likewise, I chose to focus on these texts, products of a different time of the last two decades, because I found them important and unique communicational moments worth capturing to interrogate Japanese nationhood for a multiculturalist Japanese society. These texts are noteworthy due to their use of, first, the two significant discursive Others for the construction of Japaneseness (Asia and the West); second, other discursive Others tied to the West and Asia (the English language and Japanese Americans to the West, and China/Chinese and Korea/Koreans to Asia); third, the Other as the Self (Japanese Americans and Japanese Brazilians). In addition, the case studies are placed in chronological order. Each chapter can be read out of order as a single "snapshot" and also in order as a series of "snapshots." By reading them in order, readers will be able to situate the construction of Japaneseness in Japan's social, political, and economic changes of the last two decades. If readers are interested in learning about the reception of these texts or how people in Japan reacted to the texts, please refer to articles that I wrote elsewhere (Kawai 2007, 2008, 2016).

Chapter 2 examines a governmental report proposing the adaptation of English as an official language of Japan in January of 2000. I look into the construction of Japaneseness at the nexus of nationalism and neoliberalism, analyzing how the meaning of the Japanese is created transnationally by using the English language, the West, and Asia as discursive Others. The backdrop of this proposal is globalization and neoliberalization. In both of these, the English language plays a key role. In both prewar and postwar

Japanese nationalist discourses, the Japanese language was central to defining Japaneseness. Thus the proposal of English as an official language of Japan necessitates a different meaning of being Japanese. In this chapter, I first examine how Japanese culture and communication are redefined in the report. Japanese culture and communication are intimately connected to the Japanese language and thus have been important elements, particularly for *nihonjinron* writers in the 1970s and 1980s to assert Japanese "uniqueness" in relation to the West (e.g., Yoshino 1992). Then I investigate how Japan's relationships with Asia and the West—two significant discursive Others for constructing Japan's identity—are represented in the text and situate the representation of Japanese culture and communication in the discursive triad to further contextualize the analysis.

Chapter 3 highlights the construction of Japaneseness by representing two *Nikkeijin* (people of Japanese descent) groups, Japanese Americans and Japanese Brazilians, as diasporas and using them as discursive Others. Attending to the notion of cultural memory, I explore how Japanese television dramas transnationally construct Japaneseness by remembering Japanese American and Japanese Brazilian historical experiences through World War II. The United States and Brazil were the two most popular destinations for Japanese immigration outside Asia in the first half of the twentieth century. *Nikkeijin* represented as diasporas play a unique role in constructing Japaneseness because their ambiguous position—members living away from the national homeland—makes them simultaneously the national Self and the Other (Kawai 2016b). However, Japanese American and Japanese Brazilian experiences have not been equally remembered and used for the construction of Japaneseness in the genre of television drama. In this chapter, analyzing the first major television drama series to highlight the Japanese immigration to Brazil, broadcast in 2005, and the 2010 drama series depicting the Japanese immigration to the United States, I examine different ways in which Japanese Americans and Japanese Brazilians are discursively used and discuss how the different uses of the two groups are tied to the difference in their Otherness.

Chapter 4 investigates how "hate books (*heito bon*)" construct Japaneseness by using China/Chinese and Korea/Koreans as discursive Others. When racist demonstrations targeting people of Asian descent were increasing in the early 2010s, books and magazine articles that denigrated Korea/Koreans and to a lesser extent China/Chinese became popular and turned into a literary genre. Following the two "hate South Korea (*ken kan*)" books that reached bestseller lists in 2014, a "hate book" targeting both China/Chinese and Korea/Koreans, *Jukyō ni shihai sareta chūgokujin to kankokujin no higeki* (Tragedies of Chinese and South Koreans Controlled by Confucianism) (Gilbert 2017), became one of the top ten bestselling books in 2017. The author is Kent Gilbert, a white American lawyer, who has been a TV personality in Japan since the 1980s and started to be known as a far-right Japanese nationalist "spokesperson" in the 2010s. The book in which a white American male degrades China/Chinese and Korea/Koreans on behalf of Japanese far-right nationalists demonstrates interlocking relationships among Japanese nationalism, Japanese racism, and Western racism. In this chapter, referring to David Theo Goldberg's (1993) notion of the grammar of racialized discourse, I look into the grammar of Japanese racialized discourse embedded in Gilbert's 2017 bestseller and its sequence published in 2018 titled *Chūkashisō wo mōshinsuru chūgokujin to kankokujin no higeki* (Tragedies of Chinese and South Koreans Swallowing Sinocentrism). I examine what kind of meaning of the Japanese the two texts create by pejoratively representing and differentiating China/Chinese and Korea/Koreans from Japan/Japanese with the use of historical resources, Confucianism and Sinocentrism, as well as identifying Japan/Japanese with white America/Americans.

While chapters 2, 3, and 4 focus on the construction of Japaneseness itself in texts, chapter 5 takes a different approach to this issue, spotlighting a case of intercultural interaction. Examining trans-East Asian friendships that Japanese university students form when they participate in study-abroad programs in the West, I investigate the ideas of Asia and the West—significant discursive Others for Japaneseness—that are implicated in such relationships and thereby illuminate problems and possibilities for transformation embedded there. Due to the Japanese government's study-abroad campaign to increase globally competitive Japanese individuals, the number of Japanese university students participating in short-term study-abroad programs has more than doubled in the 2010s (MEXT 2020). Western Anglophone countries such as the United States and Britain are the most popular destinations for Japanese university students. Despite Japanese people's worsening perceptions about Korea and China in the 2010s, students who have studied in Western countries often say that they became most friendly with students from China, South Korea, and Taiwan. In this chapter, I start with a discussion of the ideas of Asia and the West in prewar and post-war Japan. Then analyzing interviews that I conducted with fourteen Japanese university students who had studied in Western countries for one or two semesters between 2013 and 2018, I discuss how the ideas of Asia and the West operate in their trans-East Asian friendships made in the West and what challenges and chances for transformation can be found there.

The conclusion chapter summarizes the five chapters and suggests academic and social contributions as well as future research directions. I argue the importance of using transnational critique as a perspective for understanding and transforming Japanese nationhood. The construction of Japaneseness is inexorably underway, and thus its meaning is always in process. The global spread of the new coronavirus in 2020 and its consequences will certainly impact the construction of Japaneseness. The communicational practices analyzed in this book are just a handful of such practices made and moments captured in the last two decades. In addition, Japaneseness constructed in the texts will certainly overlap with but not be completely identical to people's more diverse ideas of Japaneseness. However, examining these practices with transnational critique will provide a glimpse into not only how Japaneseness is constructed in relation to various discursive Others but also the connection and disconnection between what it meant to be Japanese in post-war pre-globalization Japan (i.e., Japaneseness constructed in *nihonjinron*) and what it does in a globalizing Japan and after. Understanding these is indispensable for reimagining Japan as a multiculturalist society.

NOTE

1. Superdiversity refers to the diversification of immigrants' backgrounds, such as their country of origin, migration channels, education, employment, and legal status, starting in the 1990s (Vertovec 2007). This concept was constructed in the contexts of Britain and other European countries.

Chapter 1

Japaneseness, Western and Japanese Concepts of Race, and Modalities of Racism

Differentiation[1] among people and discrimination against some based on a particular kind of difference are not strictly modern phenomena. However, over time, the concept of race, conceived in the West in the modern era, has influenced the ontological understanding of relations among different groups and their political, economic, and cultural relationships on a global scale. Although notions equivalent to the Western idea of race have been constructed in local and global socio-historical, political, and economic contexts (e.g., Takezawa 2005, 31–35), the impact of Western race theories on local ones is undeniable, considering that Western knowledge has been privileged and seen as "legitimate" and "universal" across the world. Discussing the main lessons to be learned from the expansion of race and racism research, Les Back and John Solomos (2009) state that "there is a need for greater theoretical clarity on key concepts" (23). The local concept of race is undoubtedly an important one that requires clarification for the further understanding and theorization of race and racism.

This chapter examines the interrelationships among Japaneseness, the Western and Japanese concepts of race, and the obfuscation of racism in contemporary Japanese society. The Japanese words for race, *jinshu* and *minzoku*, were key concepts in the construction of modern Japan's national identity (Yamamuro 2000, 9–10) as they permitted it to differentiate itself from its significant discursive Others: Asia and the West. The two concepts were generated in the late nineteenth and early twentieth centuries, respectively, when Japan was transforming itself into a modern nation-state by incorporating, challenging, and appropriating Western knowledge, including its theories of race. *Jinshu*, consisting of the two words 人*jin* (human) and 種*shu* (species), is the Japanese translation of the word "race." It was used interchangeably with the notion of *bunmei* (civilization) to argue Japan's commonality with Asia and their united defiance of Western political practices based on the latter's racial order (Yamamoro 2000, 9). *Minzoku*, a combination of 民*min* (people) and 族*zoku* (family or tribe), is a concept constructed under the influence of the German concept of *Volk*, displacing that of *jinshu* when self-representing the Japanese (Kawata 1999, 457–58, 2009, 138; Morris-Suzuki 1998, 87; Yoon 1994, 42–44). Often used with the concept of *bunka* (culture), it differentiated the Japanese from other people in Asia and produced a Japanized "racial order" (Yamamuro 2000, 9). Put simply, in the concept of *jinshu* the Japanese shared "a common fate" with people in Asia as a nonwhite and thus "inferior" race; reading the Japanese as a *minzoku* made it possible to change this fate by leaving the Western racial order while retaining a racialized notion of the Japanese nation.

In public discourse, as ruling elites and public intellectuals shifted Japan's self-portrayal from that of a multiethnic empire to a small, homogeneous nation after its defeat in World War II, Japanese people generally have avoided using the term *minzoku* to refer to themselves as *Nihon minzoku* or *Yamato minzoku* (Oguma 2002). However, the term *minzoku* remained in the phrase *tan'itsu minzoku* (a single race/ethnic nation), a very influential ideological phrase in Japanese self-reference. Even so, with the *minzoku* of the *tan'itsu minzoku* left unspecified, the link between the Japanese and the concept of *minzoku* has been nebulous (e.g., Okamoto 2011, 77–78; Stewart 2002, 81). Instead, in general Japanese simply called themselves *nihonjin*, literally meaning Japan (*nihon*日本) human (*jin*人) (Yoon 1994, 283–88).[2] They used the words *jinshu* and *minzoku* mainly for groups other than the Japanese themselves and for discussing racial/ethnic discrimination and conflicts outside Japan (e.g., Kanbe 2007; Stewart 2002, 55–83; Yoon 1994, 3–16).

Not calling the Japanese *jinshu* or *minzoku* does not mean that the racialization of Japaneseness disappeared or that racism ceased to exist in postwar Japan. Scholars who have critically examined dominant discourses on Japaneseness have pointed out that the exclusivity of the idea of Japaneseness created the prevailing assumption that the Japanese are a race (e.g., Yoshino 1992, 22–32; Befu 1993, 114–16). Visible minorities or people of European and African descent in Japan have long endured discriminatory and exclusionary practices, such as refusals of entry to or service in restaurants, bars, or shops, to which the racialized idea of the Japanese is closely connected (Arudou 2015). Yet people of Asian descent, who constitute the dominant majority of non-Japanese citizens in Japan, have suffered from a more complex and intense dynamic of exclusion and assimilation, which is exemplified by pressure to use a Japanese-style family name in public (Kawai 2016a).

Moreover, racist comments, especially against Asian minorities, are often casually made in public. For example, in 2001, a conservative national newspaper, *Sankei Shimbun*, published on its front page an essay written by former Tokyo Governor Ishihara Shintaro in which he insisted that Chinese people have criminal DNA (Ishihara 2001). In 2013, a conservative Lower House member remarked at a public meeting that "there are swarms of [*uyouyo iru*] South Korean prostitutes in Japan" and posted on his blog the following comment: "Many South Korean 'comfort women' are still in Japan. That makes me wonder if South Korea is exporting them to Japan" (*Japan Times* 2013). In 2009 and 2010, the far-right nationalist group *Zaitokukai* (Citizens Against the Special Privileges of Ethnic Korean Residents in Japan)[3] vandalized a Korean elementary school in Kyoto, calling the children "cockroaches" and "spies" (Fackler 2013). In the following years, the *Zaitokukai* and other similar far-right groups held anti-Korean demonstrations numerous times across Japan including Korea-towns in Tokyo and Osaka, carrying placards that included comments such as "Good or Bad Koreans: Kill Them All" (Ishibashi 2013). A governmental survey found 1,152 cases of such demonstrations between April 2012 and September 2015 (*Mainichi Shimbun* 2016).

Despite these manifestations, the presence of racism has been obscured in Japan. The dominant Japanese view has been that racism is a foreign, not a domestic issue (e.g., Iesaka 1986, 1–2; Stewart 2002, 60). Aside from politicians' remarks and *Zaitokukai*, cases similar to those described above generally receive limited coverage in mainstream Japanese media and, consequently, limited attention from the public. In addition, although mainstream Japanese media report incidents of this type as problematic, they usually do not associate them with racism. For example, the comment tweeted by a member of the Greek national team for the 2012 Olympics that "with so many Africans in Greece, at least the mosquitoes of West Nile will eat home-made food" (*Guardian* 2012) was denounced as racist internationally, and mainstream Japanese media also reported it as a racism case (e.g., *Mainichi Shimbun* 2012).[4] Meanwhile, although the Japanese media criticized the statements made by the Japanese right-wing politicians and far-right groups' demonstrations as inappropriate and discriminatory, they often did not depict them as racist or just called "hate speech."

The Japanese government has played a key role in obscuring racism. This is exemplified in the first report that the Japanese government submitted in 2000 to the International Convention on the Elimination of All Forms of Racial Discrimination (ICERD) committee after joining the convention in 1995. Refuting a concern raised by the committee that Japan's legal system is not adequate to deal with racial discrimination, the Japanese government claimed that existing laws such as the Penal Code and the Civil Code could handle racial discrimination cases: "We do not recognize that the present situation of Japan is one in which discriminative acts cannot be effectively restrained by the existing legal system and in which explicit racial discriminative acts, which cannot be restrained by measures other than legislation, are conducted" (Ministry of Foreign Affairs 2000). This argument was reiterated in its 2013 report despite the rise of those racist demonstrations (Ministry of Foreign Affairs 2013).[5]

In 2016, Japan's first "anti-hate speech" law, the Act on the Promotion of Efforts to Eliminate Unfair Discriminatory Speech and Behavior against Persons Originating from Outside Japan, was belatedly introduced under pressure from anti-racism activists. However, as the title of the law clearly shows, it aims to simply promote "efforts" to eliminate hate speech and crimes. As it neither bans racist demonstrations and institutionalized discriminatory practices (e.g., refusing to rent an apartment to a foreign citizen) nor criminalizes these actions, it is not a comprehensive anti-racism law. Thus after this much overdue legislation, racist demonstrations continue to be held, although their number and frequency have decreased (*Tokyo Shimbun* 2017).

The purpose of this chapter is threefold. First, it discusses how the Japanese concepts of race, *jinshu* and *minzoku*, were constructed and have shaped the dominant meaning of the Japanese in different historical contexts, transnationally intertwining with Western notions of race, nation, *Volk*, and ethnicity. The Western concept of race itself has been interrelated with other concepts, such as ethnicity, nation, and class (e.g., Omi and Winant 2015; Sollors 2002). Examining the local Japanese concepts of race in relation to the dominant Western ones is important since the latter, which are seen as "universal" knowledge, have been constitutive of the former. In addition, the focus is on the dominant ideas of the Japanese concepts of race. Although Japanese intellectuals, academics, politicians, and activists have used *jinshu* and *minzoku* to imagine the Japanese in various ways, they have not been equally influential in the construction of Japaneseness and racism in Japan. Second, it suggests that obscured racism in contemporary Japan is linked with the conceptual presence and nominal absence of *jinshu* and *minzoku* in defining Japaneseness today. The concepts of race and modalities of racism are inseparable, and both of them are not fixed but are rather changeable in different historical, political, economic, and social contexts (e.g., Omi and Winant 2015). In thinking about the current modality of Japanese racism, it is indispensable to examine how the Japanese concepts of race are implicated in the construction of Japaneseness. Lastly, it explores how obscured racism in Japan overlaps with and diverges from racisms in the West.

WESTERN AND JAPANESE CONCEPTS OF RACE

Race and *Jinshu*

The word "race" entered European languages including English in the sixteenth century, initially with the meaning descent or lineage (Hannaford 1996, 4–6). However, the concept of race is a modern one constructed in the eighteenth century under the influence of the European Enlightenment, which emphasized rationalism and empiricism, and also promoted "objective" observation and classification of natural and social phenomena. Enlightenment thinkers believed that humans were "objectively" classifiable into distinct groups based not only on physical characteristics such as skin color or facial features but also on cultural values, behaviors, and products (Hannaford 1996, 187–233). Academics and intellectuals proposed countless versions of racial categorization, among which the typology proposed by Johann Friedrich Blumenbach (Caucasians, Mongolians, Africans, Americans, Malays) was the most influential in the eighteenth century (Blumenbach 2000, 28–29; Jackson and Weidman 2004, 19–20).

Classifying humans cannot be completely "objective" because differentiation, a critical aspect for classification, is necessarily a "subjective" process. Étienne Balibar (1991b) argues that "the criteria used for differentiation can never be 'neutral' in a real context" because "[t]hey contain within them sociopolitical values" (56). The values influencing the criteria inevitably entail a hierarchical relationship between the West (or whites) and the non-West (or nonwhites) since the idea of race is tightly connected to modernity, colonialism, imperialism, nationalism and capitalism, in all of which the West has played the central role.

Using the word *jinshu* as a concept started in the late nineteenth century when the Western understanding of race came to Japan. Blumenbach's taxonomy of five races frequently appeared in primary and secondary school textbooks until the 1920s (Takezawa 2005, 36). Fukuzawa Yukichi (1835–1901), a leading intellectual of the period, is said to have popularized the term, thereby introducing the most influential idea of racial classification in modern Japan (Morris-Suzuki 1998, 85; Yamamuro 2000, 56). For example, in his 1869 book *Shōchū bankoku ichiran* (Pocket Guides to the Countries of the World), following Blumenbach's typology but replacing the geographical labels assigned to the five categories with color terms (Yamamuro 2000, 56), Fukuzawa (1959) characterized racial groups as follows: "[The white race] are beautiful in their facial and physical features. They are bright and the most civilized. They are the most superior race . . . [The yellow race] have a short nose and slanted eyes. Although they are resilient and diligent, they are less talented and progressed . . . [The black race] have a flat nose and unusually large eyes. They are physically very strong but are lazy and the least progressed" (462–63).

Japanese academics did not simply accept Western racial knowledge. They appropriated it and created a Japanese version by distinguishing the Japanese from minority groups such as Okinawans, the Ainu, and the *burakumin* or descendants of Japan's former outcaste class in terms of skin color, bone structure, personality, and cultural products, as well as representing them as "savage" in contrast to the "civilized" Japanese (Tomiyama 1994; Kurokawa 2004). As Western race theorists depicted the white race as "advanced" or "civilized" as opposed to the "backward" or "primitive" races in Africa, the Americas, and Asia, so the Japanese counterparts adopted a similar strategy, putting the Japanese in the place of the white race in its own racial hierarchy. This use of *jinshu* overlaps with that of *tōyō* or "the East" by appropriating the Western notion of the Orient, a backward and exotic space without history (Tanaka 1993). According to Stefan Tanaka (1993), Japanese historians in the late nineteenth and early twentieth centuries constructed the idea of *tōyō* to dissociate Japan from the Orient by orientalizing China as Japan's past while at the same time preserving a sense of "oriental uniqueness." As in the case of *tōyō*, they applied the notion of *jinshu* "to understand and incorporate [Western] knowledge into their received knowledge and institutions" (Tanaka 1993, 16).

In the late nineteenth and early twentieth centuries, under the influences of Social Darwinism and eugenics, the Western concept of race became more "scientific" and more tightly integrated into the notion of nation against the backdrops of intensifying imperialism and nationalism. Darwin's theory of natural selection posits that organisms are mutable because variations within organisms better suited to compete for scarce resources outreproduce other variations and thus survive. Simplifying the theory and applying it to human society, Social Darwinists justified racial, gender, class, and other inequalities as reflecting "the survival of the fittest" (e.g., Hofstadter 1944, 31–50).

Rooted in Social Darwinism, eugenics, a term first coined by the British scientist Francis Galton in the 1880s, is the idea that "the State can and should intervene in demographic development by encouraging some groups to breed and/or preventing other groups from doing so" (Garner 2010, 71). The key difference between Social Darwinism and eugenics is that the former opposes applying any forms of state or institutional intervention in favor of laissez-faire, whereas the latter advocates intervention (e.g., Degler 1991, 42). Eugenics is premised on degeneration or "reverse natural selection," the antithesis of natural selection, which, eugenicists argue, does not work for humankind because civilization preserves and multiplies the "unfit" such as the poor, the disabled, criminals, people of color, and immigrants (Galton 1999 [1869], 158; Suzuki 1993, 55). Eugenicists found this situation threatening since strengthening national power was an imperative in the face of intensifying imperial competition at the time. Using genetics and statistics, Galton contended that not only phenotype but also intellectual and mental abilities are heritable, and therefore, "artificial selection" or discouraging intermarriage between the superior race or group and the inferior counterpart and encouraging marriage among the superior race are vital imperatives (Galton 1999 [1869], 57–63; 2000 [1909], 79–83).

These theories, surely influencing the notion of *jinshu*, were modified in Japanese contexts. Japanese eugenicists stressed environmental factors more than genetic ones, contending that the Japanese *jinshu* can be altered by raising living conditions, strengthening the body, providing better education, and raising moral standards (Tomiyama 1994, 46–47). This idea derived from a desire to deessentialize the "racial inferiority" that Western race theories attributed to the Japanese. Moreover, changing the Japanese body was indispensable to implement *fukoku kyōhei* ("enrich the country and strengthen the military"), Japan's state policy for strengthening its military and economic power to vie with Western imperial countries.

One example is Takahashi Yoshio's 1884 work, *Nihon jinshu kairyōron* (A Treatise on Improving the Japanese Race), which is known for advocacy of *kōhaku zakkon* or intermarriage between the yellow race and the white race as a means of competing against the latter.[6] Takahashi's argument was based on the eugenicist idea of artificial selection from the viewpoint of an "inferior" race, as shown in the following statement: "Intermarriage with the superior race will produce a better result for an inferior race" (Takahashi 2001 [1884], 568). However, Takahashi also pressed for physical exercise, education, and better living standards and lifestyle habits to improve the quality of the Japanese race.[7]

An additional example is Unno Kotoku's *Nihon jinshu kaizōron* (A Treatise on Remodeling the Japanese Race). In this book published in 1910 (Unno 2010 [1910]),[8] a quarter century after Takahashi's treatise, Unno emphasized the environmental aspect more than Takahashi. Identifying three types of competition for survival—body, knowledge, and nation—Unno contended that the Japanese cannot compete with Europeans and Americans in terms of individual physique and knowledge, but they can surpass them in *kokkashin* (national spirit), which centers on a quasi-familial relationship between the imperial family and the Japanese people (Unno 2010 [1910], 89–90). Unno urged the Japanese to remodel themselves by strengthening their bodies and improving their knowledge by means of artificial selection, such as encouraging reproduction among those thought to be "fit," to make Japan a stronger rival to the West. Unno's notion of *jinshu* is already interchangeable with *minzoku* in the sense that national spirit—a Japanese cultural characteristic—is highlighted as a significant marker of differentiation from people in the West.

Nation, *Volk*, and *Minzoku*

The concept of *minzoku* is tightly related to the notion of nation. The English word "nation," coming into the language via French, was recorded as early as the fourteenth century, initially meaning "a 'breed' or 'stock' of people who share a common descent" as well as implying "foreign," "barbarian" or "gentile"—the Other or the "them" (Fenton 2010, 16). However, it came to be associated more with the "us" as nationalism, prevailing along with imperialism and making the nation-state system the normative governing principle of the world.

Kokumin came into use earlier than *minzoku* as a Japanese word for nation. The term, consisting of the words 国*koku* (country) and 民*min* (people), was used to refer specifically to samurai in a feudal domain (*han*), thus excluding other classes such as peasants, artisans, and merchants in the Tokugawa era (1603–1867) (Doak 2007, 166). In the 1870s and 1880s, participants in the Freedom and Popular Rights Movement (*Jiyū minken undō*)—a movement that mobilized former lower-ranking samurai, affluent landowners and merchants, and urban intellectuals—popularized the term *kokumin* as a civic or political idea of the nation by incorporating those previously excluded groups (Yasuda 1992, 64). Christians, a religious minority, also supported the concept of *kokumin* with enthusiasm, seeking to realize a nation comprised of individuals and thereby to secure their freedom of religion (Doak 2007, 184–90). Although government officials introduced a more feudal term, 臣*shin* (subject) 民*min* (people), this coinage was not successful, so they appropriated the concept of *minzoku* instead, incorporating the meaning of *shinmin* and conflating *kokumin* with *minzoku* (Yasuda 1992, 64–65).

The term *minzoku* entered into use between the late 1880s and the early 1890s and was popularized in the ensuing two decades when Japan started to establish itself as an imperial nation-state (Koyasu 2006, 17; Yasuda 1992, 66; Yoon 1994, 47). During this period, Japan won wars against China and Russia, started to colonize Taiwan and Korea, and turned a particular dialect spoken around Tokyo into the national language, a necessity in constructing a nation as an "imagined community" (Anderson 1991, 37–46). An alternative concept to replace *jinshu* was necessary because in the idea of *jinshu* the Japanese as yellow could not escape from the "common fate" of all people in Asia, whereas *minzoku* allowed them to differentiate themselves from other Asians. Furthermore, it rendered invisible regional, class, gender, and other differences within Japan by imagining diverse groups of people as Japanese (Yoon 1994, 47).

The aftermath of World War I also contributed to popularizing the term *minzoku*. Japan, attending the 1919 Paris Peace Conference as the only non-Western major power, proposed including a "racial [*jinshu*] equality clause" in the Covenant of the League of Nations. However, U.S. President Woodrow Wilson, backed by Britain and Australia, rejected the proposal. Japan had demanded that all member states be guaranteed "equal and just treatment [*kintō kōsei no taigū*]" regardless of "their race [*jinshu*] or nationality [*kokuseki*]" (Ministry of Foreign Affairs 1919, 203). However, Japan's main concern was not racial equality as a universal principle applicable to all peoples including the Koreans and Chinese whom Japan colonized and subjugated; Japan promoted racial equality to secure its gains in China during World War I and to resolve anti-Japanese immigration policies in the Anglo-Saxon territories, seeking to have the West acknowledge Japan's status as a great power (Shimazu 1998). It is not difficult to see the connection between further adoption of the term *minzoku* in self-reference to the Japanese and rejection of the proposal, which was perceived in Japan as the West's "unwilling[ness] to acknowledge Japan as an equal on the basis of race" (Shimazu 1998, 171).

As mentioned earlier, the dominant notion of *minzoku* drew influence from the German concept of *Volk*. Ruling elites and pro-establishment intellectuals used *Volk* as a reference partly because they saw similarities between Germany and Japan as "latecomer" modern nation-states (Kawata 1999, 457; Koyasu 2006, 13–14). *Volk* became a concept in nineteenth-century European romanticism, a reaction against the modernity, universalism, and human rationality that were stressed in the Enlightenment (Mosse 1964, 13–18). Thereafter *Volk* was incorporated into the concept of *Nation*—a loanword from French—as a way to differentiate the German nation from its significant Others, the French and the Jews, who were viewed as embodying modernity and rationality (Hutton 2005, 7–8; Mosse 1964, 13–30). Language, culture, and the land were stressed as critical elements of the German *Volk*. The *Volk* were primarily conceptualized as a linguistic cultural group and yet racialized by treating their language and culture as "biological" traits and the group as "plants" rooted in the homeland (e.g., Hutton 2005, 18–20).

Likewise, the dominant prewar meaning of the Japanese *minzoku* was "a group of people who share 'traditions' based on natural environment [*fūdo*], history, and culture," which were regarded as eternal, fixed entities constitutive of the essence of Japaneseness (Yasuda 1992, 72). For example, Shiga Shigetaka, the chief editor of the nationalist magazine *Nihonjin*, stressed Japan's geography, landscape, and climate in defining Japaneseness (*kokusui*) and claimed that "the Japanese [*Yamato*] *minzoku* has created, developed, purified, inherited, and preserved it [Japaneseness] from ancient times until the present day" (Shiga 1980 [1888], 99–100). Language was also a key element of the Japanese *minzoku*, which is exemplified in statements made by Ueda Kazutoshi, who studied linguistics in Germany and later became a key figure in constructing Japan's national language (*kokugo*) at the turn of the twentieth century. Ueda called the national language "Japanese spiritual blood" indispensable for Japan's fundamental national character (*kokutai*) (Ueda 1968 [1894], 110), comparing the Japanese language to blood, a biological material indispensable to life, which pertained to the racialization of the Japanese as a group with a common language—a blood-tie. In the notion of *minzoku*, the blood, an invisible entity, took the place of "visible" phenotypic characteristics such as facial features and skin color. As a result, *minzoku* sustained the meaning of *jinshu* while removing the word *jinshu* itself.

Localized in Japanese sociopolitical contexts, *minzoku* was not simply a copy of the concept of *Volk*. The localization was inevitable considering the differing Others invoked in constructing each concept: the French and the Jews for *Volk*; the West and Asia for *minzoku*. Nationalist intellectuals popularized the dominant idea of *minzoku* in the course of criticizing the government's superficial and excessive Westernization policies as exemplified by "Rokumeikan diplomacy" (Yasuda 1992, 66).[9] Thus while the notion of *kokumin* was mainly for constructing the "we" domestically or internally, *minzoku* was a concept directed more at the outside world.

Hozumi Yatsuka, a constitutional law scholar who studied law in Germany, was very influential in generating the dominant meaning of *minzoku* by connecting it to the idea of *kokutai*, or national character (Yasuda 1992, 67). The term *kokutai* was spread through the Imperial Rescript on Education (*kyōiku chokugo*) published in 1890 (Oguma 1995, 50), in which it was defined as being "united in loyalty and filial piety" to the emperor for generations (Meiji Shrine n.d.). The imperial family was extremely important in Hozumi's assertion of Japanese uniqueness over the West because of *bansei ikkei* or the male-line continuity of the emperors and its "purity" compared with the European monarchies which were "mixed" through intermarriage (Yasuda 1992, 67). Linking the idea of *kokutai* to *minzoku*, Hozumi argued that the Japanese *minzoku* were "a group tied in blood" (*kettō dantai*) or kin to each other because they were descendants of the imperial family and children of the emperor, the father of the Japanese *minzoku* (Hozumi 1910 [1897], 1–27). Hozumi's conceptualization of *minzoku* had a great impact on the dominant prewar nationalist ideology—Japan as a family state (*kazoku kokka*). Sakai Naoki (1996) argues that the three unities of language, culture, and nation formed an integral part of Japan's prewar nationalist ideology (131–45). The prewar emperor system, a political structure in which the emperor possessed supreme power in military and civil government, was supported by and simultaneously materialized these three unities (131–34). The notion of *minzoku* is epitomized in the three unities, in which the Japanese are defined as a people who share "spiritual" (i.e., language) and "physical" (i.e., "children" of the emperor) blood ties, equating nation with state, culture (or ethnicity), and race

According to Kevin Doak (1997, 2007, chapter 6), prior to the consolidation of the dominant idea of *minzoku*, especially from 1925 to 1935, intellectuals used the word in various ways when discussing the Japanese nation. The leftist use of *minzoku* as people struggling under imperial rule was contextually tied to the 1919 Paris Peace Conference that circulated the notion of national self-determination or *minzoku jiketsu* in Japanese (Doak 2007, 230–33). Leftist intellectuals who followed a Stalinist line posited "a national struggle (*minzoku tōsō*) with 'dominant nations' (*shihai minzoku*) and 'dominated nations' (*hi-shihai minzoku*)" (234). Liberals meanwhile conceptualized *minzoku* as "a subjective consciousness" constructed by the people, not as an essential nature or a consciousness imposed on them by the state (233). These ideas, however, were never completely detached from the dominant notion of *minzoku* (Doak 1997, 291–99). The politician Oyama Ikuo, whom Doak introduced as a leftist exemplar, considered that "society was largely interchangeable with an ethnically determined sense of nationality" (292). Such a formulation, which was obviously influenced by the principle of national self-determination, was useful in opposing imperialism but simultaneously had a close affinity with the dominant idea of *minzoku*. Hasegawa Nyozekan, whom Doak referred to as a liberal exemplar, also ended up concluding that "it was difficult to imagine an ethnic nationalism that the state could not use to its own profit," again conflating nation with state and ethnicity (295).

The dominant self-representation was deployed to differentiate the Japanese from the Asians as well as to create a hierarchical relationship between them. Defining the Japanese as not a *jinshu* but a *minzoku* was supposed to draw clear boundaries between the Japanese and other groups lumped together as yellow. However, the presence of the Asian colonized would pose an increasingly complicated conundrum. As Japan stepped up the Second Sino-Japanese War (1937–1945), it strengthened its colonial assimilation policies to further exploit the colonial population as laborers and soldiers. This situation created a dilemma: how to incorporate the Asian colonized as Japanese while barring them from becoming Japanese completely. Assimilation policies that Japan imposed in Korea and Taiwan included Japanese language education, Japanizing their names, and encouraging intermarriage specifically between Japanese men and Korean or Taiwanese women. However, at that time, empirical studies on mixed-blood offspring of Japanese and the Asian colonized became popular due to increasing possibilities of intermarriage (Sakano 2009, 189–90), often expressing reluctant or negative opinions on it (192–93). In addition, the contention that the Japanese *minzoku* were already "racially" mixed with neighboring Asian *minzoku* groups was influential among academics and intellectuals; but this was felt to be somehow resolved in the idea that the Japanese had been "racially purified" in the course of historical processes while accepting their mixed origin (Sakano 2005, 247). Consequently, the Asian colonized were both de-differentiated and simultaneously differentiated: having some blood ties with the ancient Japanese, thereby legitimating Japanese colonial rule over them, yet not purely Japanese (Oguma 1995, 371). Just as imperial Japan's territory was divided into *naichi* (mainland Japan) and *gaichi* (the colonies), the Japanese *minzoku* was conceptually bifurcated into the "authentic Japanese" and the "quasi-Japanese" in a hierarchical relationship (Koyasu 2006, 17).

Ethnicity, Nation, and Japanese (*Nihonjin*) as *Tan'itsu Minzoku*

After World War I, the concept of race lost ground to a notion of ethnicity that found cultural explanations for differences among groups designated as "races." In English, the word "ethnic" had referred to "foreigners" or "heathens" in the fifteenth century (Fenton 2010, 14). Although use of the word had become rare by the late eighteenth century and was considered obsolete, academics in particular revived it during World War II when "race" was increasingly linked to Nazi racial policies (Sollors 2002, 98). In the 1920s and 1930s, anthropologists and sociologists such as Franz Boas and Robert Park conducting research in the United States had already started questioning strictly biological explanations of differences among human groups and incorporating the concept of culture (Jackson and Weidman 2004, 129–59; Malik 1996, 149–77). In the mid-1930s, the term "ethnic group" was proposed to replace "race" by the biologist Julian Huxley and the anthropologist Alfred Cort Haddon. They argued that a key idea of race, shared ancestry or common descent is scientifically unverifiable (Fenton 2010, 54–55). In the 1950s and 1960s, UNESCO issued four statements on race, opposing the idea that social categories of race reflect biological differences (UNESCO 1969).[10] However, the terms "race" and "ethnic group" continued to be used interchangeably until the 1960s (Fenton 2010, 56) when ethnicity started to become a crucial social science concept in the contexts of African and Asian decolonization and the intensification of anti-colonial and anti-racism movements in the West (e.g., Guibernau and Rex 2010, 1; Jenkins 2008, 17–18).

In contrast to the concept of race, which is seen as negative and ideologically charged, ethnicity is generally regarded as a positive (or at least "neutral") and egalitarian notion (e.g., Eriksen 2010, 5–9; Jenkins 2008, 22). Ethnicity is usually associated with cultural differences and race with physical and biological differences, as exemplified in Thomas Eriksen's (2010) statement: "Notions about cultural uniqueness and social solidarity tend to be stronger with respect to ethnic categorization, while the idea of biological, nowadays dubbed 'genetic', difference is stronger in racist thought and practice" (9). The positive connotation of ethnicity partly derives from a particular view of culture—culture as somehow apolitical and thus harmless (Jenkins 2008, 14). Also it has to do with how categorization is viewed: ethnicity entails voluntary categorization or identification with a group, in contrast to race which denotes an involuntary, imposed categorization of a group (Banton 1983, 106).

However, the neutrality or egalitarian-ness of the concept of ethnicity is dubious, considering that ethnicity generally implies minority groups while today majority groups are not usually presumed to be "ethnic" (Fenton 2010, 14, 22; Guibernau and Rex 2010, 3–4). In the United States where use of the term "ethnicity" began earlier (Jenkins 2008, 11), the word "ethnics" came to be "used around the Second World War as a polite term referring to Jews, Italian, Irish, other people considered inferior to the dominant 'WASP' group (White Anglo-Saxon Protestants)" (Erikson 2010, 4). Ethnicity overlaps with race, which, as Richard Dyer (1996) argues, is often seen as "something only applied to non-white peoples" (1).

Replacing the concept of race with that of ethnicity does not necessarily mean superseding another key idea of race—viewing group differences deterministically as immutable. Ethnicity theories are roughly categorized into primordialism and instrumentalism. The former, despite variations in definition, presumes that ethnic boundaries are "given" and cultures are fixed and possessed by ethnic groups (Spencer 2006, 76–77). An extreme version claims that "there is a biological aspect to the formation of ethnic bonds" (76). The latter argues that ethnic groups are formed strategically to achieve collective political goals, often viewing culture as "invented" or constructed (Fenton 2010, 3). Étienne Balibar (1991a) contends that "culture can also function like a nature" (22). If ethnicity is conceptualized primordially and as an attribute only of minority groups, it is not so farfetched to suggest that "in many ways, 'ethnicity' is 'race' after an attempt to take the biology out" (Chapman 1993, 21). Ethnicity can function like race while superficially eluding the negative connotations of race.

Furthermore, ethnicity's positive connotation is tied to its close relationship with nation (and nationalism), which is also viewed as more legitimate than race (and racism). Both ethnic groups and nations are characterized by culture and common descent (e.g., Fenton 2010, 12–23). Therefore, as in ethnicity theories, a central debate over nation and nationalism is between primordialists and constructionists (or modernists). Typically represented by Anthony Smith, the former explain nations as innate and "eternal" beings, while the latter, often represented by Ernest Gellner and Benedict Anderson, view them as modern inventions (e.g., Calhoun 1997, 30; Pecora 2001, 25–29).

Although the nation's association with the state is usually mentioned as its most significant difference from ethnicity (e.g., Fenton 2010, 12–23), ethnicity (and race), nation, and state are very much intertwined in the world governed by the normative principle of "one state-one nation." Granted that ethnicity is just one potential recourse among several to construct a nation-state (Calhoun 1997, 20–23), it is still a very powerful one because the modern state is "preoccup[ied] with political and cultural homogeneity" (Parekh 2006, 184) and ethnicity is inseparable from the production of culture. The nation does not simply construct the state but also is constructed by the state (184), in the process of which one particular group's "invented" collective culture and "imagined" common descent—ethnicity—often represents that of the nation-state, excluding, subordinating or assimilating other ethnic groups. In some states, for instance, the United States, the white race as an aggregation of European ethnic groups represents the nation, assuming the role of the dominant "ethnicity" by referring to Western civilization, Western canons, and Christianity as constitutive of their core values. Thus, if ethnicity, of the majority group, is defined primordially, ethnic, racial, and national categories become identical, producing a very exclusive meaning of the group.

With the end of World War II, *minzoku* was dissociated from its prewar *Volk*-ish connotations. According to Oguma Eiji, until the mid-1950s, leftist intellectuals and politicians, who were very influential in the postwar turmoil, were the main users of the word *minzoku*, whereas rightists avoided it as they were concerned about the word's (or their own) tight association with prewar militaristic nationalism (Oguma 1998, chapter 21; 2002, chapters 5–9). Using it interchangeably with the terms *minshū*—consisting of the two words 民*min* (people) and 衆*shū* (the masses)—and *kokumin*, the leftists revived their prewar use of the Japanese *minzoku* as a collegial group of people united in their struggle against foreign occupation as well as the state authority and the emperor system. The context of this shift was overwhelming U.S. political, military, economic, and cultural control over Japan by the Supreme Commander for the Allied Powers (SCAP) or the General Headquarters (GHQ) of the Allied Powers until 1952. In leftist discourse, the Japanese *minzoku* were portrayed as an oppressed group suffering from U.S. imperialism, similar to the colonized peoples of Africa and the rest of Asia (1998, 535, 541; 2002, 368–70). They even paralleled the Japanese with the Koreans—based on the logic that both nations are divided (Okinawa and Japan; North Korea and South Korea) under foreign control and thus their right to national self-determination is infringed—while making no substantial self-criticism about Japan's military invasion and colonial role in Asia (1998, 541–42; 2002, chapter 9). Such comparison would not have been possible without separating *minzoku* from its prewar meaning.

Oguma (1998) further argues that defining the Japanese *minzoku* as a "colonized" people whose national self-determination is unfulfilled contributed to constructing the myth of the Japanese as a 単一*tan'itsu* (single) *minzoku* because the right to national self-determination presupposes the principle of "one nation-one state" (535). Moreover, the leftists used the phrase *tan'itsu* (single) *minzoku* in a positive sense as opposed to 多*ta* (multi) *minzoku*

(Oguma 2002, chapter 7). From the end of World War II until the 1950s, the Japanese were divided by large socio-economic and cultural gaps between poor and rich as well as urban and rural. The leftists regarded a *tan'itsu minzoku* positively as an ideal to be realized by reducing these gaps among the Japanese, as opposed to *ta minzoku*, which was seen as a characteristic of the empire, a relic of the past that needed to be abandoned. However, as the Allied occupation ended and Japan's economic recovery was back on track, the leftist influence waned and their rhetoric of the Japanese as an oppressed *minzoku* lost its potency. By the 1960s, the term *tan'itsu minzoku* came to designate an essential trait of Japanese society, losing its critical nuance and becoming an idea largely advocated by rightists (556).

The use of *minzoku* since the 1960s can be summarized into three points. First, the word *minzoku* has been avoided in reference to the Japanese, who have come to call themselves simply *nihonjin* or Japanese people. Second, despite the rejection of the term *minzoku*, the idea of Japan as a *tan'itsu minzoku* nation has prevailed. Third, *minzoku* has been used primarily to describe ethnic conflicts outside Japan, ethnic minorities, and indigenous people, overlapping with the concept of ethnicity.

Regarding the first point, Yoon Keun-Cha (1994) contends that avoiding *minzoku* and using only *nihonjin* in self-reference to the Japanese produced "a hollowing-out of *minzoku* from Japanese identity," creating "the perception that the Japanese are not *minzoku*, and therefore, Japan does not have *minzoku* problems" (6). Yoon also argues that the avoidance has obscured Japan's colonial past and prewar nationalism based on the emperor system epitomized in the notion of *minzoku* and has made it harder for the nation to self-critically disengage itself from these (13). This "hollowing-out of *minzoku* from Japanese identity" is tied to the second point. Okamoto Masataka (2011) postulates that in the notion of *tan'itsu* (single) *minzoku*, the *minzoku* has been "nameless" or left unspecified (77–78). This "nameless *tan'itsu minzoku*" view, coined by Okamoto, is demonstrated in remarks commonly heard from Japanese young people: "I don't know what *minzoku* I belong to" and "I have never thought I belong to a *minzoku*" (77). Japan's imperial and colonial past when the Japanese were a *minzoku* has been made ambiguous by denying that the Japanese are a *minzoku* and—as mentioned in the third point—by reserving the term *minzoku* for minorities and indigenous peoples, primarily outside Japan. Furthermore, in the course of popularizing the idea of Japan as a *tan'itsu minzoku* nation, the prewar idea of *minzoku* has been retained in the meaning of the Japanese without requiring the Japanese public to look into its role in Japan's colonial rule and military invasion in various parts of Asia. Obscuring the Japanese as a *minzoku* thus has contributed to making Asia—a significant discursive Other in constructing the prewar concept of *minzoku*—invisible.

The public discourse on Japaneseness known as *nihonjinron* (literally meaning "discussions of the Japanese") filled in for what was "hollowed out" in Japanese identity. The *nihonjinron* discourse was particularly popular during the 1970s and 1980s in conjunction with internationalization discourse, which John Dower (1993) portrays as "the contradictions between opening outward and turning inward" or the "discordant clamor, with fanfare about 'internationalization' mingling with paeans to 'racial spirit' and 'being Japanese'" (33). The backdrop was Japan's ascendant position as an economic power-house and intensifying accusations from the West, especially the United States, of the Japanese market being unfairly closed to Western competitors (31–32). Numerous academic and journalistic *nihonjinron* books were published, with some selling millions of copies during that time.[11] Scholars have criticized *nihonjinron*, for instance, as "works of cultural nationalism" (Dale 1986), "cultural determinism or cultural reductionism" (Yoshino 1992, 10), "an ideology" (Befu 1993, 126) or "narcissistic preoccupation with so-called traditional values" (Dower 1993, 32).

The *nihonjinron* literature constructed Japanese identity against that of the West by appropriating and applying Western Orientalist ideas to Japan (Yoshino 1992, 11–12). American anthropologist Ruth Benedict's 1946 work *The Chrysanthemum and the Sword* strongly influenced the *nihonjinron* discourse (Aoki 1991, 29). Benedict characterized Japanese culture as collectivistic, hierarchical and thus less free, and in turn constructed (white) Americanness by defining American culture as individualistic, egalitarian and thus freer (Yoneyama 2003, 28–36). Affirming these characteristics as "our" difference, *nihonjinron* writers often explained Japanese cultural uniqueness, using characteristics such as conformity, groupism or collectivism, vertical or hierarchical social structure (*tate shakai*), homogeneity, mutual psychological dependence among in-group members (*amae*), and a high-context or indirect communication style (e.g., Yoshino 1992, 10–22). These characteristics were posited against those that are regarded as most prevalent in the West, especially the United States: individualism, horizontal or "egalitarian" social structure, psychological independence, and a low-context or explicit communication style.

Despite *nihonjinron*'s seemingly apolitical characterization of Japaneseness, it had highly political implications. First, the construction of Japaneseness largely in comparison with the West intensified the invisibility of Asia. Second, equating nation with ethnicity and viewing it primordially, the Japanese continued to be defined as a racialized ethno-national group. The central premise of *nihonjinron* was "equivalency and mutual implications among land, people (i.e., race), culture, and language," or the idea that "only those who practice the culture also speak the language and have inherited Japanese 'blood' from their forebears who have always lived on the Japanese archipelago" (Befu 1993, 116). This premise corresponds to Japan's prewar unities of language, culture, and nation. Therefore, and finally, such political and ideological meaning of Japaneseness became invisible because the Japanese were portrayed primarily as an apolitical cultural group. The Japanese as *nihonjin* were depoliticized and dehistoricized while sustaining the prewar dominant idea of the Japanese *minzoku*.

Since *nihonjinron* lost its initial popularity in the 1990s, the essentialized idea of Japaneseness has persisted. According to Iwabuchi Koichi (2007), as internationalization discourse shifted to globalization discourse in the 1990s, *nihonjinron* transformed itself to fit the latter by diversifying the discursive Other and incorporating non-Western areas among the Others (198–223). This change is connected to the increase of the "real" Others, namely people from various parts of Asia and Africa, in Japan starting in the 1980s. In this "*nihonjinron* in the globalization era" (221–23), the Japanese were represented in a slightly different manner, for example, as people who speak not only Japanese but also English or are skilled in direct communication such as debate (see chapter 2). However, the boundaries of the Japanese stayed intact by treating *gaikokujin* or non-Japanese as the "disposable" Other to accentuate not only Japanese "uniqueness" but also "globalness." In the 2000s, with the rise of Asian economies, the construction of Japaneseness has entered a new phase: Asia, particularly China and Korea, is emerging as the significant Other. How does such a conceptualization of the Japanese relate to the dominant attitude toward racism in Japan?

OBSCURED RACISM

Racism needs to be discussed in relation to the concept of race. David Goldberg and John Solomos (2002) define racism broadly as "an expression of racially predicated or manifested social and political relations of domination, subordination, and privilege" (4). In other words, racism refers to an ideology—ideas and practices—based on sociopolitical power relationships involving "race." Moreover, racism is not monolithic, as Goldberg (1990) claims that "the presumption of a single monolithic racism is being displaced by a mapping of the multifarious historical formulations of *racisms*" (xiii). Different racisms exist not only because racism as an ideology is necessarily constructed and practiced in specific local and historical contexts but also because the concept of race is not monolithic, and modalities of racism depend on how race is conceptualized.

Although racism theoretically does not mean ideas and practices solely based on the "biological" notion of race, this tends to be assumed in general understandings. In Japan, translated as *jinshu* (race)-*shugi* (ism) or *jinshu sabetsu* (discrimination), racism is usually understood with the concept of *jinshu*. One possible factor for such a tendency is the dominant role of the United States in discussing race and racism issues. For example, António Guimarães (1999) claims that "social scientists frequently took the US pattern of race relations as a standard for comparison and contrast in their understanding of race in other societies" (315). This is also the case for the Japanese public, who often equate *jinshu* with racial categories based on phenotype (e.g., the black, the yellow, and the white) (e.g., Kanbe 2007, 30–31), and *jinshu-shugi* or *sabetsu* with white racism against black people. Another possible factor is how the concept of racism was generated. The term "racism" first appeared in English regular usage in the 1930s when the concept of race started to be challenged (Miles 1989, 58–59). It gained prominence after 1945 in tandem with the rise of international initiatives (e.g., UNESCO's statements on race) to prevent atrocities like Nazi Germany's eugenic racism committed against Jewish people (59–60). Thus "racism and anti-racism are often intermingled, even inseparable, tendencies" since "the concept of racism was conceived by those who oppose it, by anti-racists" (Bonnett 2000, 9–10).

Problematizing race and racism is tied to racism becoming obscured. In the 1980s, scholars in Western Europe started to identify a racism based on not "biological" but cultural differences. Labelled as, for example, "new racism" (Barker 1981), "neo-racism" (Balibar 1991a), "differentialist racism" (Taguieff 1999), and "cultural racism" (Rattansi 2007), this is "a racism whose dominant theme is not biological heredity but insurmountability of cultural difference" (Balibar 1991a, 21). Exaggerating and essentializing cultural difference, the new racism based on "pseudo-biological culturalism" (Barker 1981, 23), "claims to reject the old hierarchies of race while, at the same time, insisting on the inherent incompatibility between groups of human beings" (Lentin 2011, 92). Moreover, the shift from "biological" to cultural racism is inseparable from the establishment of the concept of ethnicity in the 1960s and 1970s. Discriminatory practices against an ethnic group on the basis of cultural difference can be perceived and claimed as not constitutive of racism based on the reasons that, first, the group is not a race, and second, the issue is not "biological" inferiority but cultural difference. In short, cultural racism has made it more difficult to pinpoint and attack racism.

Racism in Japan and cultural racism function similarly but differ in how each racism came about. In the Japanese case, racism has been made invisible in the course of redefining the Japanese from a *jinshu* to a *minzoku* and from a *minzoku* to *nihonjin* in which culture has been the central element. Likewise, the shift from race to ethnicity has made racism ambiguous by defining former racial groups as ethnic or national groups and highlighting culture as the marker of difference. However, the two racisms differ because the accompanying conceptual shifts occurred in different contexts. On the one hand, the concept of ethnicity was proposed through self-criticizing racism and the concept of race (even if it meant or functioned to avert criticism from racialized groups). On the other hand, the term *minzoku* was generated to challenge the Western concept of race and later came to be avoided in self-reference to the Japanese without scrutinizing its role in racializing themselves and people in Asia as well as subordinating the latter. Put differently, cultural racism is a result of at least viewing "biological" racism as "our" problem and thereafter camouflaging it as something else, whereas for the Japanese, a people of color, racism has been not "our" problem but "their" problem. Although it is important to acknowledge Japan's role between the two world wars in challenging Western racism and changing the Western political norm based on racial inequality into one based on racial equality (Füredi 1998), this role must be scrutinized in tandem with Japan's use of anti-racism rhetoric as a way to legitimize its colonial rule in Asia and suppress anti-colonial grievances. Racism has not been an issue for the Japanese as the victimizer as much as it has been for the Japanese as the victimized. This explains why in Japanese racist discourse, "biological" differences can be publicly and unrepentantly stressed, as seen in the remark made by former Tokyo Governor Ishihara. Such speech is not often controlled because there has not yet been sufficient discussion about scrutinizing and confronting the meaning of race in Japan and Japanese racism.

While cultural racism was drawing attention in Europe, scholars in the United States began to highlight a new form of racism: color-blind racism (e.g., Bonilla-Silva 2010; Omi and Winant 2015). The ideology of color-blindness, the "central racial component" of neoliberalism (Omi and Winant 2015, 211), started to become influential in the 1980s under the Reagan presidency (212). This kind of racism sustains itself by disguising itself as something else. In color-blind racism, race is made "formally" irrelevant by stressing "formal" equality among racialized groups and attributing racial inequality to individual responsibility, and thereby perpetuating racism.

Color-blind racism and cultural racism have similar consequences—obscuring and dodging accusations of racism. However, the two racisms differ in the ways that they produce consequences: Cultural racism emphasizes culture and differences, while color-blind racism emphasizes the insignificance of race and the principle of racial equality despite the great relevance of race and the prevalence of racial inequality. Racism in Japan has a similar function, but it parts company with color-blind racism because race is viewed not simply as insignificant but as nonexistent inside Japan as a *tan'itsu* (single) *minzoku* state.

However, discussion of color-blind racism provides useful insights into racism in Japan. Referring to color-blind racism as "racelessness," Goldberg

(2002) identifies its three effects: dehistoricizing race; silencing public awareness or serious discussion of racism; and preventing public policy intervention (217). These effects are very close to those of the nameless *tan'itsu* (single) *minzoku* view. First, "formally" dissociating the Japanese from *jinshu* and *minzoku* has depoliticized and dehistoricized the meaning of the Japanese. Second, it has become harder for the Japanese public to recognize racism as "our" problem because if Japan is a nation-state where only the Japanese reside, racism cannot be an important domestic issue. Consequently, racism has been obscured and trivialized, as indicated in the Japanese government's reports submitted to the ICERD committee.

In addition, the Allied occupation of Japan led by the United States also played a role in shaping the dominant view of racism in Japan. During the occupation, the Supreme Commander for the Allied Powers (SCAP) banned or censored any discussion of race and racism in the Japanese media (Koshiro 1999, 62–65). SCAP was concerned about Japanese media criticizing racism against minority groups in the United States since it "questioned America's moral position and amounted to a defiance of American prestige" (62). SCAP censored every comment on race and racism including references to the Japanese as a "colored race" and self-criticism of Japanese racism in all media, including newspapers, journals, and films. In the wake of this policy, criticism of both Western and Japanese racisms virtually vanished from the dominant discourse in Japan (Sakai 2008, 196–97).

An intriguing twist, however, is that SCAP approved including a racial equality provision in the Japanese Constitution, while censoring discussions of race and racism. Article 14 of the Constitution, which was formulated following a draft composed by SCAP officials (the GHQ draft) and issued on February 12 in 1946, prohibited discrimination (*sabetsu*) based on "race [*jinshu*], creed, sex, social status, or family origin." Before publication of the Constitution on November 3 in 1946, various governmental and non-governmental groups and individuals proposed constitutional drafts. What drew SCAP's attention to racism in Japan was a draft proposed on December 26 in 1945 by a private group of intellectuals called *Kenpō kenkyū kai* (the Constitutional Research Association) (Koshiro 1999, 103). Their draft contained a clause to ban discrimination on grounds of "*minzoku* and *jinshu*" (Kenpō kenkyū kai 1945), an idea that Suzuki Yasuzo, a constitutional scholar and a key member of the association, drew from the Soviet Constitution (Hara 2006, 642–43). The Japanese Communist Party's (1946) draft published on June 29 in 1946 contained a similar clause to prohibit political, economic and social privileges based on "*jinshu, minzoku*, sex, religion, status, and family origin." However, the word "race" in the GHQ draft (Supreme Commander for the Allied Powers 1946)[12]was translated simply as *jinshu* in Article 14 of the Japanese Constitution.

The use of race or *jinshu* reflected the different motives of SCAP and the Japanese government. By "race," SCAP meant mainly the *burakumin* or descendants of Japan's former outcaste class, whom SCAP officials viewed as a prime example of Japanese racism; the provision was not intended for people of colonial Asian descent such as Koreans and Chinese or for rectifying white racism toward people of color (Koshiro 1999, 107–108). For Japanese ruling officials, excluding the term *minzoku* in Article 14 was convenient because *jinshu*, primarily referring to the phenotypic categories of black, yellow, and white, implied white racism, whereas the inclusion of *minzoku* might hold the Japanese accountable for their own racism against Asian peoples. The two parties' conflicting *and* complicit motives, entangled with the linguistic, conceptual complication of race, *jinshu,* and *minzoku*, de-substantiated the provision, and accordingly "the 'race [*jinshu*]' provision [of Article 14] changed virtually nothing since there was no clue as to whose racial status was being protected" (107). This exclusion of *minzoku* may explain why in postwar Japan discrimination (*sabetsu*) in public discourse has been associated with *jinshu sabetsu, buraku sabetsu*, or *josei* (women) *sabetsu*, all of which are banned under Article 14, and far less so with *minzoku sabetsu*, which can refer to discrimination against Chinese and Koreans.[13]

CONCLUSION

Constructed transnationally in conjunction with Western notions of race, nation, *Volk*, and ethnicity, the concepts of *jinshu* and *minzoku*, have been tightly connected to the production of Japaneseness. Representing the Japanese as *nihonjin* and a nameless *tan'itsu* (single) *minzoku* amounts to obscuring racism in Japan. Such self-portrayal enables the following logic, which is also entailed in the Japanese government's attitude toward racism discussed at the beginning of this essay: Japan is the place where only the Japanese live; and therefore racism cannot be an issue in Japan. In today's world where racial equality is officially upheld as an international political norm, obscured racism is perhaps the default modality. However, obscured racism in Japan has its own specificity, although it has similarities with its Euro-American counterparts such as cultural racism and color-blind racism.

Race and racism must be comprehended not simply as words or fixed ideas but as transmutative and interrelated with other concepts. This is not the same as conflating the concepts of race and racism or crudely equating, for example, race with ethnicity and racism with nationalism. It means carefully looking into how race and racism have been produced and reproduced by replacing the term "race" with another while retaining its meaning and thereby making racism invisible while perpetuating racial power relationships. Paying close attention to the transformation of the concept of race and its different versions is critical in keeping racism from being obscured.

Investigating local concepts of race in relation to Western race theories is indispensable for advancing the understanding of race and racism. For example, racist practices against Chinese and Korean peoples are often not viewed as racism in Japan partly because, for Japanese people, racism or *jinshu-shugi* (*sabetsu*) is based on the concept of *jinshu*—constructed as the Japanese equivalent of the Western concept of race—and thus refers to racism directed to different *jinshu* groups but not to peoples in the same *jinshu* group. Such an interpretation of racism also contributes to obscuring racism against people of Asian descent who constitute approximately three-quarters of the foreign-citizen population in Japan today, or even more if naturalized Japanese citizens are included. Non-Western discourses on race and racism are affected not only by local contexts but also transnationally by Western discourses on race and racism. By the same token, examining the connection between Japanese concepts of race and those constructed in East Asia is necessary. The Chinese characters for the term *minzoku* were adopted into the Chinese, Korean, and Vietnamese languages shortly after it started to be used in Japan (Kawata 2009, 136). It is thus relevant to ask how the Japanese concept of *minzoku*, along with Western theories of race, influenced Chinese, Korean, and Vietnamese concepts of race. How were their versions of racial hierarchy created in specific local and historical contexts by appropriating Western and Japanese race theories and producing their own concepts of race? How can the trajectories of their race concepts explain present-day racisms in those areas?

As Asia is becoming a significant Other for the construction of Japaneseness today, the Japanese are being forced to confront the past when the Japanese were officially *minzoku*. Besides those anti-Asian racist speeches of far-right groups such as the *Zaitokukai*, the recent intensification in denying or dismissing Japan's imperial and colonial atrocities, and the sharp increase in books and tabloid and magazine articles attacking and degrading China and Korea can be situated in this changing construction of Japaneseness (see chapter 4). To combat racism in Japan, it is crucial to become aware of the Japanese concepts of race, their historical trajectories intertwined with those in the West, and linkages with the meaning of the Japanese.

NOTES

1. Chapter 1 was originally published with the title "Deracialised Race, Obscured Racism: Japaneseness, Western and Japanese Concepts of Race, and Modalities of Racism" in *Japanese Studies* (volume 35, issue 1) in 2015.

2. The word *nihonjin* itself was used interchangeably with *nihon jinshu, nihon minzoku*, and *Yamato minzoku* before World War II.

3. *Zaitokukai* is a far-right group established in 2006. Its purpose is to abolish privileges held by *zainichi* Koreans (people of colonial Korean descent) in Japan (https://www.zaitoku814.com/blank-1). According to the former *Zaitokukai* website (http://www.zaitokukai.info/), as of January 2018, the group had 14,400 members and chapters in thirty-three of the forty-seven prefectures in Japan. As of April 2020, the numbers of members and chapters are not specified in the group's new website (https://www.zaitoku814.com/).

4. The title of this newspaper article includes the words *jinshu sabetsu* or racism.

5. According to the 2013 report, "The Government of Japan does not believe that, in present-day Japan, racist thoughts are disseminated and racial discrimination is incited, to the extent that the withdrawal of its reservations or legislation to impose punishment against dissemination of racist thoughts and other acts should be considered even at the risk of unduly stifling legitimate speech" (see Ministry of Foreign Affairs 2013, 20).

6. Takahashi (2001 [1884], 555) refers to Galton's heredity studies.

7. Takahashi (2001 [1884]) discusses these environmental issues in chapters 3 and 4.

8. A revised edition was published in 1911 (Unno 1991).

9. The Rokumeikan was a Western-style government guest house built for Japanese elites to socialize with foreign dignitaries. The building itself and the elites punctiliously followed European cultural customs for clothing, food, drink, music, and manners. Rokumeikan symbolized the Japanese government's effort to show that Japan was as "civilized" (i.e., Westernized) as the West and to claim equal status with Western nations.

10. The statements were published in 1950, 1951, 1964, and 1967.

11. For example, Nakane Chie's 1967 book *Tateshakai no ningen kankei*, Doi Takeo's 1971 book *Amae no kōzō*, and Ezra Vogel's 1979 *Japan as Number One*.

12. Article 13 of this draft states that "No discrimination shall be authorized or tolerated in political, economic or social relations on account of race, creed, sex, social status, caste or national origin."

13. For example, I searched the database of *Asahi shimbun*, a major national newspaper, by the key words "*sabetsu*," "*jinshu*," and "*minzoku*." In the postwar Showa era (1945–1989), the newspaper published 765 articles with the words "*sabetsu*" and "*jinshu*," whereas the number of articles with the words "*sabetsu*" and "*minzoku*" was merely seventy, about half of which were international news reports. The rest, domestic news stories, mainly concerned discrimination against Ainu people and *zainichi* Koreans (people of colonial Korean descent).

Chapter 2

Neoliberal Nationalism and Japaneseness

In[1] January 2000, English was proposed to be adopted as an official language of Japan in the governmental report "The Frontier Within: Individual Empowerment and Better Governance in the New Millennium" (*Nihon no furontia wa nihon no naka ni aru: Jiritsu to kyōchi de kizuku sinseiki*) published on a governmental website in Japanese and English.[2] The report was prepared by the Commission on Japan's Goals in the Twenty-First Century (CJGTC), an advisory commission to the then prime minister Obuchi. Although it contained other equally contentious proposals, such as inviting immigrants to Japan (CJGTC 2000c, 23; 2000d, 12–13) and reducing the number of primary and secondary school days from five days a week to three days (2000c, 19; 2000d, 9), the proposal of adopting English as an official language of Japan drew far more media attention than the others, triggering heated popular debates (e.g., Kawai 2007).

The report "The Frontier Within" exemplifies Japan's neoliberal nationalism (e.g., Watanabe 2001, 241–45), constructing a "new" meaning of the nation under today's globalization. The purpose of this report is "to elucidate Japan's challenges and policies as it moves into the next century from a medium to long-term viewpoint" (CJGTC 2000b, 1). A major factor behind the report is globalization, which is listed as the first out of five issues that pressure Japan to transform itself (CJGTC 2000c, 2000d). Most dominantly used as a common language in global political, economic, educational, and cultural settings, English is often perceived as "the key language of globalization" (Phillipson 2003, 1) and the language of neoliberalism that enhances both national and individual economic competitiveness and benefits (Kubota 2016, 468–70). Many nation-states stress English language education because perceived deficiencies in English language ability are often equated with their inability to survive escalating global competition, which is inseparable from globalization and neoliberalism. Simultaneously the same nation-states need to promote their national languages, which often play a major symbolic role in nationalism. The Japanese language has been a strong symbol of Japanese cultural nationalism since the country's emergence as a modern nation-state in the late nineteenth century, and Japanese "uniqueness" has been often explained as deriving from the language (e.g., Befu 1993; Yoshino 1992). When English is recommended as an official language of Japan, a different story of the nation needs to be told.

Neoliberalism and globalization are in a very close relationship, which is observable in the often-used term "neoliberal globalization." Intensifying the transnational movement of commodities, people, and ideas, globalization involves numerous dimensions, such as economic, technological, informational, cultural, legal, and political among many others. Contemporary globalization literature demonstrates contradictory views of globalization: on the one hand, it is understood positively as increasing cultural hybridity, nurturing transnational connection and solidarity, and providing opportunities for global justice and human rights; on the other hand, it is negatively seen as homogenizing local cultures (i.e., Westernization or Americanization), intensifying capitalism and its negative consequences such as the gap between rich and poor, and promoting transborder criminal activities such as human trafficking (Turner and Holton 2016). Associated with the latter view of globalization, neoliberalism plays an ideologically significant role in rationalizing and promoting globalization (e.g., Bowles 2013; Saad-Filho and Johnston 2005, 2–3).

Neoliberalism is not simply an economic principle but a political and cultural ideology. Concerned with power, inequality, and social reality, ideology offers a particular worldview or a common picture or map of reality, seducing people to make sense of the world, their communities, their interpersonal relationships, and themselves based on this worldview and thereby defining what is "natural" or "common sense" (Grossberg et al. 1998, 21, 177–201).[3] Ideology in this sense is inseparable from representation (Grossberg et al. 1998, 178–84; Hall 1988) or "the production of meaning through language" (Hall 2013, 2), which involves constructing people's identity, worldview, and social reality (e.g., Kidd 2016, 11; Webb 2009, 10). In the neoliberal worldview, it is assumed that the world is the market in which people—atomized individuals who are detached from historical and socioeconomic contexts—have the "freedom" to pursue their interests, whereas social problems are "personal" issues for which each individual is responsible (e.g., Brown 2015; Clarke 2005; Giroux 2004; Wilson 2018). Put simply, neoliberalism privatizes humans, decontextualizes human relations, and thereby "hide[s] the effects of power" (Giroux 2004, 75).

Likewise, nationalism is a political and cultural ideology constructed transnationally through communicating with the Other. Nations as imagined communities (Anderson 1991) are realized by persuading people to share the map of meaning or reality (i.e., nationalism) through which they interpret the world in a particular way. Anderson (1991) argues that nations are "distinguished, not by their falsity/genuineness, but by the style that they are imagined" (6). The discursive Other or difference plays a critical role in how nations are communicated and consequently what kind of common picture or map of reality is created because "without relations of difference, no representation could occur" (Hall 1990, 229).

As discussed in chapter 1, historically Japaneseness has been constructed by using the two significant discursive Others: Asia and the West. The meaning of Japan/Japanese has been constructed by differentiating itself from both Asia and the West and creating a power hierarchy in which Japan places itself above Asia but below the West. In postwar Japan, until the 1980s, the public discourse on Japaneseness known as *nihonjinron* had played a significant role in defining what it means to be Japanese despite later criticisms from scholars in various disciplines (e.g., Befu 1993, 2001; Fujimoto 2001; Sugimoto and Mouer 1995; Yoshino 1992). Japanese cultural nationalism practiced as *nihonjinron* was tightly connected with Japanese culture and communication, which have been often generalized and characterized as high contextual, collectivistic, and homogenous in contrast to those of the West, especially white America (e.g., Aoki 1991; Yoshino 1992). However, considering that in parallel with the rise of other Asian economies, Asia has reemerged as a significant discursive Other in Japanese nationalism, it is indispensable to look into the triadic relationship involving Japan, Asia, and the West.

Neoliberalism has an ambivalent relationship with nationalism. Neoliberalism undermines nationalism because in the world as the market where people are not social but private beings, the national boundaries and unity that nationalism attempts to establish and maintain become more fragile. At the same time, neoliberalism depends on nationalism to sustain a nation cut into private pieces and torn between haves and have-nots due to neoliberal policies, often triggering neoconservative reactions such as attacking, excluding, and/or assimilating foreigners, feminists, racial and ethnic minority groups, and sexual minorities, who are often viewed as anomalies to national unity and traditions (e.g., Harvey 2005, 81–85; Watanabe 2007a, 16–17).

Thus, how does neoliberalism, a very influential ideology or worldview, in the era of globalization, impact nationalism, another very powerful one? How does Japanese cultural nationalism negotiate with neoliberalism? To be more specific, how do individualism, the neutralization of power relations, and decontextualization which characterize the neoliberal worldview, affect the portrayal of Japanese culture and communication and Japan's discursive relations with Asia and the West?

This chapter looks into the impact of neoliberalism on a Japanese nationalism discourse and its implications for constructing a multiculturalist Japanese society. Using Stuart Hall's (1988, 1997, 2013) notion of representation as a methodological lens, I investigate how Japanese culture and communication, which were utilized to distinguish Japan from the West in *nihonjinron*, are represented in "The Frontier Within." Furthermore, I examine Japan's discursive relationship with Asia and the West in the text, situating the representation of Japanese culture and communication within the triad. This two-step analysis is necessary to dig into an attempt of reconstructing Japaneseness, for as Hall (1990) argues that representation requires relations of difference, constructing the meaning of Japan/Japanese involves referring to Asia and the West, and therefore focusing exclusively on the ways in which Japanese culture and communication are represented will end up using a similar logic to that of neoliberalism—decontextualization (Comaroff and Comaroff 2001, 13).

NEOLIBERALISM AND NATIONALISM

Neoliberalism is not simply a return to classical laissez-faire liberalism represented by Adam Smith's notion of the invisible hand. Neoliberalism began as a response to the crisis of classical liberalism and the emergence of the Keynesian welfare states, state socialism, and socialist movements in the West triggered by the world economic crisis during the interwar period in the first half of the twentieth century (e.g., Foucault 2008; Cahill and Konings 2017). Neoliberalists regarded the challenge of these "collectivists" (Hayek 2014 [1945]) as threatening to liberalism, individualism, and capitalism.

Neoliberalism as a cultural and political ideology provides a worldview different from that of classical liberalism. Classical liberalism assumed that a civil society consists of atomistic and rational individuals who pursue their interests freely, and thus a just society is produced by free market exchanges (e.g., Conway 1995). Unlike classical liberalists, who believed that state intervention in the market—which is natural and self-sufficient—should be as limited as possible, the market for neoliberalists is to be made through the state's active involvement in producing a market-friendly environment and thereby securing competition, "the essence of the market" (Foucault 2008, 121). In the neoliberal world, the human is enterprise and capital (Foucault 2008). The enterprise plans a project, thinks about tactics to realize it, and invests capital in it. Likewise, neoliberalism seduces each human to become a project in which one needs to incessantly invest in oneself to multiply one's own value or human capital to survive competition. In short, the neoliberal society is "an enterprise made up of enterprises" (Dardot and Laval 2014, 255). This explains why neoliberalism aggressively applies market logic to areas traditionally considered unfit for it such as education, medical care and social welfare.

Accelerating the individualization of people, neoliberalism promotes "hyper-individualism" (Wilson 2018, 3) and deteriorates the social. Neoliberal humans are abstract individuals detached from various personal and social conditions and contexts, and therefore social issues such as poverty and unemployment are not examined structurally but viewed as "personal" problems for which each person is responsible (e.g., Clarke 2005; Giroux 2004). In addition, "responsibilized" for their actions, humans as enterprises are urged to "[undertake] the correct strategies of self-investment and entrepreneurship for thriving and surviving" (Brown 2015, 133). Thus the neoliberal society, dominated by the economic sphere and logic, diminishes the political sphere and turns *homo politicus* into *homo oeconomicus* (Brown 2015, 107–111). In the neoliberal world filled with "power-evasive strategies wrapped up in the individual choice and the virtues of self-reliance," power differences are seen as "natural" and thereby become "invisible" (Giroux 2004, 70), and the past is separated from the present and subsequently forgotten (Shibuya 2003, 159–162). By privatizing and commercializing people and society, neoliberalism obscures social injustices and legitimates power hierarchies by viewing humans strictly as "private and present beings" rather than "social and historical beings" whose success or failure depends on their "effort" at this moment.

Emphasizing the importance of advancing individual freedom, neoliberalism is not only endorsed by neoliberal elites who are benefited by neoliberalization but also attracts a wide range of people, including feminists (Rottenberg 2014) and social activists who fight against totalitarianism that suppress individual freedom, such as fascism and dictatorship (Harvey 2005, 40–43). This can be explained using Antonio Gramsci's (2000) notion of hegemony, that a certain idea becomes hegemonic not merely through domination but by gaining the "voluntary" consent of groups who may be adversely affected by the idea. The prevalence of neoliberalism indicates that its hegemonic power has successfully persuaded various groups as well as nation-states to support the ideology willingly. Referring to Foucault's notion of rationality, some scholars view the power of neoliberalism more strongly and argue that neoliberalism is a political rationality that "tends to structure and organize not only the action of rulers, but also the conduct of the ruled" (Dardot and Laval 2013, 4) or "legitimately govern[s] as well as structure[s] life and activity as a whole" (Brown 2015, 117).

Neoliberalism is in a conflicting and compatible relationship with nationalism. On the one hand, neoliberalism, due to its transnational dimension, threatens nationalism, prioritizing the individual over the national and tolerating the movement of cultures, ideas, and people beyond nation-state borders so as to secure "free" economic activities and maximize profits. On the other hand, the neoliberal nation-state strengthens nationalism as a means of sustaining the social crumbling under neoliberal policies. Neoliberalism polarizes the nation into the rich and the poor, the "superior" and the "inferior," or winners and losers. Such polarization shakes national unity, and therefore culture and nationalism are deployed to "glue" the nation back together without solving the socioeconomic divide. Thus neoliberalism cultivates neoconservatism, an ideology that calls for the cultural restoration of the nation jeopardized by neoliberal policies (e.g., Harvey 2005, 81–86; Watanabe 2007a, 16–17). Neoconservatism is tied to cultural chauvinism, xenophobia, racism, and sexism because neoconservatives, desiring to maintain existing hierarchical relations among various cultural and socioeconomic groups, attack and/or assimilate those who try to transform such relations, for example, racial or ethnic minority groups who seek fair treatments, feminists who reject "traditional" gender roles, and sexual minorities who question heterosexual norms and values (e.g., Harvey 2005; Watanabe 2007a).

JAPANESE NATIONALISM AND ITS OTHERS

As discussed in chapter 1, inseparable from the two Japanese concepts of race, *jinshu* and *minzoku*, Japanese nationalism has been transnational by creating two significant discursive Others—Asia and the West—outside while simultaneously assimilating and excluding ethnic minority groups, such as the Ainu, Okinawans, and Koreans inside. Since Japan emerged as a modern nation-state in the late nineteenth century, the question of Japanese nationalism has been "how to become modern while simultaneously shedding the objective category of Oriental and yet not lose an identity" (Tanaka 1993, 3). Although Japan had to dissociate itself from the category of Asia, which was portrayed as stagnant, despotic, and backward by Western Orientalism (Said 1978), Japan needed Asia to claim its identity in contrast to the West. Japan's task thus has been to be Asian and not to be Asian at the same time. In order to solve the dilemma, Japan conceptualized Asia as Japan's past, secured the source of its identity, and asserted Japan's superiority over other nations in Asia as the only nation that had achieved a comparable "progress" with the West (Morris-Suzuki 1998; Tanaka 1993). Despite its efforts to assimilate itself, Japan—a nation of color—was not completely accepted as a member of the West. Instead of challenging the Orientalist representation of Asia, however, Japanese nationalism used and reinforced the Orientalist images of Asia to differentiate itself from Asia and the West simultaneously.

After World War II, Asia as a key discursive Other has been gradually made invisible in tandem with the avoidance of the use of the term *minzoku* in self-reference to the Japanese. Stripped of its colonies, Japan was placed under the control of the Supreme Commander for the Allied Powers (SCAP) led by the United States. People in Japan's former colonies, Korea in particular, were barred by the Allied nations from playing a substantial role in the process of rectifying Japan's colonial and war responsibilities. Moreover, Japan was spared from dealing with the decolonization processes of its former colonies due to the U.S. occupation and later, the Cold War. This also tied into the fact that the Allied countries—imperial and colonial forces themselves—avoided confronting Japan on its imperialism and colonialism because doing so would mean confronting their own problems (e.g., Dower 1999, 469–74). Taking advantage of being excused from facing its imperial past, Japan erased Asia as a significant discursive Other on the surface until the 1990s. This is exemplified in the Japanese cultural nationalism of the 1970s and 1980s, when *nihonjinron* constructed Japanese cultural identity as high contextual, collectivistic, homogenous, and hierarchical as opposed to its Western, especially white American, counterparts, which were defined as individualistic, direct, heterogeneous, and egalitarian (see chapter 1). Yet, the invisibility of Asia does not equate to the absence of Asia. Keeping the West as the superior Other sustains the structure of the superior Self (Japan) over the subordinate Other (Asia) (Tai 1999, 89). Japan's superiority over Asia is supported by using the West as its point of reference and arguing that Japan has progressed (i.e., westernized) more than Asia.

CONTEXTS AND TEXT

The text that I attended to is the report "The Frontier Within: Individual Empowerment and Better Governance in the New Millennium" (*Nihon no furontia wa nihon no naka ni aru: Jiritsu to kyōchi de kizuku sinseiki*). The report was published in January 2000 on a governmental website (http://www.kantei.go.jp/jp/21century) in Japanese and English. The Commission of Japan's Goals in the Twenty-First Century (CJGTC), which prepared the report was formed in March 1999 with sixteen members—professors,[4] business executives, journalists, and other professionals—appointed by Keizo Obuchi, the then prime minister.

Contexts

"The Frontier Within" is a key neoliberal text produced in Japan's symbolic and material contexts of the 1990s (e.g., Watanabe 2001, 241–45). This report is said to have emulated the report "*Kokorozashi aru hitobito no tsudou kuni* [Japan, a Country of People with Great Ambitions]," published by the Japan Association of Corporate Executives (*Keizai dōyūkai*) in 1999 (Watanabe 2001, 241).[5] In the 1990s, influential economic policy reports proposed that Japan should adopt a U.S.-style neoliberal socioeconomic system based on "free" market policies, a small government, more flexible labor markets, and self-reliance.[6] In Japan, neoliberal economic policies, such as selling off state-owned enterprises, deregulating financial, real-estate, and labor markets, and cutting social welfare budgets, were proposed in the 1980s following Reaganomics and Thatcherism.

However, Japan's substantial economic neoliberalization was implemented somewhat later in the early 1990s, following the end of the Cold War and the burst of Japan's bubble economy (Watanabe 2007b, 296–99). Japanese companies moved their manufacturing operations outside of Japan in an effort to utilize cheap labor, thereby increasing the number of unemployed and underemployed people in Japan. The income gap between the top and the bottom quintiles widened from ten times in the early 1980s to 168 times in 2002 (*Asahi Shimbun* 2005a). The percentage of non-regular employment doubled from 16.4 percent to 32.6 percent between 1985 and 2005 (Ministry of Health, Labour and Welfare 2012). Consequently, the notion that "all Japanese are middle-class," which had been popularized in the 1970s and 1980s, was replaced with that of Japan as an unequal society (*kakusa shakai*) in the 2000s (e.g., Tachibanaki 2006).

Meanwhile, neoconservative reactions started to emerge in the middle of the neoliberalization of Japanese economy and increasingly loud voices from Asian countries to challenge Japan's unwillingness to confront its colonial and imperial past. In 1997, a group of neoconservative academics, writers, and educators denounced current Japanese history textbooks as "masochistic" and demanded scaling back or eliminating descriptions of Japan as a colonial and military aggressor, such as the Nanjing Massacre and the "comfort women" issue.[7] A junior high school history textbook edited by their group, the Japanese Society for History Textbook Reform (*Atarashii rekishi kyōkasho wo tsukuru kai*), became a bestseller in 2001. Furthermore, in 1999, a new law was introduced to grant legal recognition to the national anthem *Kimigayo* and the national flag *Hinomaru*, which had been heavily used as symbols to promote Japanese imperialism until the end of World War II. Taking advantage of the flag anthem law, the Ministry of Education directed public schools to raise the flag and play the anthem at school assemblies. In an extreme case, the Tokyo Board of Education reprimanded about 200 public school teachers who refused to stand up to show respect for the flag and the anthem in 2004 (*Japan Times* 2006).

Text

The report "The Frontier Within" is comprised of six chapters. The first chapter, titled "Overview" and written by the CJGTC members, raises key issues that are subsequently discussed in detail in the remaining five chapters by five subcommittees comprised of an additional thirty-three professionals beyond the sixteen CJGTC members. I focused on analyzing the first chapter of the report and complemented the discussion with other chapters for further elaboration. The first chapter is particularly important because, authored by the CJGTC members, it shows the commission's position clearly and serves as the governing principle for the following chapters. I analyzed the Japanese version but referred to the English version for direct quotations. When the English version did not seem to convey the words and meanings of the Japanese version sufficiently, it was supplemented with the Japanese version. The report is ninety-five pages long in the English version (PDF file format); the first chapter is twenty-one pages long.

Using the notion of representation (Hall 1988, 1997, 2013), I examined how the report represents, first, Japanese culture and communication, and second, Japan in relation to Asia and the West to contextualize the representation of Japanese culture and communication. Representation, or "the production of meaning through language" (Hall 2013, 2), implies "the active work of selecting and presenting, of structuring and shaping: Not merely the transmitting of an already-existing meaning, but the more active labour of *making things mean*" (Hall 1988, 64; emphasis in original). Moreover, representation is not neutral, but rather a power-laden process in which meaning is "accomplished" as a result of "a struggle over meaning" (Hall 1988, 78). In the dynamic process of representation, Japaneseness is not permanently connected with particular meanings (e.g., collectivistic) but can be disconnected and reconnected with other meanings (e.g., individualistic) in different contexts.

JAPANESE CULTURE AND COMMUNICATION

English-Speaking Japanese

In the text, the Japanese are defined as people who speak English. The commission suggests that "in the long term, it may be possible to make English an official second language [of Japan]" (CJGTC 2000d, 10). According to the report, all Japanese people are supposed to acquire English language ability, which is designated as constitutive of "global literacy" (4), for the sake of the nation. For example, it is posited that "this [making English as an official language of Japan] is not simply a matter of foreign language education. It should be regarded as a strategic imperative" (10). The significance of English proficiency for Japan's national competitiveness is further explicated in the following statement: "[The] mastery of global literacy by the people of a country will determine whether the country's power in the international politics of the twenty-first century will wax and wane—and is also likely to determine whether the country rises or falls" (4). For Japanese people who speak Japanese as their first language, mastering English—a language linguistically very different from the Japanese language—requires a larger amount of time and financial investment than simply passing a class in formal education. Becoming an English-speaking Japanese in Japan means becoming an enterprise that must constantly spend time and money to acquire and maintain English language ability.

Depicting the Japanese as English-speaking people is possible here because English is defined as the international language and a tool, which is less threatening to Japanese nationalist sentiments (Kawai 2007). Throughout the report, English is regarded not as a foreign language spoken in specific countries, such as the United States and Britain, but as "the international lingua franca" (e.g., CJGTC 2000d, 4, 13, 20; 2000j, 20). In addition, English is portrayed not as a cultural entity that may affect Japanese culture or a complex instrument that requires training for operating it, but as a humble tool like a hammer or a can opener that everybody should be able to use easily: "English is the most basic tool [*dōgu*] that is necessary for Japanese people to obtain global information, express ideas, do business, and do things together with people around the world" (CJGTC 2000c, 20).

The Japanese are encouraged to become English speakers because English is a tool that will enable them to know the world while the Japanese language is not. The commission posits,

> Of course the Japanese language, our mother tongue, is the basis for perpetuating Japan's culture and traditions, and study of foreign languages other than English should be actively encouraged. Nevertheless, knowledge of English as the international lingua franca equips one with a key skill for knowing and accessing the world. (CJGTC 2000d, 10)

Put differently, in order to know the world, fluency in English—the international language—is crucial since Japanese or other foreign languages do not let people reach the world as much as English does. Although it is claimed that "Japanese is a wonderful language" (2000j, 20) and is useful for knowing Japan, the Japanese language does not provide a means for Japan to survive globalization, which is referred to as "an age of mega-competition" (2000d, 3), demonstrating the tight relationship between globalization and neoliberalism.

From High Contextual to Low Contextual Japanese Communication

To imagine the Japanese as English speakers, their communication style also has to be redefined. Japanese communication, which has been depicted as high contextual, is recommended to become low contextual in the report. High contextual Japanese communication is one of the key cultural concepts on which *nihonjinron* has depended to assert Japanese uniqueness. Current Japanese communication is described as implicit and indirect: "Japan has relied on a time-consuming process of reaching consensus . . . , rules have not been made explicit, and nonverbal communication [*ishin-denshin*] has been prized" (CJGTC 2000c, 12; 2000d, 3).[8] *Ishin-denshin*, which refers to intuitive communication or communication that occurs without involving explicit verbal communication, has been defined as a unique characteristic of Japanese communication by *nihonjinron* writers (Yoshino 1992, 12–17) and communication scholars (e.g., Tsujimura 1987). *Ishin-denshin*, "harmonious" decision-making styles, and implicit rules are all tied to high contextual communication in which meanings are not expressed overtly in verbal messages but are implied implicitly with verbal and nonverbal cues.

The commission contends that Japanese communication should become low contextual because high contextual communication adversely affects Japan in today's world. It is posited that "these [high contextual communication] practices will put Japan at a disadvantage in the age to come. Japan needs to base its systems and rules on standards that are explicit and internationally acceptable" (CJGTC 2000d, 3). Globalization is the factor behind this call for change as the issue of Japanese communication is discussed in the subsections "globalization" and "global literacy" in the report.

Due to their high contextual communication, the Japanese are depicted as lacking in communication skills. It is claimed that "The Japanese themselves are painfully aware of the inadequacy of their communication skills" (CJGTC 2000d, 4). Communication skills are defined as "the ability to express oneself in two-way exchanges, particularly debates and dialogues involving multiple participants on each side, along with clarity in the exposition of ideas, richness of content, and persuasiveness" (4). In short, communication skills specifically refer to low contextual and instrumental ones. If globalization means diversifying the world and increasing interactions with people with different cultural backgrounds, what is equally needed is the ability to understand various kinds of communication styles and messages. What is stressed here, however, is the need to *express oneself* directly and explicitly and persuade others—low contextual communication—rather than to understand others with different perspectives through learning various communication styles.

Low contextual communication is advocated in the report because it is necessary to "convey their country's [Japan's] good points and its real situation to the rest of the world" (CJGTC 2000d, 4). In other words, the Japanese need to master low contextual communication in order to strengthen Japan's national power, not to enhance mutual understanding among people around the world. It is further posited in the report,

> Prewar [before World War II] Japan was oriented toward power politics and was prepared to exercise military force as a last resort. In the postwar period, Japan shifted to "money politics" devoting all its energy to building up its economic power. Today, however, "word politics," which uses language as a weapon, is rapidly gaining importance in international relations. (CJGTC 2000j, 17)

Low contextual communication skills are important for pursuing "word politics" in which language is viewed as a weapon. In neoliberal globalization, in addition to bullets, guns, and money, communication skills become a significant source of power. The commission clearly states that "people with superior powers of expression are worth several [military] divisions in terms of national power" (17). Now it is becoming useful for the nation to produce "communication soldiers" who attempt to defeat others with "word power" (18) as well as military and corporate soldiers. *Word power* is defined as "the ability to acquire information, map out ideas, and deliver proposals based on information and ideas, as well as the ability to debate and influence decisions, and possibly even the ability to mobilize people and organizations to implement decisions" (18).

The low contextual communication skills emphasized in the report are tied to neoliberalism and English. Bonnie Urciuoli (2008) contends that in the neoliberal world, "communication skills, in particular, are fetishized as surefire techniques that can transform users and bring in the bucks (or pounds or euros)" (213). As Ryuko Kubota (2011) argues, what is valued is "effective" oral communication skills that "are supposed to make individuals competitive in the knowledge economy in which information-based activities involving technology and communication take precedence over physical labor" (249). In non-English-speaking countries, neoliberalism promotes fetishizing not only such communication skills but also English because "the communication skills necessary for global competitiveness are skills in English—a language that has global dominance" (249).

Furthermore, the communication modes described in the report correspond to what Sonja Foss and Karen Foss (2003, 4–5) call conquest and conversion in which the goal of communication is winning and changing others' perspectives, respectively. Conquest and conversion, preferred modes in the dominant American culture, can lead to perceiving the world as adversarial and contentious (8–9). If the spread of English globalizes not only the language itself but also its preferred communication modes (e.g., Cameron 2002; Kubota 2002), the modes disseminated around the world will be conquest and conversion. For example, in Japan, English language education—instead of Japanese language education—is considered to develop "logical" thinking, self-expression, and debate skills (Kubota 2002, 18). There is nothing wrong with the two modes of communication. People use different communication styles depending on the context. What is problematic, however, is that other communication modes or styles are regarded as "deficient" or "inferior" to the dominant ones. Portraying the Japanese as high contextual *and* "poor" communicators indicates that low contextual communication is seen as "better" and "more desirable."

From Collectivistic to Individualistic Japanese

Collectivism is also targeted as a Japanese cultural characteristic that needs to be changed. In the report, the Japanese are depicted as having a "tendency to regard the harmony of the institutions to which one belongs as paramount" (CJGTC 2000d, 7), and it is claimed that "Japanese society still tends to frown on displays of individual excellence" (8). The commission contends that overemphasizing groupism or collectivism has worked to suppress Japanese people's individuality and creativity: "[T]his system [groupism or collectivism] has not functioned effectively, however, as a basis for enabling individuals to give full rein to their abilities and creativity, and has even become a drag" (7).

In the report, Japanese people are encouraged to become individualistic because collectivistic culture is not suitable for dealing with neoliberal globalization, which accelerates economic, political, and cultural competitions and the diversification of the world. The commission, designating the twenty-first century as "the century of the individual" while calling the twentieth century "the century of the organization," claims that "In the twenty-first century, whose salient feature will be diversity in the context of the trends globalization and the information-technology revolution, the bedrock imperative is that the Japanese empower themselves as individuals, that they possess a robust individuality" (CJGTC 2000d, 7–8).

Although individualism was defined as a Western cultural trait in *nihonjinron*, it is neutralized in the report as a universal value that any people are supposed to follow. It is postulated that "the Japanese will be fundamentally liberated from the material scarcity that has hung heavy over its history right down to the twentieth century. Individual freedom and empowerment, so far enjoyed by only a handful of people, will be within reach of the great majority" (CJGTC 2000d, 7). This statement implies that individualism is a luxurious value that only affluent people are allowed to appreciate. It is argued that the Japanese have been collectivistic, not because this is a Japanese cultural characteristic as argued in *nihonjinron*, but because Japan was poor in the past. Today Japan has become a rich country and thus the Japanese can also enjoy individualism.

The "new" Japanese under neoliberal globalization are defined as "the tough and yet flexible [*takumashiku shinayaka na*] individual . . . [who] acts freely and with self-responsibility, self-reliantly supporting him or herself" (CJGTC 2000d, 8). Moreover, the self-responsible individual or enterprise who continues to invest in oneself to survive competition self-responsibly is an integral part of the neoliberal worldview. This neoliberal individualism is further explicated with the notion of "fair disparity [*kōhei na kakusa*]," which "appreciates [individual] performance and growth potential, accepting differences and disparities in individual abilities and talents as a given" (2000c, 19; 2000d, 9). Although appreciating individual performance and growth potential despite inequalities of abilities and talents sounds nice, when people are viewed as essentially unequal and yet are supposed to be self-responsible and self-reliant, this individualism simply indicates the survival of the fittest—the most popular motto of Social Darwinism.

The *tough and yet flexible individual*, however, is not completely free because "once a consensus has been formed, everyone should obey it" (CJGTC 2000d, 8). The notion of the *tough and yet flexible individual* indicates the necessity to advocate individualism while sustaining the nation. Becoming more individualistic does not imply becoming "less" Japanese. It is claimed in the report that "given the interplay of diverse interests crossing the line between the domestic and the international, the general public will need to develop a deeper awareness of what Japan's own national interest is" (17). That is, Japanese people are urged to be more individualistic and more conscious of being members of Japan simultaneously. Just as a flexible labor market promoted under neoliberal economic policies provides a convenient labor force that corporations can use and disuse at any time (Harvey 1990, 141–72; 2005, 74–75), this "flexible" national identity is meant to produce convenient nationals who do not rely on the nation-state and yet collectively work for it when necessary.

From Homogeneous to Heterogeneous Japanese

Japanese homogeneity, an important cultural concept employed to explain Japanese uniqueness in *nihonjinron*, is also discarded. This can mean dropping "racial purity" as a characteristic of the nation. In stating that "Japan's present social systems were created on the presumption of homogeneity" (CJGTC 2000d, 10), the commission practically admits that Japan has long ignored the presence of various ethnic minority groups in Japan such as the Koreans, Chinese, Okinawans, and Ainu. It is claimed in the report that Japan has to change the premise that Japan is a homogeneous, racial/ethnic society:

> To respond positively to globalization and maintain Japan's vitality in the twenty-first century, we cannot avoid the task of creating an environment that will allow foreigners to live normally and comfortably in this country. In short,

this means coming up with an immigration policy that will make foreigners want to live and work in Japan. (CJGTC 2000d, 13)

Put differently, under globalization Japan has to diversify itself and become multicultural by "importing" diversity outside of Japan, *not* by acknowledging heterogeneity within itself. Diversifying Japan is necessary because "achieving greater ethnic diversity within Japan has the potential of broadening the scope of the country's intellectual creativity and enhancing its social vitality and international competitiveness" (13). In short, Japan should open its doors to immigrants because they are necessary if Japan wants to survive intensifying political, economic, and cultural competitions. This suggestion, however, implies that Japan should welcome immigrants as long as they are useful for Japan. The commission explicitly states that Japan wants only "foreigners who can be expected to contribute to the development of Japanese society" (13). As in the use of English as a tool, foreigners are treated as if they were "flexible tools" that can be imported to serve Japan's national interests and be discarded when they are no longer useful. A heterogeneous Japan simply implies a version of conservative multiculturalism (McLaren 1994, 53–55) or "corporate multiculturalism" (Davis 1997, 41) that corporations accommodate and exploit gender, racial, religious, and other differences to stay competitive under globalization in which they need to go beyond national borders to a far greater degree (Yoneyama 2003, 22).

Likewise, despite the claim that a heterogeneous Japan will be no longer represented solely by men, the inclusion of Japanese women cannot be celebrated without reservation. The commission admits that Japanese society has been dominated largely by men: "men in their prime were primarily responsible for realizing [Japan's] stability in the twentieth century. They headed the household, worked themselves to the bone to drive economic growth and ran politics, economics, and society" (CJGTC 2000g, 67; 2000h, 7). It is posited that such a system "led to the undervaluation of women, children, and older people" (7). What is striking is that why children and older people have been undervalued is further explained in subsequent paragraphs, whereas for women the commission remains silent.

Moreover, when the commission specifically refers to women, they are consistently associated with production and reproduction labor. In the section titled "Falling Birthrates and Aging Populations," it is argued that "we should systematically promote opportunities for women to be involved in society and the workplace on a major scale" (CJGTC 2000d, 6). It is also stated in the report that "in a graying society [*kōreika shakai*], women and older people are expected to make up increasingly large shares of the labor force" (CJGTC 2000e, 41; 2000f, 6).[9] In neoliberal capitalism characterized by "flexible accumulation," however, women (and migrants) have been used as a cheap, "flexible" source of labor (e.g., temporary, part-time, and contract workers), allowing companies to maximize profits by replacing male full-time workers (Harvey 1990, 141–72; 2005, 74–75). Furthermore, women's participation in the workforce does not seem to change the situation that they will be likely to remain largely responsible for rearing children. The commission postulates that "mothers (or fathers) should be able to concentrate on childcare for a certain period before returning to work" (CJGTC 2000g, 73; 2000h, 11). Including fathers in parentheses indicates that men are seen as secondary players in childcare; it is still women that are expected to concentrate on childcare.[10]

Yuval-Davis (1997) argues that nationalist narratives in relation to gender relations are differentiated in three major dimensions: genealogical, cultural, and civic dimensions. In genealogical nationalist narratives, the myth of common origin and blood among the people is stressed, which leads to highlighting women's role as biological reproducers who supply people in "the 'genetic pool' of the nation" (22). In cultural nationalist narratives, language, religion, and other customs are viewed as significant boundaries that distinguish one nation from others. Women are defined as cultural reproducers who are supposed to protect the boundaries including the "traditional" womanhood of their nation. In civic nationalist narratives, in principle any women who obtain citizenship can become members of the nation regardless of their origin or culture because they are not expected to play a role of biological and cultural reproducers. Women's citizenship, however, does not guarantee complete integration into the nation because they are implicated in relationships between their ethnic, racial, and transnational communities and the country in which they have citizenship.

By portraying the Japanese as English speakers and proposing that Japan invite more immigrants to Japan, the commission seems to incorporate a civic dimension into Japan's nationalist narrative that stresses the genealogical and cultural dimensions. Yet associating women with low birthrates and childcare indicates that the genealogical and cultural dimensions are not completely cut off. Japan has been struggling with shrinking birthrates and an aging population since the 1990s. The total fertility rate declined from 1.57 in 1989 to a record low of 1.26 in 2005 (Cabinet Office 2019a, 5), and the percentage of the population aged 65 or over, which was 12.1 percent in 1990, surpassed 20 percent in 2005 (Cabinet Office 2019b, 4). As of 2018, the total fertility rate was 1.43 and the population aged 65 or over was 28.1 percent of the total population (Cabinet Office 2019a, 5; 2019b, 4). When Japanese society was made up of younger populations, women were encouraged to stay at home and engage in domestic work. Now that Japan is aging rapidly, it desperately needs women as a "flexible" labor force and simultaneously expects them to bear Japanese children and play a larger role in domestic work including child rearing than men. Like foreigners, Japanese women are also regarded as "flexible" tools that can be used to repair Japan.

THE WEST, ASIA, AND JAPAN

The West That Matters in the Past and the Present and Future

The West overtly appears in historical contexts in the report, seen as an overwhelmingly powerful Other with which Japan had tried to catch up in the past. The commission posits that "nineteenth-century Western civilization, having gone through the Industrial Revolution, became extremely powerful, and the Western powers seemed well on their way to dominating the entire globe as the world's only major players" (CJGTC 2000j, 3). Despite "breathtaking political, economic, and social disparities between Western countries and Japan" (CJGTC 2000d, 20) in the nineteenth century, Japan's rise as "an industrial power" (CJGTC 2000j, 3) showed that "with sufficient application any nation could acquire the affluence and strength that had been regarded as the monopoly of Western civilization" (3). Here Japan is described as a nation that was politically and economically far behind the West but challenged Western political, economic domination and narrowed the gaps with the West on its own. However, the report fails to discuss how Asia was affected by Japan's applications of Western "civilization," such as imperialism and colonialism, in pursuing its prosperity.

In the past context, the West is seen as the role model for Japan, whereas, according to the report, this is not the case in the present context. The commission contends that under globalization, "the 'catch up and overtake' model" that Japan has followed since the nineteenth century does not work and thus "Japan must now seek a better model. But the world no longer offers ready-made models" (CJGTC 2000d, 2). Since the nineteenth century, Japan has tried to compete with the West by absorbing Western "civilization," but today the political, economic, and social gaps with the West that the Japanese felt in the nineteenth century do not exist. Currently Japan is "affluent, and its citizens enjoy a high standard of living . . . It [Japan] is deeply engaged with the world as a major power . . . Things are very different from a century ago" (20).

However, clearly the West is still the model that Japan looks up to, considering that the "new" Japanese are imagined as a people who speak English, communicate low contextually, and become individualistic. Although these are designated as "international standards," they are not universal cultural characteristics but preferred and privileged ones particularly in

Anglo-American culture. The disappearance of the West in the present context simply means that the West has been replaced with the "international" or "global" and has become invisible.

Asia that Matters in the Present and Future

Asia matters more in the present and future context despite its visible appearance in the past context. It is admitted in the report that Japan has "a more recent history of colonial rule and invasion" with Asia (CJGTC 2000j, 7), and in the first half of the twentieth century, "Japan forced its self-serving goals and order on surrounding countries, pursued aggrandizement of the Japanese empire at huge cost to other countries, and brought war and calamity to the Asia-Pacific region" (3). At least referring to Japan's colonial and wartime past is necessary because Asia in the present and future are "important trading partners" (CJGTC 2000j, 7). The commission claims,

> The firmest foundation of Japan's foreign relations will continue to be its alliance with the United States and the trilateral cooperative relationship including strong ties with an increasing integrated Europe . . . In the twenty-first century, however, we should further strengthen cooperative relations within East Asia, a region of great potential for the future and one with which we have geographical proximity and deep historical and cultural ties. (CJGTC 2000d, 19)

Apparently, the West is still primarily important for Japan. During the Cold War, Japan could neglect Asia and look largely toward the West because taking advantage of the war as a key U.S. ally, Japan was able to have the upper hand over Asia economically. Today, however, Japan cannot afford to overlook Asia's growing economic power, which is described as follows: "A vast frontier beckons in the realm of economic cooperation among Japan, China, and Korea" (19).

Although Japan's colonial and wartime past is seemingly recognized in the report, its postcolonial relations with Asia are what Japan wants to eliminate. It is contended that "to say that we can freely build the future, ignoring the constraints of the past and the present, is disingenuous and is liable to lead us to deceive both ourselves and others" (CJGTC 2000j, 2). That statement, however, is immediately set off by the following argument:

> Of course, being constrained by the past and being ruled by the past are not identical. What we were in the past and what we are now are not identical. Our present identity is the product of our evaluation and screening [*senbetsu*] of our historical experience. The past that we affirm is the identity that we continue to confirm, whereas the past that we condemn is the identity that we try to slough

> off. The weight of historical continuity is great, but at the same time it is true in every age that it is people who shape history; their perceptions and will are important factors that constitute history. (CJGTC 2000i, 110; 2000j, 2)

In short, recognizing the past is a step of forgetting the past. Once Japan acknowledges its colonial and wartime responsibility, it can forget this responsibility and create a history that is not "tainted" by the particular portion of Japan's past. The commission also claims that "we should increase the amount of school time devoted to the study of Korean and Chinese history and the history of these countries' relations with Japan" (CJGTC 2000d, 19). This suggestion is important. Yet if history is shaped by Japan's identity that is constructed through Japan's filtering of its historical relations with Asia, what kind of history will be taught at school?

On the other hand, the Meiji era (1868–1912), during which Japan established itself as a modern nation-state and an imperial power by adopting Western "civilization" and "successfully" modernizing itself, continues to be remembered as an important part of Japan's past:

> Our Meiji-era forebears greeted the twentieth century with that kind of resilient optimism. The most impressive aspect of the report of the Iwakura mission[11] is its "can do" approach to Japan's future, its optimism in the best sense. Though the mission's members saw firsthand the breathtaking political, economic, and social disparities between Western countries and Japan, they had the "practical imagination" to believe that Japan could achieve modernization in its way. We need to bring the same resilient optimism and practical imagination to the twenty-first century. (CJGTC 2000d, 20)

While Japan hopes to eliminate its past as a colonizer in Asia, it wants to keep its past as the nation-state that westernized itself ahead of other countries in Asia. The latter is positively depicted as "a great achievement in terms of world history" because "Western civilization was synonymous with the world [in the nineteenth century]," and "emerging from the ranks of non-Western countries, Japan dedicated itself to modernization in the latter half of the [twentieth] century" (CJGTC 2000j, 3). That, however, is not possible because the two pasts are inseparable: colonizing Asia was an essential process of westernizing Japan. In order to narrow the political, economic, and social gaps between Japan and the West, mimicking the West and securing colonies from which Japan was able to exploit natural, material, and human resources were crucial.

This contrast of eliminating Japan's colonial past while keeping its past in which Japan "successfully" westernized itself is related to Homi Bhabha's (1990) argument that "it is this forgetting [of the history of the past]—a minus in the origin—that constitutes the *beginning* of the nation's narrative" (310). Deleting some historical events while highlighting others is an integral part of constructing the nation (Renan 2011 [1882]). Neoliberal ideology, which individualizes and decontextualizes people and society, also accelerates the national "amnesia." In constructing a particular worldview for the nation, the past is chopped into chunks, and then certain chunks are picked up while the others are thrown away. According to the commission's argument, Japan determines what chunks are to be kept because the story of Japan is supposed to be told by the Japanese alone. Admitting Japan's past as an imperial and colonial power in Asia in the report thus does not necessarily lead to reflecting its past in a real sense because it is just a step of erasing the particular portion of the past and recomposing Japan's national story.

Furthermore, Asia is naturalized or neutralized in the present context. According to the report, today's Asia "has been seamed by underground *katsu dansō* [active fault lines], not only *dansō sen* [the fault lines] of the cold war that divided the world into Eastern and Western blocks but also the North-South fault line separating rich and poor" (CJGTC 2000i, 115; 2000j, 7). The Cold War and the gap between the haves and the have-nots under neoliberalization are regarded as fault lines (*dansō sen*)—nature—not as human-made. The commission applies this analogy to contentions involving Japan and countries in Asia, Korea and China in particular, over territorial and historical issues: "there have also been numerous fault lines of geography and history that have made it difficult to reconcile the past and the future" (CJGTC 2000j, 7). Treating the disputes as fault lines that "naturally" divide Japan and Asia obscures the facts that it is Japan that invaded countries in Asia and caused territorial conflicts, and it is Japan that has repeatedly downgraded or even denied Japan's colonial and wartime atrocities in Asia, which led to controversies over history with Asia.

CONCLUSION

Neoliberalism is problematic for constructing a multiculturalist Japanese society since it renders power relations invisible and contexts intangible, thereby making equitable relationships with others difficult. When the world is seen through a neoliberal lens, what happened can be forgotten, the present and future is decoupled from the past, and people, events, and ideas are understood in isolation, being individualized and detached from others.

In the neoliberal story of Japan, "old" Japanese cultural and communicational characteristics, such as high contextual communication, collectivism, and homogeneity, are laid aside. Instead, the "new" Japanese are represented as people who speak English, have low contextual communication skills (especially conquest and conversion modes), become *tough and yet flexible individuals* who are self-responsible enterprises and simultaneously nationalistic, and diversified by inviting "useful" human resources from the outside. In the neoliberal worldview that decontextualizes social events and relations and thereby naturalizes power differences, English is neutralized as the international language, low contextual communication as an international standard, and individualism as a universal value to be pursued. Thus the West as "*both* the organizing factor in a system of global power relations *and* the organizing concept or term in a whole way of thinking and speaking" (Hall 1992, 278; emphasis in original) is made invisible in the present context. In addition, foreigners and women are decontextualized as flexible and convenient tools for diversifying and stimulating Japanese society, while ethnic minority groups in Japan are forgotten.

As neoliberalism further prevents viewing people, events, and ideas in relation to others, Japan's detachment from its colonial relations with Asia has become more consolidated. This does not mean that such an attitude toward Asia is a new development, but that the neoliberal worldview has made it easier to legitimate the attitude. For example, during five years in office (2001–2006), former Japanese prime minister Koizumi Junichiro repeatedly made official visits to Yasukuni Shrine which honors Class-A war criminals despite strong criticisms especially from China and Korea. Prime Minister Koizumi justified his visits by arguing that "each country has its own history, traditions, and way of thinking" (*Asahi Shimbun* 2005b). Also he contended that visiting the shrine is "an issue of freedom of mind" and even accused China and Korea of interfering in Japan's domestic affairs (Yoshitake 2006). Koizumi's statements and behaviors resonate with the commission's argument that "our [Japan's] present identity is the product of *our* evaluation and screening of *our* historical experience" (CJGTC 2000i, 110; 2000j, 2; emphasis added). What is problematically common between the two is to view Japan as an atomized and individualized entity. Japan's history has been implicated with histories in Asia, especially China and Korea, and the West. It is impossible for any country to have its own history independent of those of other countries. Japan's identity can be problematic when it is constructed without historically, critically, and self-reflexively relating itself with Asia and the West. Neoliberalism, however, makes it more difficult to see this relationality.

As another example, in 2013, Prime Minister Abe Shinzo expressed his skepticism about inheriting the 1995 Murayama statement (*Japan Times* 2015) in which the then prime minister Murayama Tomiichi stated his "feelings of deep remorse" and "heartfelt apology" over Japan's aggression and colonial rule in Asia (Ministry of Foreign Affairs 1995). Prime Minister Abe argued that "the definition of 'aggression' has not been established 'in either academic or international terms'" (*Japan Times* 2015). And unlike his predecessors, he has refused to mention Japan's aggression in Asia since he took office in 2012, notably at the national memorial service for the war dead marking the end of World War II to be held on August 15 every year (Inoue 2017). This attitude of Prime Minister Abe, an avid supporter of the Japanese Society for History Textbook Reform, overlaps with far-right activists and writers' attack on former "comfort women," denial of the Nanjing Massacre, and the legitimation of Japan's colonial rules in Asia (e.g., Gilbert 2017; Hyakuta 2017; see chapter 4).

Since the publication of the report, neoliberalism and neoconservatism have jointly operated in Japan's political, economic, educational and immigration policies and practices. For example, first, while making visits to Yasukuni Shrine, a very strong symbol of prewar Japanese militaristic nationalism and imperialism, Prime Minister Koizumi pursued neoliberal policies including the privatization of the postal and highway systems, cutting government spending, and a drastic labor market deregulation.

Second, while English language education has been strengthened, neoconservative education policies have been implemented. In 2011, the Ministry of Education (MEXT) introduced English classes as a required "activity" for fifth and sixth graders in primary school. English will be included as a formal subject for them in 2020. In 2013, responding to Prime Minister Abe's request, the MEXT published "*Kyōkasho kaikaku jikkō puran* (Action Plans for School Textbook Reform)" with the following new rules: primary and secondary school textbooks must mention the Japanese government's positions on contentious historical issues; they should not deviate from the Fundamental Law of Education, which the first Abe administration revised in 2006 to include as a purpose of education nurturing "an attitude that respects tradition and culture and love of the national homeland that has fostered them" (MEXT 2013a). Another 2013 MEXT policy paper on English education entitled "*Gurōbaruka ni taiōshita eigo kyōiku kaikaku jisshi keikaku*" (Action Plans for English Language Education Reforms to Cope with Globalization) discussed not only reforming English language education but also enhancing Japanese language, culture and history education to strengthen Japanese identity (MEXT 2013b).

Third, in 2012, the Japanese government introduced a points-based immigration system to recruit highly educated and skilled professionals and allow them and their family members to stay in Japan practically permanently after the minimum three years. The number of professionals whom Japan accepted through the points-based immigration system was 14,924 in 2019 (Ministry of Justice 2020). At the same time, the government expanded the foreign technical trainee program and nearly quadrupled the number of foreign "trainees," who are permitted to work in Japan temporarily (from three to five years), during the last ten years from 86,826 in 2008 to 410,972 in 2019 (Ministry of Justice n.d., 2020). The trainee program was introduced in 1993 as a way of "international contributions" to transfer industrial skills and knowledge to developing countries. However, it has been a loophole exploited in order to hire foreign workers especially from China and Southeast Asian countries as cheap labor to fill empty jobs in the farming, fishing, construction, and food industries. Recruiting "useful" foreigners from outside of Japan as "flexible tools" to heterogenize Japanese society and stimulate Japanese economic vitality, the Japanese government has divided them into the more useful and the less useful, and tried to retain the former, who are far smaller in number and less threatening to the homogeneity of the Japanese nation. In addition, the use of women as "flexible tools" also accelerated. While the employment rate of women (aged fifteen to sixty-four) continued to rise from 57.0 percent in 2001 to 69.6 percent in 2018 (Cabinet Office 2019c), in the World Economic Forum's gender equality ranking, Japan dropped from 80th in 2006 to 94th in 2010 and to 121st in 2020 (World Economic Forum 2020, 201).[12]

Neoliberalism as an ideology makes it more difficult to view nations, cultures, histories, ideas, and people not in isolation but as interconnected. At the same time, neoliberal values, such as decontextualization, marketization, the neutralization of power differences, and individualism, strengthen neoconservatism, which is often expressed at the cost of less powerful Others. In order to resist such neoliberal ideology as well as parochial nationalism, it is crucial to see different nations and people more holistically, contextually, and transnationally by transcending temporal, spatial, and cultural borders without losing sight of specific contexts.

NOTES

1. An earlier version of chapter 2 was published with the title "Neoliberalism, Nationalism, and Intercultural Communication: A Critical Analysis of a Japan's Neoliberal Nationalism Discourse under Globalization" in *Journal of International and Intercultural Communication* (volume 2, issue 1) in 2009.

2. The report has six chapters in total. Initially two chapters (chapters 1 and 6) of the report were translated into Korean and Chinese and appeared on the website. As of August 2005, the Chinese and Korean versions were no longer available. The two chapters were translated into Chinese and Korean probably because in preparing for the report, the CJGTC exchanged ideas with politicians, government officials, journalists, and researchers in South Korea (in total eighteen people) and China (twenty-one) as well as the United States (sixteen) (CJGTC 2000a). In these two chapters, the proposal that Japan adopt English as an official language is mentioned.

3. For a historical overview of different approaches to ideology, see Cash (2014).

4. Their fields of expertise are political science, economics, psychology, bioscience, and music (CJGTC 2000b).

5. This report contains neoliberal policies very similar to those found in "The Frontier Within." *Keizai Dōyūkai*, then a very influential economic organization of top executives from large business corporations, regularly proposes socioeconomic policies in its reports.

6. Examples include "the Hiraiwa report" prepared by the Economic Restructuring Council in 1993 and the report by the Economic Strategy Council in 1999. These advisory councils to the prime minister were chaired by top business leaders such as Hiraiwa Gaishi, a former chair of the Japan Federation of Economic Organization (*Keidanren*), a most powerful economic organization in Japan, and included academics such as Takenaka Heizo, a neoliberal economist, who later became one of the most influential ministers in the Koizumi administration (2001–2006).

7. The term "comfort women" refers to girls and women who were "'recruited' in a variety of ways that often included violence, deception, and coercion" (Muta 2016, 621) to provide sexual services to Japanese soldiers during the Asia-Pacific War.

8. The term "*ishin-denshin*" is translated as nonverbal communication in the English version.

9. In the English version, the phrase "a graying society" is not translated.

10. In the English version, the word "fathers" is not in parentheses.

11. This refers to a two-year diplomatic journey (1871–1873) headed by Iwakura Tomomi. The members of the mission, government officials, and scholars visited Europe and the United States to collect information to help Japan's modernization.

12. The Global Gender Gap Report was first published in 2006.

Chapter 3

Remembering Japanese Americans and Japanese Brazilians for Japaneseness

This chapter examines how Japanese television dramas construct Japaneseness by representing Japanese Americans and Japanese Brazilians as diasporas and making cultural memories of their experiences through World War II. The United States and Brazil were the two most popular destinations for Japanese immigration outside Asia. Between the late nineteenth century and the first half of the twentieth century, about 270,000 Japanese migrated to the United States (Spickard 2009, 23) while 190,000 Japanese to Brazil (Masterson 2004, 113). Treated as "enemy aliens" and confronted with blatant state racism and discrimination, their diasporic experiences were closely connected to World War II.

Television drama serves as an important educational vehicle through which people learn cultural memory (Popular Memory Group 2011 [1998]) and ideologies such as nationalism (Thornham and Purvis 2005). Cultural memory, which is tied to identity and culture, is intertwined with nationalism (Nora 1989). Nationalism as an ideology defines national identity or what it means to be a member of a nation in relation to various discursive Others. Remembering emigrants and their descendants as diasporas can become a useful discursive way for nationalism "back home" by arbitrarily highlighting their maintenance of ethnic and national belongingness and construction of nostalgic memories about the homeland. National memories of its emigrants and their descendants play a unique role in nationalism because their ambiguous and ambivalent position—members living away from the national homeland—can make them simultaneously the national Self and the Other (Kawai 2016b). Although Japan's collective views of *Nikkeijin* (people of Japanese descent), such as Japanese Americans and Japanese Brazilians, have changed with Japan's rise as a world economic power and consequent transition from a migrant-sender to a migrant-receiver in the 1980s, these views have consistently served Japan's own interests (White 2003, 320).

Such a discursive use of *Nikkeijin* is problematic in today's era of accelerated human mobility in which ethnic return migration and diasporic homecoming have become more frequent (e.g., Tsuda 2009a). In the 1990s, the acute labor shortage in Japan and hyperinflation in Brazil triggered a massive return migration of Japanese Brazilians to Japan. At its peak in 2008, more than 300,000 Japanese Brazilian return migrants or one-fifth of their entire population (1.5 million) were living in Japan. No official statistics are available for Japan's Japanese American population. The dismantling of Japanese American communities and the stigmatization of their ethnicity due to the internment during World War II promoted their assimilation to mainstream U.S. society and culture (e.g., Spickard 2009, 157–60). However, under the influence of U.S. multiculturalism and the advancement of digital technology such as the internet, more recent and later-generation Japanese Americans have reclaimed their ethnic ancestry and created transnational connections with Japan by studying the Japanese language and by visiting, studying, and working in Japan (Tsuda 2016).

It is an important task to scrutinize the ways in which Japanese nationalism discursively uses *Nikkeijin* because these practices are entangled with the Japanese government's immigration policies, Japanese people's views of *Nikkeijin*, and *Nikkeijin*'s experiences in Japan. The Japanese government encouraged Japanese Brazilian return migration to Japan by relaxing the Immigration Control Act in 1990 and offering *Nikkeijin* special visas to work without restrictions in Japan. In the late 1980s, Japanese government officials were concerned about the rapidly increasing number of undocumented Asians entering Japan in search of work. In order to resolve the labor shortage and curtail the inflow of non-Japanese Asians, the government invited *Nikkeijin* to return, assuming that *Nikkeijin* were racially Japanese and would keep Japan as a *tan'itsu minzoku kokka* (a single race/ethnic nation-state) intact (Nojima 1989, 98). This racialist idea throws *Nikkeijin* living in Japan into a more intensified dual politics of inclusion and exclusion due to their ambiguous position as both Japanese and non-Japanese (e.g., Kondo 1990; Yamashiro 2011).

In addition, Japanese Brazilians tend to have less favorable experiences in Japan than Japanese Americans (Tsuda 2009b). Takeyuki Tsuda argues that this is "mainly a product of the different international positions of Brazil and the United States in the global hierarchy of nations" (227). While Japanese Americans stay in Japan largely as professionals and students, many Japanese Brazilians have worked at factories regardless of their educational background. The global hierarchy of nations (and languages) is responsible for this occupational pattern. Japanese Americans have far more opportunities to obtain an office job without sufficient Japanese cultural and linguistic knowledge because the Japanese are familiar with American mainstream culture and English. In contrast, Japanese Brazilians' lack of proficiency in Japanese and knowledge about Japanese culture has been frequently problematized, and they have endured socioeconomic and cultural marginalization in their ancestral homeland (e.g., Tsuda 2003). Yet the contrasting experiences of the two groups in Japan cannot be explained solely in terms of today's global hierarchy of nations but must also take into consideration the Japanese imaginations of the two *Nikkeijin* groups.

In this chapter, I refer to the concept of cultural memory and explore the role of Japanese memories of Japanese Americans and Japanese Brazilians in constructing Japaneseness and the problematic relationality between the two *Nikkeijin* groups and the Japanese in Japan. Analyzing two Japanese television drama series, I look into different ways in which the two peoples' historical experiences are diasporically remembered to educate the Japanese audience what it means to be Japanese. In the following sections, I first discuss how diaspora, nationalism as an ideology and a narrative, and memory are conceptually interrelated and the ways in which television drama—a form of narrative—serves as an educational vehicle for nationalism and national memory construction. Then after clarifying narrative strategies shared in the two drama series, I comparatively examine how the two media texts construct Japaneseness.

DIASPORA, NATIONALISM, MEMORY, AND TELEVISION DRAMA

Diaspora and Nationalism "Back Home"

The concept of diaspora has been used to investigate diverse issues concerning migration by highlighting linkages between a real or imagined homeland and a hostland (e.g., Stierstorfer and Wilson 2018, xvii; Vora 2018, 1577–78). Diaspora is closely related to nationalism because these "lands" often overlap with nation-states, and nationalism is also involved in "boundary-maintenance," a core element of diaspora (Brubaker 2005, 5–7).

Understood as both undermining and reinforcing nationalism, diaspora's relationship with nationalism has been ambivalent since the 1990s when the term "diaspora" became popularized. On the one hand, scholars discussed diaspora in relation to concepts such as heterogeneity, diversity, and hybridity (Hall 1990, 235) and transnationalism (e.g., Bauböck and Faist 2010). Diaspora's transnationality, or being connected to multiple nation-states by "living here and remembering/desiring another place" (Clifford 1997, 255), was viewed to have subversive effects on nationalism, which tends to essentialize the identities and cultural practices of its nationals.

On the other hand, other scholars pointed out diaspora's close affinity with nationalism, exemplified by notions of long-distance nationalism (Anderson 1992) and transnational nationalism (Ang 2000, chapter 4). Diasporic identities can be expressed in an essentialized way or their ethno-national solidarities with the homeland can be overemphasized as a way of defending against negative experiences such as exclusion and alienation in the hostland. With respect to this strong connection between diaspora and nationalism, some theorists problematized the concept of diaspora itself. For example, Floya Anthias (1998) argued that the idea of diaspora presupposes a homogenous and primordial notion of community by neglecting its intersection with gender. Yasemin Soysal (2000) also criticized the concept's "insistence on privileging the nation-state model and nationally-defined formations" (2) even though people's sense of belonging has become diversified in today's globalizing world.

The two different positions on the relationship between diaspora and nationalism can be reconciled by seeing diaspora not as an entity but as "a category of practice, project, claim and stance" (Brubaker 2005, 13)—that is, a matter of communication. If diaspora is referred to as a substantial group, the two theoretical views are a contradiction, whereas if it is seen as a discursive practice, they simply indicate different modes of practice. Diaspora "does not so much *describe* the world as seek to *remake* it" (12; emphasis in original), in the process of which not only people away from their "homeland" but also those in the "homeland" can participate. Highlighting diaspora's essentialized sense of belonging, nationalism "back home" can use it to offer a particular view of the nation in the process of imaging and reimagining itself.

Imagining a nation needs the Other. Michael Billig (1995) contended that nationalism "was always an international ideology" (53) and "the national community can only be imagined by also imagining communities of foreigners" (79). Diaspora can be a useful discursive resource for nationalism "back home," serving simultaneously as the Other and the national Self (Kawai 2016b). In addition, diaspora's transnational connection is convenient to add a "global flavor" to nationalism. Nationalism in the homeland can strengthen itself by highlighting the ambivalence of diasporic identities as well as the discrepancy between the place in which a population physically resides and the place to which they feel they belong.

Nationalism as an Ideology and a Narrative

Established nations as "imagined communities" (Anderson 1991) are constructed and maintained discursively through ordinary cultural objects and mundane communicational practices (Billig 1995). Although Benedict Anderson stressed the roles of newspaper and national language for emerging nations in the nineteenth and the twentieth centuries, popular cultural texts play a major role in today's nationalism. According to Stuart Hall (1996), national narratives are "told and retold in national histories, literatures, the media, and popular culture" (613). People become nationals not only by consciously studying their national language, history, and literature at school but also by unconsciously learning the meaning of their nation while enjoying popular cultural texts such as films, novels, and television programs at home.

Nationalism, ideology, and narrative are closely related. A narrative is "an ordered account created out of disordered material or experience" (Abrams 2010, 106). Without creating a narrative or choosing and bringing certain events together into a coherent whole, it is difficult to view them as experience. Narrative, a mode of representation, portrays events (or actions) and characters (or entities) involved in the events in a certain manner (e.g., Abbott 2008, 13–20; Herman 2009, 17), "shap[ing] and defin[ing] our reality for us in ways that might be limiting, showing us only a version of events, and excluding the experience of many" (Thomas 2016, 7). In short, narrative involves arbitrarily choosing and sequencing events, representing them along with their characters, constructing a reality, and thereby influencing how people view the world and themselves. Likewise, nationalism as an ideology shapes people's worldview and identity by offering a certain way of understanding the nation and its members. Narrative is one strategy with which ideology operates (Thompson 1990, 61–62). Selecting and ordering certain events and people from a particular perspective, national history narrated in primary or secondary school textbooks is a prime example of nationalism as a narrative as well as an ideology. Combining two narrative forms—history and television drama—, historical television drama can create a certain idea of the nation and educate people about it in an accessible way.

Memory, Narrative, and Historical Television Drama

Memories can be "held" by an individual or by a group (Halbwachs 1992). Referring to the latter, sociologists tend to use the term "collective memory" or "social memory," whereas scholars in media studies, literature, and cultural history are more likely to use the term "cultural memory" (Rigney 2016, 66). As opposed to collective memory research that pays more attention to the roles of individuals and institutions engaging in memory construction, cultural memory research focuses on closely reading cultural artifacts and practices by taking into account "the role of culture in the production of collective memory" and thereby attempts to answer the question of "how culture mediates collective memory and gives it substance, form, and social reach"

(Rigney 2016, 67). Although cultural remembering occurs on several levels (e.g., nation, ethnicity, gender, religion), it is more political and ideological when cultural texts mediate national level memories.

Memory is concerned not only with the past but also with versions of the past seen from the present because it involves remembering, which necessarily takes place in the present (Halbwachs 1992, 46–51). Broadly memory is "an umbrella term for all those processes of a biological, medial, or social nature which relate past and present (and future) in sociocultural contexts" (Erll 2011, 7). Memory constructs collective identity and exercises political power because it brings different times (past and present) and different peoples together by inviting them to join the repetitive act of remembering and forgetting (Assmann 2011, 2–3).

Thus, memory is crucial to construct a nation, which involves forgetting some things about the past while remembering others (Renan 2011 [1882]) and requires a shared identity and culture. People become nationals by learning and remembering certain incidents as national events and certain people as national heroes/heroines, and yet what they remember and how they remember depend on present social, political and economic contexts. For this process, narrative is indispensable because "memory itself is dependent on the capacity for narrative" (Abbott 2008, 3). Both memory and narrative play key roles in constructing and thereby understanding identity and the past. Catherine Riessman (2008) argues that "narrative constitutes past experience at the same time as it provides ways for individuals to make sense of the past" (8). Understanding who we are as a nation involves remembering certain events as the national past, which necessitates choosing some events and characters over others, sequencing them into a coherent story, and depicting them in a certain way—narrative.

Television, characterized by its accessibility, is an important vehicle for this. Although newer media technologies including VCR, DVD, the internet, and smart phones have challenged television, "the supposed 'death of TV' is actually myth rather than a reality" because people keep watching television programs using other kinds of media (Bignell 2013, 282). Television drama, due to its narrativity, serves as "a primary generator and the most everyday source of such [identity] narratives in contemporary culture" (Thornham and Purvis 2005, 28). By watching television dramas, people learn what it means to be, for example, a woman, a man, gay, poor, and a national. Furthermore, television is a key site for history to be constructed and consumed (de Groot 2016), and historical television drama, which costs more for production and is, therefore, regarded as the most prestigious kind of programming, usually is involved in producing national memories (Bignell 2013, 20). The two drama series about Japanese American and Japanese Brazilian historical experiences broadcast in Japan's major television stations are two such examples.

TWO PEOPLES OF JAPANESE DESCENT AND TWO DRAMA SERIES

Japanese Immigration to the Americas

Most Japanese immigration to the Americas took place between the late nineteenth century and the first half of the twentieth century. Dismantling the Tokugawa samurai government that lasted for about 250 years, in 1868, Meiji Restoration began transforming Japan into a modern nation-state with a constitutional monarchy. Limited employment, inflation, and heavy taxes caused by the government's militarization, industrialization, and a series of wars drove especially farmers to seek opportunities outside Japan (Iino 2000, 13–17). Large-scale immigration to Hawaii began in the late 1880s following the Japanese government's legalization of ordinary Japanese people going abroad. After the United States annexed Hawaii in 1898, Japanese immigrants moved from Hawaii to the U.S. Pacific Coast, seeking better employment opportunities.[1] In Hawaii, they worked mostly as contract laborers on sugar cane plantations, while those on the mainland were employed as railroad workers, field hands, servants, and service providers in restaurants and small businesses including brothels (Iino 2000, 17–22; Ichioka 1988).

The number of Japanese immigrants on the U.S. mainland rapidly increased until the U.S. government enacted the "Gentlemen's Agreement" in 1907–1908 to restrict Japanese immigration against the backdrop of the "yellow peril" discourse that viewed Asian immigrants as culturally inassimilable, cheap laborers who were stealing jobs from white people, or in short, a menace to the white nation (Spickard 2009, 29–33). Unlike the 1882 Chinese Exclusion Act that banned Chinese immigration, the U.S. government adopted a more nuanced tactic to achieve the same end by making it appear that Japan would "voluntarily" bar its nationals from immigrating to the United States (Ichioka 1988, 69–72). Japan's defeat of Russia in the Russo-Japanese War (1904–1905) intensified the "yellow peril" discourse and anti-Japanese sentiments that led to the agreement, but it also provided Japan with a face-saving opportunity (Iino 2000, 29–30). Until the 1924 Immigration Act stopped Japanese immigration, however, the Japanese immigrant population in the United States continued to rise because wives and children of Japanese immigrants were still allowed to enter.

The 1907–1908 agreement shifted the flow of Japanese migration to Brazil. Brazil accepted Japanese immigrants, given the serious labor shortage on plantations following the abolition of slavery in 1888. Although Brazilian authorities were reluctant to receive nonwhite immigrants, the Japanese government persuaded them by claiming that its nationals were the "whites" of Asia (Lesser 2003, 5). Japan's rise as an imperial power particularly after the

Russo-Japanese War was also helpful in reinforcing the image of Japan as a "Westernized" nation (Lesser 2007, 5). Japanese immigrants worked mostly as contract laborers on coffee plantations, planning to return to Japan after making enough money to secure their families' future. Nevertheless, the vast majority of them ended up permanently settling in Brazil, owning land in *colônias* (colonies) or ethnic agricultural enclaves in which they grew cash crops such as cotton, rice, and sugar (Masterson 2004, 77–79).

Unlike Japanese immigration to Hawaii and North America, which was undertaken by private agencies, the Japanese government was much more directly involved in Japanese immigration to Brazil. The government provided loans to new emigrants, funding travel costs, purchasing real estate, constructing the infrastructure for Japanese colonies through state companies, and even selecting crops for them to grow (Endoh 2009, 170–86). Japan's Brazilian migration, called *ishokumin* or migration-colonization, was part of its imperial and colonial projects in which Japan sought to expand its economic and political domain not only in Asia but also globally (Endoh 2009, 191). Thus officials in the Ministry of Education ensured that the settlers of children learned the same curricula as children in Imperial Japan, by sending teachers to Brazil or checking the curriculum and textbooks used in the schools (Endoh 2009, 181). Expected to "outshine the Japanese in Japan" by the government (Endoh 2009, 186) and becoming a minority in Brazil, Japanese settlers stressed emperor worship as the central expression of Japaneseness even more than the Japanese in Japan did (Maeyama 1979, 594).

Two Television Drama Series

The two drama series, *Haru to Natsu* (*Haru and Natsu*) and *99 nen no ai* (*99 Years of Love*), tell the story of a Japanese family who immigrated to Brazil and the United States, respectively. *Haru and Natsu* (5 episodes; 390 minutes) was the first major television drama series to feature Japanese Brazilian historical experiences. It was broadcast for five consecutive nights from October 2 to 6, 2005 on NHK, Japan's state-funded television station, attracting a large audience with a viewer rating of 18 percent, the highest rating among the television programs aired that week (Video Research Ltd. n.d.a). The drama *99 Years of Love* (5 episodes; 570 minutes) aired from November 3 to 7, 2010 on TBS, a major commercial television station, which can be viewed in most prefectures in Japan. Its average viewer rating was 15 percent (Oricon 2010).

The two *Nikkeijin* groups have not been treated equally in the genre of television drama. In contrast to the dearth of drama series portraying Japanese Brazilian historical experiences, one drama series featuring those of Japanese

Americans has been produced each decade since the 1970s.[2] Except for *99 Years of Love*, Japan's national public broadcaster NHK created all the drama series about the two groups, demonstrating the close connection between constructing memories about *Nikkeijin* and constructing Japanese nationalism. Although several television dramas that included Japanese American and Japanese Brazilian historical and contemporary characters has been broadcast after 2000, *Haru and Natsu* and *99 Years of Love* were the only serial dramas.[3]

The two drama series are original stories authored by a popular drama script writer, Hashida Sugako. She has written numerous television dramas including the NHK morning drama series *Oshin* (1983–1984) that attracted an average audience rating of 52.1 percent, the highest rating recorded for a television drama in Japan (Video Research Ltd. n.d.b). *Haru and Natsu* is the story of two sisters, Haru Takakura who migrated to Brazil with her family and Natsu who had to remain in Japan with an uncle's family due to her illness. Their father Chuji went to Brazil in the mid-1930s because as the second son of a poor farmer in Hokkaido, he was ineligible to inherit the family's land. The drama narrates the sister's separate lives in the Brazil and Japan from the 1930s to 2005. The drama *99 Years of Love* has a similar narrative structure. The story starts with Chokichi Hiramatsu, the second son of a poor farmer in Shimane, immigrating to the United States to support his family in the 1910s. Covering the century from the 1910s to 2010, the drama describes lives of Chokichi, his picture bride Tomo, and their four children who are separated between the United States and Japan shortly before Japan's attack on Pearl Harbor in 1941.

I analyze how the two *Nikkeijin* groups' historical experiences are remembered in the two drama series to construct Japaneseness by examining events and characters—two key elements of narrative. First, I pay attention to narrative strategies for main characters adopted in the two narratives because for the construction of Japaneseness, the characters necessarily play significant roles. Then I examine Japaneseness constructed in the two drama series by focusing on main characters and historical events selected to depict *Nikkeijin* and Japanese experiences.

NARRATIVE STRATEGIES FOR NATIONAL MEMORY CONSTRUCTION

Both drama series adopt two narrative strategies to use Japanese American and Japanese Brazilian historical experiences for the construction of Japanese national memory. Firstly, their main characters are first-generation Japanese immigrants who are still alive at the time of their broadcast in 2005 and 2010.

Secondly, both series overlap and blur the experiences (i.e., events) of the two *Nikkeijin* groups and those of the Japanese in the first half of the twentieth century. The two strategies clearly show the two dramas' involvement in constructing Japanese national memories, relating the past (i.e., the first half of the twentieth century) with the present (i.e., early twenty-first century) and bringing different peoples (i.e., *Nikkeijin* and Japanese of the past and the present) together.

First-generation Immigrants as Main Characters

The first strategy is necessary to make the stories more relevant to the Japanese audience. The dominant idea of Japaneseness has been premised on "equivalency and mutual implications among land, people (i.e., race), culture, and language" (Befu 1993, 116). In other words, people are recognized as "fully" Japanese when they are born to two Japanese parents and grow up in Japan, immersed in Japanese culture and language. Thus, first-generation *Nikkeijin* who spend many years outside of Japan are considered as "less" Japanese, but they are "more" Japanese than later generations. The Japanese government's attitude toward *Nikkeijin* manifests this idea of Japaneseness: while first-generation emigrants are Japanese, their Japaneseness decreases with each generation (Roth 2002, 25–26). The 1990 revision of the Immigration Control Act enabled *Nikkeijin*—but not other foreign nationals—to work without restrictions in Japan, but only to the third generation.

Moreover, both drama series employ a narrative structure in which the main characters recall their past lives at the present time after 2000—a process of relating past to present. The stories develop as the main characters in their 1970s meet for the first time in several decades and narrate to each other their past lives in Brazil or the United States and Japan. In *Haru and Natsu,* having first-generation characters play leading roles is not difficult since Japanese immigration to Brazil peaked in the 1930s. The story starts with Haru's return to Japan in 2005 for the first time in seventy years to find her sister Natsu and unfolds as the sisters reflect on their lives in Brazil and Japan.

However, in *99 Years of Love*, the main characters have to be second-generation Japanese Americans because the peak of Japanese immigration to the United States was one generation earlier than to Brazil and also because Japanese immigration stopped after the U.S. government passed the 1924 Immigration Act. Yet second-generation Japanese Americans are generally more familiar with the English language and American culture, and their identities are more hybrid and transnational (e.g., Ichioka 2006; Takahashi 1997). In order to include a first-generation immigrant as a main character and avoid contending with the more dynamic identities of second-generation Japanese Americans, *99 Years of Love* brings in a first-generation Japanese immigrant as the bride of Chokichi's first son, Ichiro. Ichiro's wife, Shinobu, comes to the United States to study at the university in Seattle that Ichiro attends. With their son Ken-Yamato, she survives Ichiro who dies serving as a U.S. soldier during World War II. The drama begins in 2010 when Shinobu and Ichiro's younger brother Jiro meet his sister Sachi in Seattle for the first time in seventy years. Sachi, who was sent back to Japan before the internment, has lived in Japan since then. The story develops as they describe their lives in the United States and Japan.

Overlapping and Blurring Historical Experiences of *Nikkeijin* and Japanese

The two drama series realize the second strategy by separating the main characters between Brazil or the United States and Japan and describing their lives as "the narrative of suffering and overcoming" (Roth 2002, 31). This is an ideological narrative that Japanese politicians often used until the 1980s to insist that "Japanese and *Nikkeijin*, at opposite ends of the world from each other, were deep down one and the same" (Roth 2002, 34). This narrative corresponds to a rags-to-riches story in which both Japanese and *Nikkeijin* similarly attain a success by struggling through and overcoming World War II. The Japanese rebuilt Japan into an economic superpower, recovering it from the political, economic, and cultural turmoil following Japan's defeat in 1945; Japanese Americans and Japanese Brazilians have become the "model minority" (e.g., Lesser 2007, xxix; Spickard 2009, 156–57), conquering socioeconomic and racial/ethnic obstacles especially during the war and raising their socioeconomic status in Brazil and the United States. Japanese and *Nikkeijin*'s hardships and achievements are depicted not simply as similar and inseparable but as *Japanese* experiences (i.e., "one and the same").

In *Haru and Natsu*, Haru Takakura, the elder sister, moves to Brazil with her parents and two brothers at the age of nine in 1934. The Takakuras endure poverty and hard physical labor first as indentured laborers on a coffee plantation, and then as peasant farmers. They flee from the plantation after one of Haru's two brothers dies of malaria and realizing that as indentured servants, they will never be able to save money. They move to an American-owned farm and grow cotton. However, just when they have saved enough money to return to Japan, they are evicted from the farm due to Japan's attack on Pearl Harbor. Their life finally stabilizes after Haru marries Takuya, who establishes a successful flower farm. Likewise, Natsu, left alone in Japan with her uncle when she was seven, goes through a series of challenges. Abused by her aunt, she runs away from the uncle's house and is adopted by an old cowherd who teaches her milking and cheese-making. Yet he dies several years later and she is forced to make a living by herself. After the war, she opens a cookie factory that grows into a large confectionary company.

In *99 Years of Love*, Chokichi migrates to the United States in 1910. Initially working as a field hand, later he buys a farm and makes it prosperous with his wife Tomo and their four children. However, a few months before the outbreak of the Pacific War in 1941, Chokichi sends his two daughters, Shizu and Sachi, back to Japan to protect them from anti-Japanese violence. The rest of the family lose the farm and are forced into a concentration camp in Manzanar in 1942. There they suffer from two additional losses: Ichiro's death in the U.S. army and Chokichi's suicide upon hearing of Japan's surrender in 1945. Tomo, Jiro, and Shinobu later reclaim their family farm and expand it. Meanwhile, Shizu and Sachi are separated and taken in by Chokichi's two sisters in Hiroshima and Okinawa. Their classmates bully them as American at school and their aunts deprive them of food and force them to work. Shizu survives Hiroshima's atomic bombing and Sachi the Battle of Okinawa, but their aunts' families do not. Sachi reunites with Shizu in Hiroshima after the end of World War II, but soon Shizu dies from injuries that she sustained in the blast. Sachi is adopted by a couple who lost their sons in the war. She learns dressmaking from the foster mother and later attains fame as a fashion designer.

CONSTRUCTING JAPANESENESS

With the same ideological narrative strategies for memory construction, the two series construct different meanings of Japaneseness. The dramas use the two *Nikkeijin* groups in distinct ways by spotlighting particular historical events and by contrasting and equating them with the Japanese in Japan.

Japanese as Nationalistic and Conservative

Haru and Natsu highlights the strife between the *kachi-gumi* (victory group) who refuse to acknowledge Japan's defeat in World War II and the *make-gumi* (defeat group) who accept it. By featuring the *kachi-gumi*, the drama represents *Nikkeijin* in Brazil as nationalistic and conservative. The *kachi-gumi* was most influential in the immediate postwar period. *Kachi-gumi* members terrorized *make-gumi* by attacking them and destroying their property. Between March and September 1946, sixteen people were assassinated, and several hundreds were arrested (Lesser 2003, 11–12). However, they were marginalized by the 1950s as Japanese Brazilians ascended to the middle class and Japanese immigration resumed in 1952 after Japan's recovery of sovereignty (Lesser 2003, 12).

The movement occurred because most of these Japanese immigrants lived in isolated, rural Japanese colonies where the circulation of Brazilian newspapers was limited while Japanese language newspapers were banned (Endoh 2009, 33; Lesser 2003, 11). Under the "Brazilianization" campaign that President Getúlio Vargas undertook in 1937 to reduce foreign influence in Brazil, all foreign language schools and press were closed; even speaking foreign languages in public was banned (Endoh 2009, 32–34; Lesser 2003, 9–10; Masterson 2004, 130–34). As anti-Japanese sentiments intensified after the Vargas regime cut diplomatic ties with Japan in 1942 by joining the Allied powers, Japanese Brazilians responded by becoming more "Japanese" and establishing ultra-nationalist secret societies, which became *kachi-gumi* after World War II (Lesser 2003, 10).

In the drama, Chuji becomes extremely nationalistic after the Takakuras' eviction from the farm after the Pearl Harbor attack. He joins the *kachi-gumi* and sets fire to the property of the Nakayamas, an affluent Brazilianized Japanese immigrant family. In Episode 3, Chuji expresses his hostility against the Nakayamas: "They are no longer Japanese! They are living in a Western house, eating Brazilian food, speaking in Portuguese, and making money by trading with Americans!" In a Japanese association meeting, Chuji and other *kachi-gumi* members gets into a fight with *make-gumi* people by reiterating the Japanese military government's wartime ideological cliché: "Japan was not defeated. Japan is a divine country. Japan cannot have lost the war! How dare you call yourself Japanese [*soredemo nihonjin ka*]?" (Episode 4).

Chuji embodies prewar Japanese nationalism associated with emperor worship and excessive national loyalty. After his first son died of malaria, Chuji sends his second son Minoru back to Japan, not wanting to lose another son in Brazil. Minoru dies in World War II, fighting as a *kamikaze* pilot. When a Japanese military officer visits the Takakuras in Brazil to inform them of Minoru's death, Chuji tells his wife Shizu not to grieve by insisting: "Minoru died honorably as a child of the emperor. We should celebrate Minoru's death. Minoru, you did a great job!" (Episode 4).

In addition, Chuji's death is linked to the marriage of Crown Prince Akihito in 1959. Chuji dies after watching newsreel footage of the marriage that includes scenes of Tokyo's reconstructed and booming streetscape. After watching the film, Chuji has an exchange with Kotaro Nakayama, the patriarch of the family that he had vilified:

Chuji: Japan has won the war after all. Japan was certainly devastated by U.S. bombing. An atomic bomb was dropped in Hiroshima. But Japan has won by working hard after the war. If not, the emperor family would not survive.

Kotaro: Japan has made such a great recovery in fourteen years after the end of the war. Today watching the news, I really felt Japan's resurgence. I could not feel happier.

Chuji: I'm so happy! You have finally understood me. The Japanese are a great people [*minzoku*]! (Episode 5)

Happily coming back home, Chuji dies after offering a cup of sake to the Buddhist altar that enshrines Minoru and saying: "Minoru, you defended Japan. I am very proud of you" (Episode 5).

Contrasting the Japanese in Brazil and Japan

Natsu, representing the Japanese in Japan is portrayed in a contrastive manner. Not touched by the nationalist ideology of the 1930s and 1940s, she cares little about worshipping the emperor and just wants the war to end. During the war, she offers the milk that she produces to the military authority to protect her cows from being confiscated. When a friend says that she is doing a great thing for Japan, she responds angrily: "I'm not doing this for the country! Who the hell would be happy when the government takes away all the milk?" (Episode 4). Hearing the war has ended, she yells with joy as she can make cheese again without being forced to give up the milk.

Nationalism is not simply a discourse about the nation but "a gendered discourse" (McClintock 1996, 261). If Chuji embodies the male aspect of prewar Japanese nationalism, Haru personifies its female aspect and Natsu serves as their counter character. Haru is a dutiful daughter and wife who puts her father and husband's wishes ahead of her own. She refuses an offer of marriage from the son of the Nakayamas because of Chuji's opposition. Instead she marries Takuya, a childhood friend who worked for a while in the same coffee plantation, and helps him establish a flower farm. However, Natsu, independent, strong-willed, and ambitious, is not a "traditional" woman. She becomes pregnant by a Japanese American soldier and raises their child alone. She refuses to follow the child's father to the United States because she is afraid of losing touch with her family in Brazil and because she does not want to give up her cookie factory. Later she marries a business-savvy man so that she can expand her business.

Contrasting Japanese Brazilians (Chuji and Haru) with the Japanese in Japan (Natsu), the series revives the prewar meaning of Japaneseness characterized by emperor worship, excessive national loyalty, and a strong patriarchy. Haru and Natsu are contrasted against each other in terms of gender and nation. Haru becomes involved in flower business to support her husband's dream, whereas Natsu enters confectionary business because that is what she wants to do. Haru and Takuya grow chrysanthemums, the symbol of the

Japanese imperial family, whereas the products that Natsu has worked with since her childhood are all Western commodities—milk, cheese, and cookies. Furthermore, although both Haru and Natsu's lives follow the narrative of suffering and overcoming, the drama portrays Natsu more negatively as a lonely woman with an unfaithful husband and two self-centered sons. The story ends with Natsu on the brink of bankruptcy, selling her company and moving to Brazil to be with Haru who lives happily with her children and grandchildren. In short, the series represents Japanese Brazilians as more nationalistic, conservative, happier, and thus "better" Japanese than the Japanese in Japan. However, having Japanese Brazilians play double roles of the Other and the Self, the drama suggests that the Japanese in Japan should emulate Japanese Brazilians, who are "deep down one and the same."

Japanese as Victims

In *99 Years of Love*, three historical events represent both Japanese Americans and the Japanese as victims: the internment of Japanese Americans during World War II, the Battle of Okinawa, and the atomic bombing of Hiroshima. Following the Pearl Harbor attack in December 1941, President Franklin D. Roosevelt issued Executive Order 9066 on February 19, 1942, authorizing the forcible removal and relocation of approximately 110,000 Japanese Americans living on the Pacific Coast of the United States. Stripped of their homes and property, they were sent to ten concentration camps located in harsh natural environments such as deserts or swamps. Yet, in Hawaii, about 150,000 Japanese Americans, comprising one-third of its population, were not interned (Spickard 2009, 109). The series about Japanese American historical experiences broadcast in the past usually focus on the U.S. mainland, not Hawaii.[4]

The drama portrays Japanese Americans as victims of white racism. The internment is the pinnacle of the racism that the Hiramatsus endure. Internment scenes—how they are forced to give up their property and sent first to a foul-smelling livestock barn and then to a barbed-wired camp in the desert under armed guards—depicts the victimization of Japanese Americans. In addition to the internment scenes, the drama is peppered with scenes of the main characters confronting overt racism. For example, at school, a white student insults Ichiro who helps her from slipping and picks up her book from the ground by calling him "Jap" and saying: "Don't touch it! You are filthy" (Episode 2). Ichiro meets Shinobu when he saves her from white male students who call her "Jap" and attempt to sexually assault her (Episode 2). He also saves his sister Shizu who is dragged into a barn by white men who try to rape her immediately after the Pearl Harbor attack (Episode 2). On their honeymoon, Ichiro and Shinobu are denied service in restaurants and hotels in Seattle even though he is on leave from the U.S. military; Seattle's downtown is filled with signs saying "No Japs and dogs allowed" or "Bye bye Japs" (Episode 4).

Likewise, the drama depicts the victimization of the Japanese in Japan by referring to the Battle of Okinawa and the atomic bombing of Hiroshima. Okinawa and Hiroshima are powerful symbols of the Japanese as war victims and of Japan's subordination to the United States. The Battle of Okinawa between April and June 1945 was the last and largest Pacific island battle of World War II. More than 200,000 people (approximately 190,000 Okinawans and Japanese and 12,000 Americans) including 100,000 Okinawan civilians were estimated to have been killed. Okinawa was placed under U.S. military control after the end of the war and was a U.S. territory until its return to Japan in 1972. Today about 74 percent of the U.S. military bases in Japan are in Okinawa Prefecture, occupying about 10 percent of its land (Okinawa Prefectural Peace Memorial Museum n.d.). Hiroshima is well known around the world as the city where the United States dropped the first atomic bomb on August 6, 1945. The bomb killed approximately 140,000 people, about 40 percent of the city population and demolished almost every building in a two–kilometer radius (Hiroshima City n.d.).

Depicting the Japanese in Japan as war victims, the drama obscures the role as victimizers who caused massive damages to people in East and South East Asia by invading, and colonizing there, killing them, and exploiting them as labor force, soldiers, and "comfort women." It also masks the fact that the Japanese government exacerbated the number of casualties in the Battle of Okinawa by continuing the losing battle and sacrificing the Okinawan people. Okinawans are an ethnic minority whose kingdom was officially annexed by Japan in 1879. Since then the Japanese government has assimilated them as Japanese and simultaneously subordinated them as "less Japanese" (e.g., Oguma 1998). The drama sets up the situation that Chokichi's two sisters move to Okinawa and Hiroshima for marriage and then take in his two daughters, Shizu and Sachi, there in order to opportunistically incorporate into the story the two places and the two significant historical events. And because the drama fails to describe the asymmetrical relationship between Okinawans and the Japanese, Okinawans' heavy wartime casualties are whitewashed as Japanese ones in the same manner that the Japanese government's assimilation policies attempted to made Okinawans into Japanese.

Japanese as a People Accepted by White Americans

In *99 Years of Love*, Japanese Americans and the Japanese in Japan are portrayed not simply as victims but as people who nevertheless remain loyal to the United States and eventually gain acceptance from white Americans. The main historical event for this representation is the 1944 rescue of a trapped U.S. battalion in France by the 442nd Regimental Combat Team consisting entirely of Japanese American soldiers. Racial minority soldiers usually trained and served separately from their white counterparts since racial segregation was the norm in the U.S. military then (e.g., Osher 2000, 585). The 442nd fought fierce battles to liberate French and Italian towns from German occupation. Best-known for their heroic action that resulted in 800 casualties to rescue 211 men of a Texas battalion in the Vosges Mountains, France, the 442nd is the most decorated unit for its size with the highest casualty rate in U.S. military history (e.g., Niiya 2001, 164; Okihiro 2013, 54).

The War Department created the 442nd to counter Japan's accusation of U.S. racism and to present itself as a democratic leader that valued freedom and equality (e.g., Niiya 2001, 163). The Japanese American Citizens League (JACL) was also involved in the creation of this regiment. The JACL, an organization established in 1930 by second-generation Japanese Americans, stressed loyalty and assimilation to white America and enthusiastically cooperated with the U.S. government to incarcerate Japanese Americans and encourage them to volunteer for military service (e.g., Spickard 2009, 125–27). The War Department and the War Relocation Authority administered questionnaires to the interned Japanese Americans in 1943, following the JACL's petition to President Roosevelt in which they called for reinstating the draft for Japanese American citizens (e.g., Collins 2001, 260). Responding to the call for volunteers, about 10,000 Japanese Americans in Hawaii answered, whereas only 1,200 mainlanders did, despite that the numbers of eligible male citizens in the two places were comparable (Fujitani 2011, 191–92).[5] The disparity derived from different kinds of treatment that the two groups had received from the U.S. government: Most of the mainlanders had been interned before joining the military while those in Hawaii were not.

The questionnaire included two "loyalty questions" that asked them whether they would be willing to serve in the U.S. military and swear unqualified allegiance to the United States by renouncing loyalty to Japan.[6] Their affirmative answers to the questions made them become eligible to leave the camp or to be drafted.

In the drama, Ichiro is drafted after answering "yes" to the loyalty questions. His mother Tomo asks her two sons to answer "no" because she does not want them to be drafted and fight against Japan. Ichiro explains his decision:

> We have been called "Jap" and insulted. But I can serve as an American soldier by answering "yes" to the questions. When I go to the war, I want to show our pride as *Nikkeijin*. I want to make Americans accept us. I will never let them call

us "Jap." I answered these questions "yes" because I thought about my family and other *Nikkeijin* and wished such a day would come. I will defend the United States, the place where my parents have decided to settle. (Episode 4)

Ichiro dies while serving as a 442nd solider in the rescue mission of the Texas battalion in France. Before carrying out the mission, Ichiro speaks in front of the exhausted and demoralized 442nd soldiers after having fought a series of difficult battles incessantly:

> We are American soldiers, so we can't disobey the order. If we have to do it, it is our responsibility to show that we can do what other American soldiers can't do. We can do it because we have the Japanese spirit [*Yamato damashii*]. We are American but different from them. Let's show that we can rescue them because we are Japanese American. Let's show that we fight for America more than they do. (Episode 4)

With their morale restored by the speech, the soldiers chant "Go for broke! Go for broke!" the motto of the 442nd and also the title of a top-earning 1951 Hollywood movie about them.

The notion of hyperidentification (Fujitani 2011, 187) explains Ichiro's words and actions. Modern nationalism, intersecting with racism, simultaneously includes and excludes racial and ethnic minorities. The universalist discourses of U.S. nationalism imply that everybody has an equal chance to become American and realize the "American Dream" or raise socioeconomic status through educational and occupational achievements. However, contradicting this message, the exclusionary discourses of U.S. racism tell minorities that they have a lesser chance due to their racial and ethnic backgrounds, which cannot be overcome by individual efforts. Hyperidentification is "one reasonable response to the contradictory ways in which national subjects are interpellated as both equal and less than the same" (Fujitani 2011, 187). Hyperidentification occurs when racial and ethnic minorities make extraordinary efforts to gain acceptance from the national majority group and attain full membership in the national community. The 442nd's heroism and sacrifice does not indicate the trait of Japanese Americans but their response to the intersecting and contradictory discourses of U.S. nationalism and racism.

However, the twist is that the drama equates trying hard to be accepted as American with stressing Japanese identity. Ichiro believes that Japanese Americans can become more American than white Americans because they are *Nikkeijin* or have the Japanese spirit. That is, becoming more Japanese means becoming more American. Japanese first-generation immigrant intellectuals used this logic to rationalize their unnaturalizable status and the necessity of assimilation to American society (Azuma 2005) as well as differentiate themselves from Chinese immigrants (Ichioka 1988, 176–96). Although this logic is a diasporic response to their experiences of exclusion and marginalization as a racial minority, Japanese nationalism can easily appropriate it for itself by redefining it as the strength of their loyalty to Japan.

The Japanese in Japan are also depicted as a people accepted by Americans. The opening scene centers on Ichiro Suzuki, a Japanese professional baseball player. After a notable eight-year career in Japan, he played for the Seattle Mariners in Major League Baseball (MLB) (2001–2012 and 2018–2019), the New York Yankees (2012–2014), and the Miami Marlins (2015–2017). As a ten-time MLB All-Star (2001–2010) and a ten-time Gold Glove Award winner (2001–2010), he was the most successful Japanese baseball player exported to the United States. The series starts with the scene in which Shinobu and Jiro meet Sachi at Safeco Field, the home stadium of the Mariners in 2010 for the first time after being separated in 1941. Sachi visits Seattle with her grandson who wants to see Ichiro play. Sitting in the stadium packed with American baseball fans cheering for Ichiro, Shinobu and Jiro have the following conversation:

Shinobu: Ichiro is a hero for all Americans!
Jiro: I can't believe they cheer for a Japanese. What a difference from the time when we were younger.
Shinobu: This is so unbelievable. I still remember they had detested and insulted us as "Jap." (Episode 1)

Despite Ichiro's long absence from Japan, the mainstream Japanese media has portrayed Ichiro as "a hero who is still loyal to Japanese traditions, and as a symbol of Japan's brighter future" (Nakamura 2005, 471). Moreover, the Japanese media's "recurring references to Ichiro being accepted by the American people" indicate "an evident 'desire for approval'" from them (473). Since the MLB is considered the best baseball league in the world, for baseball players in Japan, joining an MLB team is the pinnacle of a career. Ichiro, who not only has become an MLB player but also proved a Japanese could play better than many American MLB players, is a powerful representation of the Japanese in Japan as a people who are respected and admired by Americans. The series engages in memory construction by connecting the two Ichiros—Ichiro Suzuki (i.e., the present) and Ichiro Hiramatsu (i.e., the past)—and representing the Japanese as a people who have overcome hardships and been accepted by Americans in line with the narrative of suffering and overcoming.

CONCLUSION

Using Japanese Americans and Japanese Brazilians and representing them as diasporas, the two drama series created different meanings of Japaneseness while making Japan's cultural memories of World War II. Both series appropriated *Nikkeijin*'s historical experiences for Japanese national memory construction by employing the two narrative strategies: having as main characters first-generation Japanese immigrants who are still alive after 2000, and overlapping and blurring *Nikkeijin* and Japanese histories. However, the two *Nikkeijin* groups were used differently for the construction of Japaneseness. On the one hand, comparing Japanese Brazilians with the Japanese in Japan and treating the former as "better" Japanese, *Haru and Natsu* revived the prewar meaning of Japaneseness closely tied to emperor worship and excessive national loyalty. On the other hand, *99 Years of Love* equated Japanese Americans with the Japanese in Japan as victims who gain recognition and acceptance from the victimizer. The former exoticized Japanese Brazilians by highlighting and celebrating their excessive nationalism, whereas the latter emphasized the continuity or identification between Japanese Americans and the Japanese in Japan. Put simply, Japanese Brazilians are who the Japanese in Japan *should become* but Japanese Americans are those who the Japanese in Japan *have become*.

The different uses of the two peoples are tied to the difference in their Otherness. The United States has been the most significant Other and also the ideal Self that postwar Japan has desired to become (Yoshimi 2007). Having led the Allied occupation of Japan (1945–1952) and still having 131 military-related facilities and areas across Japan (Ministry of Defense 2019), the United States has had a tremendous political, economic, and sociocultural impact on Japanese people's lives and mind since 1945. Like *Nikkeijin*, the United States is also the Other *and* the Self in constructing Japaneseness, but Brazil is predominantly the Other.

The drama series used the difference to construct Japaneseness in the era of globalization in which national borders are eroded, and, therefore, nationalism becomes more intensified (e.g., Giddens 1994, 5) and still is expected to incorporate some kind of "globalness." Japaneseness was constructed in a more nationalistic and simultaneously global manner, for which using Japanese Americans and Japanese Brazilians as diasporas was useful. These uses of *Nikkeijin* for Japanese national memory construction are problematic because they homogenize and essentialize Japaneseness by neglecting their more complex identities and feelings toward their ancestral homeland. The meanings of Japaneseness constructed in the dramas are also problematic: They appropriate historical experiences of not only *Nikkeijin* but also Okinawans as Japanese ones, gloss over Japan's colonial past, and reiterate its postwar relationship with the United States as "America's model minority nation" (Fujitani 2011, 211). By becoming America's "capitalist and 'almost, but not quite' younger sibling" (210–11) under the Cold War, Japan was spared to confront its colonial and wartime responsibilities, which still hinders Japan from building conscientious relationships with other Asian countries. Remembering Japanese Americans and Japanese Brazilians is indispensable considering that a substantial number of Japanese Brazilians have settled in Japan and an increasing number of Japanese Americans are creating transnational connections to Japan. However, that must be done not to serve Japanese nationalism but rather to transform Japaneseness in a way that acknowledges the diverse identities of *Nikkeijin* and ethnic minorities in Japan and rectifies Japan's postwar relationship with the United States.

NOTES

1. Between 1901 and 1907, about 38,000 out of 42,457 Japanese people who were admitted to the United States came via Hawaii and settled largely on the Pacific coast, especially California (Ichioka 1988, 51–52).
2. The four drama series are: *Amerika monogatari* (*An American Story*) broadcasted in 1979 (4 episodes; 316 minutes), *Sanga moyu* (*Two Homelands*) in 1984 (51 episodes, 2,289 minutes), *Etorofu harukanari* (*The Far Island Iturup*) in 1993 (4 episodes, 476 minutes), and *99 Years of Love* in 2010.
3. According to the Drama Database website (http://www.tvdrama-db.com/), five TV dramas have featured Japanese Brazilian characters and eight had Japanese American characters between 2000 and 2019. Most dramas were one-time special dramas.
4. Only the 1979 drama series *An American Story* portrays the lives of Japanese immigrants in Hawaii.
5. The numbers of eligible men were approximately 23,000 on the mainland and 25,000 in Hawaii (Fujitani 2011, 191–92).
6. Question 27 asked: "Are you willing to serve in the armed forces of the United States on combat duty, wherever ordered?" and Question 28 asked: "Will you swear unqualified allegiance to the United States of America and faithfully defend the United States from any and all attacks by foreign and domestic forces, and forswear any form of allegiance or disobedience to the Japanese Emperor, or any other foreign government, power, or organization?"

Chapter 4

Using China and Korea for Japaneseness

"Hate Books," History, and the Grammar of Japanese Racialized Discourse

In tandem with the rise of far-right groups' racist demonstrations targeting people of Asian—especially Korean—descent in the early 2010s (see chapter 1), nonfiction paperback books that denigrated Korea/Koreans and to a lesser extent China/Chinese by discussing historical and contemporary political, economic, social, and cultural issues became popular and turned into a literary genre called "*heito bon* (hate book)." In 2014, two "hate books" targeting South Korea/South Koreans, *Bōkanron* (Stupid South Korea) (Murotani 2013) and *Chikanron* (Shameful South Korea) (Lee 2014), reached bestseller lists, each selling more than 200,000 copies (Nippan 2014; Tohan 2014).[1] It is estimated that more than 200 "hate books" were published between 2013 and 2014 when the popularity of this genre was at its peak (Oizumi et al. 2015, 3). Although this genre primarily attracted men over the age of forty (*Nikkan SPA* 2017), its impact cannot be underestimated. These books, which are also published by mainstream publishes and are available in regular bookstores and public libraries, constitute a more authorized form of knowledge than hateful messages publicly expressed in those demonstrations or online.

Anti-racism movements and the introduction of Japan's first "anti-hate speech" law suppressed the publication of "hate books" between 2015 and 2016.[2] These years saw the increase of *nihon raisan* (praise-Japan) books, which excessively glorified Japan and its culture (e.g., Oguni 2015; Shirona and Ikeda 2016) and were often written by "hate book" authors.[3] The overlap between the authors of hate books and praise-Japan books clearly shows the tight connection between racism and nationalism (e.g., Balibar 1991b; Kawai 2016a).

In 2017, the popularity of the hate book genre returned. A book targeting China/Chinese and South Korea/South Koreans (hereafter Korea/Koreans),[4]

Jukyō ni shihai sareta chūgokujin to kankokujin no higeki (Tragedies of Chinese and South Koreans Controlled by Confucianism), became a best-seller of the year, selling nearly 500,000 copies (Nippan 2017; Tohan 2017).[5] Depicting them solely negatively and frequently pejoratively, for example, as "less than animals [*kinjū ika*]" (Gilbert 2017, 26) and "spoiled brats [*dada-kko*]" (77), this book belongs to this genre without doubt. The publisher is Kōdansha, one of Japan's three largest publishers, and the author is Kent Gilbert, a white American lawyer and TV personality in Japan. Gilbert first came to Japan as a Mormon missionary in the 1970s and became a popular TV personality during the 1980s and 1990s. Although his popularity waned in the 2000s, he reemerged as a public figure in the 2010s, promoting far-right Japanese nationalist causes.

Gilbert's new career as a far-right Japanese nationalist "spokesperson" is said to have started with a praise-Japan book titled *Fushichō no kuni nihon* (Japan, a phoenix-like nation) published in 2013 (Yasuda 2018, 20). He coauthored it with Ueda Takahiko, his business associate and a far-right nationalist activist. Ueda also serves as the president of Jiyūsha, a book company that publishes far-right middle school history and civic studies textbooks for the Japanese Society for History Textbook Reform (*Atarashii rekishi kyōkasho wo tsukuru kai*).[6] In August 2014, Gilbert drew a wider public attention by attacking the *Asahi Shimbun*, the second largest and relatively liberal newspaper, on his blog about their reporting on the "comfort women" issue.[7]

Although Gilbert has published books since the 1980s, the number of his books surged in recent years: five books in the 1980s, nine in the 1990s, one in the 2000s, and fifty-three in the 2010s (zero between 2010 and 2012, one in 2013, zero in 2014, four in 2015, six in 2016, fifteen in 2017, eighteen in 2018, and nine in 2019).[8] His books published before 2000 were mainly about the English language, internationalization, and comparative cultural discussions. However, those published in the 2010s advocate far-right Japanese nationalist agendas: deny, whitewash and/or justify Japan's colonial and wartime aggressions in Asia by attacking what far-right nationalists call the "Tokyo trial view of history" (*Tokyo saiban shikan*) or the "masochistic view of history" (*jigyaku shikan*), which refers to a view that is critical of Japan's national past in the first half of the twentieth century.

Gilbert's books demonstrate crisscrossing, complicit, and transnational relationships among Japanese nationalism, Japanese racism, and Western racism. The books do not simply indicate his negative views about China/Chinese and Korea/Koreans. These are a collective accomplishment that involves far-right Japanese nationalists often diminishing the two Asian neighbors to elevate Japan/Japanese, the publishing industry, his Japanese office staff members serving as writing assistants, and his readers who are predominantly men in their sixties and seventies (Takaguchi 2018, 27). A newspaper article reported that it was not Gilbert but an editor of the publisher Kōdansha who proposed the idea of his 2017 bestseller because "a white person's words would sound more persuasive to the Japanese" (Takaku and Tadama 2018). A news magazine article states that his books are produced in a "book manufacturing factory" (*seisaku fakutorī*), referring to a deep involvement of his Japanese staffers in writing his books as well as the extremely quick process of publishing them, most of which Gilbert writes via dictation (Yasuda 2018).[9] Although books and articles are always intertextual and collaboratively produced by authors, reviewers, editors, publishers, and the expected readers, the degree of collaboration is far stronger in Gilbert's case.

In this chapter, I examine Gilbert's 2017 bestseller book and a sequel to the book published in 2018, *Chūkashisō wo mōshinsuru chūgokujin to kankokujin no higeki* (Tragedies of Chinese and South Koreans Swallowing Sinocentrism). Referring to David Theo Goldberg's (1993) notion of the grammar of racialized discourse, I investigate the grammar of Japanese racialized discourse embedded in his two books and ways in which China/Chinese and Korea/Koreans are used to construct a positive meaning of Japan/Japanese. Although the images of a state and its people can differ, the two often overlap, and more importantly, they are interchangeable in Gilbert's books.

Understanding this discourse is useful to problematize a variety of racist expressions, including those which do not appear explicitly racist or seem nationalist but are constitutive of Japanese racialized discourse (Kawai 2018). While insisting on distinguishing racialized discourse from national discourse (43), Goldberg (1993) admits that the two discourses are deeply related (78–79). The change of the term "racist discourse" in his original article (Goldberg 1990) to "racialized discourse" in the 1993 version shows difficulty of separating the two discourses. In addition, the difficulty can be explained by the significance of the idea of race in producing "fictive ethnicity" or the people of the nation (Balibar 1991c), which is exemplified by *minzoku*—a racialized cultural nation—that have influenced Japaneseness (see chapter 1). Considering Gilbert's strong degree of collaboration with Japanese nationalists and the feature of his books—"hate books" targeting China/Chinese and Korea/Koreans—it is crucial to see national and racialized discourses as entangled in the two texts.

Drawing on Michel Foucault's (1972) theory of the discursive field, Goldberg (1993) argues that the field of racialized discourse consists of all expressions—*statements* in Foucault's theory—that follow a common "grammar" or a system of rules governing the composition of those expressions. A "hate book" thus is an expression or statement constituting the field of Japanese racialized discourse. Analyzing racialized discourse is equivalent to a "preconceptual level analysis" (Foucault 1972, 60), which involves identifying epistemological or structural elements that govern the discursive field; or in short, a grammar. Racist expressions made in a certain place and time vary in style and "descriptive representations of others" (Goldberg 1993, 47), and yet they are coherent in their ways of perceiving racialized groups because they follow a certain grammar.

Due to its structuralist bent, Goldberg's (1993) grammar of racialized discourse may look "outdated" for some readers. Rejecting "human-centered" philosophies such as phenomenology and existentialism and pursuing an "objective science" comparable to natural science (Sedgwick 1999, 382), structuralism assumed that culture and society have "predictable regularities" (Barker 2010, 2) independent of human intentions. Later, post-structuralism (and postmodernism) criticized the premise that there are fixed social and cultural structures while furthering the idea of the death of the subject/author (e.g., Han 2014). The difference between structuralism and post-structuralism parallels Ferdinand de Saussure's (1983) distinction between the *langue* (language as system) and the *parole* (people's idiosyncratic practices): post-structuralism stressed the "parole" aspect of a culture and society, criticizing structuralism's overemphasis on the "langue" aspect of them.

Today, it is probably "outdated" to claim that a certain structure can explain an entire society or a culture as a whole, or that structure determines agency. Gilbert's books as texts will be certainly multiaccentuated (Vološinov 1973, 23), and his readers will interpret the books in multiple ways. However, analyzing the books from such a perspective is neither useful nor meaningful under the circumstances in which the writers and publishers of this genre often defend their books by arguing that they are not based on faked information (Takaku and Tamada 2018), and "hate books" continue to be published and are widely accessible in bookstores and public libraries: "hate books" have not been problematized enough despite extensive criticisms.[10]

While not endorsing structuralism's assumption and emphasis on "objectivity," I use Goldberg's grammar of racialized discourse to clarify a core problem of "hate books." Structuralism can be defined as "the study of systems it knows to be mobile but which it analyses as if they were, for the purpose of study, frozen in time" (Sturrock 2003, 22). I deliberately freeze Gilbert's books to delineate the grammar or epistemological structure of these "hate books," which will make it easier for a wider range of people to not only scrutinize both explicitly and implicitly problematic expressions to construct Japaneseness but also reject attempts to legitimize the "hate book" genre. Although identifying incorrect, distorted, and misleading information is certainly important, it is not sufficient because facts can be interpreted arbitrarily to serve far-right nationalist and racist causes. However, by understanding the grammar, it will be easier to detect ways in which certain facts are selected and manipulated to create Japaneseness at the expense of others.

In the following sections, I first discuss and expand Goldberg's grammar of racialized discourse because I feel that Goldberg does not delineate this notion sufficiently. Then I look into Western and Japanese historical relationships with and views of China and Korea in relation to Confucianism and Sinocentrism, the two main themes of Gilbert's two books. History is important for a racialized nation because its conceptual core lies in the "schema of genealogy," which involves the temporal continuity of a group (Balibar 1991c, 100). Historical narratives can thus be used as convincing recourses to essentialize both "us" and "them" and represent "us" positively. The argument that historical revisionism plays a central role in Japanese exclusionist (or racist) practices (Higuchi 2014) is explicable by this close interrelationships among history, race, and nation. Lastly, I examine the grammar of Japanese racialized discourse, a style, and representations of the two Asian neighbors deployed in his books and thereby scrutinize Japaneseness constructed there.

THE GRAMMAR OF RACIALIZED DISCOURSE

Grammar

Goldberg (1993) suggests four groups of grammatical (or epistemological) elements for racialized discourse (49). Certain elements are gathered as one group because they have been closely related with each other. However, the four groups are not mutually exclusive; they can overlap with each other, and each element does not belong strictly to just one group (51–52). Although Goldberg does not explicitly state it, this means that a certain group of elements (i.e., grammar) plays a primary role in one expression while multiple groups are simultaneously present, and that a different grammar can be made by linking elements in various manners.

The first group, which can be called *racial hierarchical classification*, includes four elements: classification, order, value, and hierarchy. This grammar was frequently used in "biological" racism, the dominant modality of racism in the West between the rise of Western race theories in the eighteenth century and its decline after World War II. The first element, classification, is a product of the European Enlightenment in which intellectuals advocated "objectively" observing and classifying natural and social entities and phenomena, including human beings, as the core of scientific method (see chapter 1). However, classifying people, which requires certain criteria, is a value-laden practice (Balibar 1991b, 56). European racial classification, differentiating and ordering humans on the basis of European values, necessarily "implied a racial hierarchy of races" (Goldberg 1993, 50), in which the white race comes on top.

The two Japanese concepts of race—*jinshu* and *minzoku*—make Japanese *racial hierarchical classification* dual-structured (see chapter 1). In Western racial hierarchization (i.e., *jinshu* hierarchization), the Japanese, together with the Chinese and the Koreans, are categorized as the yellow race, a group placed under the white race, whereas in Japan's racial hierarchization (i.e., *minzoku* hierarchization), the Japanese are differentiated from the two peoples and positioned on the top of their own hierarchy.

The second group, *racial differentiation*, comprises two pairs of elements: differentiation and identity, and discrimination and identification. Goldberg (1993) contends that hierarchy, an element of *racial hierarchical classification*, has come to be "widely considered obsolete" because of the ideas of inferiority and superiority (51). This change parallels the shift of the dominant modality of racism in the West from "biological" racism to cultural racism. As cultural racism has continuity as well as discrepancy with "biological" racism (see chapter 1), *racial differentiation* is not detached from the elements of the first group except for hierarchy. Goldberg posits that "classification enabled racial differentiation" (52). Classification, "the ordering of human groups on the basis of putatively natural (inherited or environmental) differences" (50), necessarily involves differentiating one's group from others, for which essentializing "biological" and cultural characteristics is indispensable. However, unlike racist expressions following the first group, those based on the second group do not claim the superiority or inferiority of one group to others; instead, they differentiate the former from the latter by constructing one's own and others' identities, which involves classifying and ordering people on the basis of a certain value.

Goldberg (1993) proposes the two pairs of elements to illuminate affinity and disparity between non-racist and racist identity construction practices. The first pair—creating an identity through differentiation—is inherent in any identity construction and not necessarily racist. However, it becomes racist when it is rendered at the cost of others or through otherization. More specifically, the first pair turns into the second pair when "racial differentiation begins to define otherness, and discrimination *against* the racially defined other becomes at once *exclusion* of the different" (51; emphasis in original). Here *racial differentiation* is already linked with an element of the third group—exclusion. Discrimination and exclusion are inseparable from a group identity created by not simply differentiating one's group from others but otherizing them.

The third group, which can be labeled *racial exclusion*, consists of four elements: exclusion, domination, subjection, and subjugation. Goldberg (1993) suggests that *racial exclusion* "grounds the entire superstructure of racist expressions" (52). On the one hand, this grammar itself can be highlighted as in the case of U.S. President Donald Trump's Twitter comments exhorting to four minority congresswomen in July 2019 to "go back" to their presumed countries of origin, despite the fact that all but one were born in the United States and the fourth is a naturalized citizen (Rogers and Fandos 2019). On the other hand, it operates behind all other types of grammar when a different grammar is foregrounded in a racist expression. In addition, Goldberg contends that "to succeed so long in effecting the materiality of differential exclusions, racialized discourse has to be grounded in the relations of social subjects to each other and in ways of seeing, of relation to, (other) subjects" (53). Excluding racialized others is not possible without people becoming racialized subjects. Such subjects come into existence by learning to see a group that differs from certain values as deviant and by thinking it natural to dominate and subjugate them to various forms of exclusion, such as expelling and eradicating them through assimilation from community.

Racial exclusion is thus tied to entitlement and restriction, the two elements of the fourth group, which can be named *racial control*. Entitlement entails people's rights "of accessibility (to enfranchisement, opportunity, or treatment), and of endowments (goods and the means thereto)," whereas restriction relates to the state's rights "of denial (disenfranchisement or restriction), of prohibition (to entry, participation, or services), and of alienation (of goods and the means to them)" (Goldberg 1993, 55). *Racial control* is often embedded in immigration policies and laws. For example, people with a passport issued by Western and some Asian countries are often entitled to visit many other countries without requiring a visa, while the same countries deny the right to people with a passport issued by African or Middle Eastern countries.

Style and Representations

It is possible to make an infinite number of expressions by following a certain grammar of racialized discourse. Yet racist expressions constructed at a certain time and place tend to follow the prevailing style and representations of racialized others (Goldberg 1993, 47–48). The style of racist expressions differs from representations of racialized others. Examples of the style include the "aversive, academic or scientific, legalistic, bureaucratic, economic, cultural, linguistic, religious, mythical, or ideological" (47). The popular style in the West shifted from the scientific to the cultural after World War II against the backdrop of the Jewish Holocaust experience and independence movements in Africa and Asia. Since the September 11, 2001 attacks, the religious-cultural style has become influential in the United States and many European countries.

Racist representations of others, “descriptive statements about others that delimit the way we perceive them” (Goldberg 1993, 47), overlap with stereotypes defined by Michael Pickering (2001). According to Pickering, “stereotyping imparts a sense of fixedness to the homogenized images it disseminates. It attempts to establish an attributed characteristic as natural and given in ways inseparable from the relations of power and domination through which it operates” (5). Apparently embedded in power relations, representations of racialized others affect not just perceptions but also reality.

Racist representations or stereotypes are closely related to historical narratives and images. Pickering (2001) suggests that “many stereotypes owe their resilience to the historical accretions and sedimentations of meaning and value they carry as elements within the cultural repertory available to people in their multiple relations with others” (8), which is clearly shown in Gilbert’s choice of Confucianism and Sinocentrism to racialize China/Chinese and Korea/Koreans. In the following section, I discuss Western and Japanese relationships with and views of China and Korea in relation to Confucianism and Sinocentrism. I focus on China in discussing Western view because Western dominant discourses have summarized countries and peoples in East Asia as, for example, the East, Asia, Orientals, and the yellow, often using China to represent them.

CONFUCIANISM, SINOCENTRISM, AND WESTERN AND JAPANESE RELATIONSHIPS WITH AND VIEWS OF CHINA AND KOREA

Western Relationship and View

Western images of China have been tied to Confucianism, which was not only equated with Chinese culture but also viewed as “representative of a timeless Chinese culture” (Paramore 2016, 8). The West started to have substantial contacts with China in the sixteenth century largely through Jesuit missionaries, who studied Chinese language and history as well as translated the Confucian classics. They introduced Confucianism favorably as a moral philosophy, not a religion, which offered practical reasoning for the moral and political order in China (e.g., Jones 2001, 18–19). Learning about Confucianism and Chinese society from missionaries’ writings, many European Enlightenment thinkers saw China “the model of a nation well organized on the basis of lofty reason and good conduct” (Zhang 1988, 117). Moreover, they regarded Chinese society as “a model of a moral society governed by natural reason and freed from the superstitious fetters of religion” to challenge and subvert the Christianity-based European social order (Jones 2001, 20).

In the nineteenth century, several factors, such as the first Industrial Revolution and the French and American revolutions, comparative philology, progressivism, and the intensification of European imperialism and colonialism, turned these positive views of China into mostly negative ones (Cohen 2010; Jones 2001; Mackerras 1989). European intellectuals came to regard Confucian values, such as filial piety, harmony, hierarchy, and rituals as contrary to the individualism, freedom, and equality stressed in capitalism and liberal democracy. Philosophers, philologists, and political economists at that time, such as Hegel, Herder, John Stuart Mill, and Marx, regarded Chinese (and other Asian) histories, economies, and societies as stagnant, unprogressive, inegalitarian, and thus inferior, which is exemplified in the ideas of Asiatic or Oriental despotism and Asiatic mode of production. The nexus of comparative philology and progressivism facilitated equating Chinese with ancient Egyptians as "hierographic people" and imagining Chinese society, people, and culture as obscure, irrational, archaic, and unprogressive (Goebel 1995). The idea that "China was in a state of eternal immobility and standstill . . . [became] an integral part of the traditional image of China in Western eyes" (Zhang 1988, 123). Western intellectuals often regarded Confucianism as the ideological basis that supported Asiatic or Oriental despotism, its backwardness, and inferiority to the West (Hu 1997).

This nineteenth-century Western view of China persisted in academic discourses until the late 1960s (Cohen 2010, 61) and even longer in popular discourses (Mackerras 1989, 223), although the establishment of Communist China produced a new image of China as a threat (178) while prolonging the view of China as despotic and totalitarian (272). After World War II, modernization theory played a key role in sustaining this perception of China (Cohen 2010, chapter 2; Jones 2001, chapter 5). Modernization theory was popularized after World War II against the backdrop of the independence of former colonies in Africa and Asia as well as Western interest in economic and social development there (Tipps 1973). Earlier theorists defined modernization as tied to Western social, economic, and political values such as liberal democracy, individualism, and capitalism. Applying this theory in a simplistic manner to understanding Chinese society, scholars contrasted "traditional" China and the "modern" West and perpetuated the images of China inherited from the previous century: China as backward and static, as opposed to the West as civilized and dynamic (Cohen 2010, 81). Sinologists often regarded Confucianism as a key factor in explaining China's traditionality (Cohen 2010, 79) and as inseparable from the Sinocentric tributary order. For example, calling the order the Chinese world order, John Fairbank, a very influential Sinologist in the second half of the twentieth century, argued that "From the first, the Chinese world was hierarchic and anti-egalitarian . . . The Confucian philosophy that sanctioned this hierarchic order became an orthodoxy" (1968, 5–6).

Confucianism drew positive attention in the 1980s and 1990s as a key factor for Asia's regional economic growth achieved by the "Four Asian Tigers" (Hong Kong, Singapore, South Korea, and Taiwan), which followed Japan's economic rise in earlier decades. Confucian values, which Western scholars had previously evaluated negatively, came to be called "Asian values" and viewed as positive factors for economic success (Jones 2001, 190). Simultaneously, against the backdrops of Asian region's prosperity and the liberalization of the Chinese economy initiated by Deng Xiaoping in the 1980s, Confucianism came to serve as a symbol of the Asian threat to the Western-centric world order as exemplified by Samuel Huntington's (1993) thesis of the clash of civilizations. Huntington summarized the East (except Japan) and some Southeast Asian nations as Confucian civilization, which he argued is incompatible with and hostile to Western civilization. The clash of civilization thesis has continued to be relevant. This is exemplified in the 2009 book *When China Rules the World* by Martin Jacques, a British China observer, who "provides an updated version of this Huntingtonian thesis" (Pan 2012, 29). For instance, Jacques ([2009] 2012) posits that "whatever democratic political system evolves in China will bear the heavy imprint of its Confucian past" (273).

Japanese Relationship with and View of China

Japan has had a far deeper and more direct and relationship with China and Confucianism than the West. Since ancient times, Japan has received a wide range of influence from China, including the Chinese script, Buddhism, Confucianism, legal and political systems, and arts and literature. As the most significant discursive Other that premodern Japanese elites and intellectuals attempted to emulate and overcome, China occupied the central place in Japanese cultural, intellectual, and political discourses until the nineteenth century.

Although Confucianism's role was less official than Buddhism's in premodern Japan before the institutionalization and popularization of neo-Confucianism in the Edo era (1603–1867), Confucian values have been ingrained into Japanese social and cultural fabric since ancient times. Early Confucian influences are evident, for example, in the *Seventeen Article Constitution*, which has been popularly claimed to be authored by the imperial regent Prince Shōtoku in 604, and in the centralized government system called *ritsuryōsei* established in the eighth century (e.g., Collcutt 1991, 115–16). Moreover, Confucianism in Japan has been historically conflated with not only Buddhism but also Shinto (e.g., Collcutt 1991) and Bushido (e.g., Kanno 2004; Kasaya 2014), two bodies of thought that are generally regarded as indigenous.

Premodern Japan's view of China as the most significant Other is inseparable from the tribute system, "the external expression of hierarchical relationships central to the maintenance of the Sinocentric system" (Hamashita 2008, 13). Sinocentrism or the *Hua-Yi* (華夷) order is typically explained as a hierarchical worldview that asserts China's (or *Hua*'s) centrality and superiority as opposed to the four "barbarians" (or *Yi*) residing in the north, south, east, and west of China (e.g., Danjo 2012, 19). Tributary states were required to follow particular procedures, such as obtaining the recognition and investiture of their new rulers from the Chinese emperor, paying tribute to China on a regular basis, and using the Chinese calendar. Sinocentric ideas and tributary relations in East Asia existed before the establishment of Confucianism (e.g., Wang 2013, 211). However, Confucianism came to be entangled with Sinocentrism and the tributary system because it helped Chinese rulers rationalize the system (e.g., Feng 2009). Confucian teaching envisioned a hierarchical and thus harmonious social order governed by a virtuous leader or the Son of Heaven (天子) who received the Mandate of Heaven (天命) for the ultimate purpose of creating harmony in all-under-Heaven (天下) (e.g., Chen 1991, 46–48; Wang 2013, 211). By interpreting "all-under-Heaven" as not limited to the Chinese kingdom but as the entire world, this Confucian teaching served as a powerful philosophical and ideological resource for Chinese rulers to consolidate their power both domestically and internationally.

However, in practice, the tribute system was a more complex and dynamic network of multiple relations not simply between China and tributary states but also among those states (Hamashita 2008). Chinese rulers demanded tributary relations with neighboring states not only by relying on Confucian ideas to seek for prestige but also by considering security issues on its frontier (Feng 2009, 563). The compliance of those states with this demand often did not simply indicate their belief in Chinese superiority but also their necessity to secure trade relations with China.

Japan's ambivalent view of China—admiration and rivalry—is observable in the ways in which Japanese rulers dealt with the Sinocentric tributary order. During the seventh and ninth centuries, Japan sent approximately twenty missions first to Sui China (581–618) and later to Tang China (618–907) to obtain advanced knowledge including Buddhist and Confucian writings, technology, and material goods. It is well known that according to the Book of Sui, China's official history of the Sui dynasty, Emperor Suiko's letter sent to the Emperor of Sui for a mission in the early seventh century offended him because both Chinese and Japanese emperors were referred to as the Son of Heaven, a Confucian term to be used exclusively for Chinese emperors (Todo et al. 2010, 192–93). The *Nihonshoki* (the Chronicles of Japan), an official chronicle complied in the eighth century, states that the letter used the term 皇帝 (*kōtei*) for the Chinese emperor and the term 天皇 (*tennō*) for the Japanese emperor (Aston 1956b, 139; *Nihonshoki* 1901, 383). The words related to "emperor" such as 天 (heaven) and 皇 (meaning emperor, magnificence, and imperial) were reserved for rulers in China (e.g., Wang 2013, 212). Japan's insistence on using the title of *tennō* "reflected the conception that Japan was not under the Sinocentric world order which made the Japanese emperor equal to the Chinese emperor" (Kang 1997, 43).

Formal diplomatic relations with China stopped when official missions were terminated in 894 because of Tang China's internal rebellions that eventually led to the fall of the Tang dynasty. They were finally restored five centuries later in 1403 when Ashikaga Yoshimitsu, the third shogun of the Muromachi era (1336–1573), accepted a tributary relationship to the Ming dynasty (1368–1644), receiving the title of the "King of Japan" from Emperor Yongle. The motive behind it was to consolidate the power basis of the Ashikaga shogunate and to pursue economic advantage by trading with the Ming dynasty (e.g., Toby 1985, 349). Because accepting the title "king" (王) implied submission to "the concept of universal Chinese sovereignty in the Confucian world order" (Toby 1991, 78), his decision "provoked strong criticism, particularly among the court nobles, and became a target of disapproval thereafter as it was degrading" (Kang 1997, 33).

The tributary relationship with Ming China was disrupted between the late fifteenth and sixteenth centuries due to, domestically, social upheavals caused by incessant territorial battles among samurai lords and, internationally, two military invasions of Korea in 1592 and 1597 by Toyotomi Hideyoshi, the first unifier of these lords. Tokugawa Ieyasu, the first shogun of the Tokugawa shogunate (1603–1867), which was founded by overthrowing the Toyotomi regime, attempted to establish a tributary relationship with Ming China for reasons similar to Yoshimitsu's (Toby 1991, 57–58). Eventually, the Tokugawa shogunate decided not to become a tributary state, partly so as "not to paint a portrait of the shogun as submissive and weak" (McNally 2016, 151). After conquering it in 1609, the shogunate instead used the Ryukyu kingdom (present-day Okinawa), a tribute state of Ming and Qing China, for trading and purchasing Chinese commodities.

The Tokugawa government's official incorporation of neo-Confucianism provoked nativist reactions exemplified by National Learning (*kokugaku*) or Japanese studies movements. National Learning scholars attempted to elucidate Japaneseness in relation to Chineseness through the study of Japan's history and ancient and early medieval literary canonical writings. They associated Confucianism and China with vanity, arrogance, and evil that contaminated Japan's innocence and "original" quality (Nosco 2014). Even Japanese

Confucians "found themselves walking a tightrope" to modify its foreign and Sinocentric elements to make them look more Japanese without negating its central ideas (Nakai 1980, 159). Still recognizing Chinese cultural authority was the norm for Japanese elites until the mid-nineteenth century (e.g., McNally 2016, 142; Nosco 2014, 234). Yet in the course of Qing China's defeat in the Opium War (1840–1842) and the subsequent Japan's Western-style modernization, Japanese elites and intellectuals in the mid-nineteenth century distanced themselves from Confucianism, which was "the West's marker of Chinese culture's backwardness" and thus anti-modern (Paramore 2016, 9). However, soon after the Meiji Restoration in 1868, Confucianism made a comeback among Japanese elites and intellectuals in the 1880s as a linchpin to criticize the Westernization that was rapidly changing Japanese society and culture (Collcutt 1991, 148). This is exemplified by the Imperial Rescript on Education of 1890, which blended both Shinto and Confucian values such as the divine origin of the imperial line, loyalty, and filiality (Collcutt 1991, 149–50).

In the first half of the twentieth century, Confucianism became a counter philosophy to overcome the West after the Russo-Japanese War (1904–1905) (Kurozumi 2003, 185–86), and to understand the limitations and deficiencies of Western modernity exposed in the fierce battles of World War I (Paramore 2016, 153–57). Japanese authorities also embraced it as an ideological means to rationalize their imperial ambition to expand its colonial control into China by "claim[ing] themselves as the real stewards of Asian tradition in comparison to the republicans and communists because both of these groups initially rejected Confucianism as an antithesis to their imagination of a strong, modern China" (Paramore 2016, 159). One significant example is the use of Confucianism as the ideology of Japan's colonial control of Manchuria, whose state-founding proclamation demanded that the people respect and follow Confucianism (Government of Manchukuo 1932). After World War II, Confucianism has become a taboo topic in Japanese mainstream discourses due to its close association with prewar Japan's totalitarian imperialism (Paramore 2016, 167–82).

Japanese Relationship with and View of Korea

Japan's relationship with Confucianism is closely connected with Korea. Confucianism is believed to have arrived in Japan from Paekche between the third and the fifth century (Collcutt 1991, 115; Paramore 2016, 16). Paekche was one of the three kingdoms into which the Korean peninsula was divided until it was unified by the Silla dynasty in the late seventh century. Paekche had a close relationship with the Japanese imperial court in the Yamato period (third-eighth centuries) due to their rivalry with the two other kingdoms, Silla and Koguryo, and Tang China. The *Nihonshoki* includes a passage in which Emperor Ojin invited Wani, a Confucian scholar from Paekche to Japan in 284 (Aston 1956a, 262).

Ojin's mother is Empress Jingū, whose fictious expedition to conquer Silla is highlighted in the *Nihonshoki*. Although this book is a chronicle of emperors consisting of chapters titled with their names, it dedicates one chapter exclusively to Jingū, the only emperor's wife with her own chapter. Not well known today, her story was taught in history classes at school and thus well known in prewar Japan (e.g., Allen 2003, 82). For example, the 1943 primary school history textbook published by the Ministry of Education includes the story of her attack on Silla, which is summarized as follows:

> Jingū's husband, Emperor Chuai died while trying to suppress rebellions by the Kumaso people in southern Kyushu. Finding out that Silla was supporting Kumaso, Jingū decided to attack Silla. The King of Silla, who was frightened to see her ships coming to his land, immediately surrendered and offered her a large amount of gold, silver, and beautiful textiles. She received his surrender and returned to Japan with the gifts. (19–22)

Jingū's story was used to legitimize Toyotomi Hideyoshi's invasions of the Korean peninsula in 1592 and 1597 (e.g., Elisonas 1991, 265, 276; Kang 1997, 101) and Japan's diplomatic aggression toward and subsequent colonization of Korea starting in the late nineteenth century (e.g., Allen 2003, 93; Schmid 2000, 963).

Japan's historical conflicts with Korea are inseparable from the Sinocentric tributary order, which is entangled with Confucian ideas. Hideyoshi and the Tokugawa shoguns' refusal of the title "king" and of the Chinese calendar in diplomatic letters exchanged with Joseon Korea (1392–1910), which accepted Ming China's investiture, were highly contentious issues between the two states (Toby 1991, chapter 3). Joseon Korea's official relationships with China and Japan were called the Serving-the-Great (事大) diplomacy and the Neighborly (交隣) diplomacy, respectively (e.g., Oh 1980, 38; Kang 1997, 49). In short, unlike Korea's relationship with China, its relationship with Japan was supposed to be on an equal basis. The Japanese samurai rulers rejected the title "king" because it implied a position below the Chinese emperor and also because "king" or the head of state can mean the emperor in Japan (Kang 1997, 155). However, for Korean rulers, either the shogun or the Japanese emperor should be the "king of Japan" and the Japanese emperor should not be an "emperor" comparable to the Chinese emperor. The dual power structure involving the imperial court and the shogunate as well as Japan's challenge to Sinocentrism complicated the relationship between Korea and Japan. In the 1630s, the Tokugawa government created the title "Great Prince (大君)," "a title with no clear correlate in the Chinese diplomatic lexicon," and persuaded the Joseon government to accept the disuse of the Chinese calendar in Japanese correspondence with Korea (Toby 1985, 359). Freeing itself from the Sinocentric order while mimicking it, the Tokugawa shogunate constructed Japanese version of Sinocentrism by presenting Ryukyuan, Korean, and Dutch envoys' visits to the shogunal court as if they had paid "tributary" visits to "Japan-as-central-kingdom" (Toby 1985, 1991).

The Conquer Korea Debate (*seikanron*) in 1873, which eventually led to Japan's imposition of an unequal treaty on Joseon Korea in 1876 (the Treaty of Ganghwa) and the subsequent colonization of Korea (1910–1945), was also related to the Sinocentric worldview. The debate evolved from the Korean government's refusal to accept a diplomatic letter from the Meiji government to inform Korea of the regime change in 1868. They rejected it because the letter included the Chinese character 皇 in reference to the Japanese emperor who nominally and substantially became the head of Japan and the character 勅 in reference to his order (e.g., Hatada 1969, 273; Okamoto 2008, 65–66; Kang 2012, 517).

Japanese scholars used Korea's tighter diplomatic and cultural relationship with China as a source to support the "*taritsusei shikan*" (literally, the subservient view of history) or the "*teitai shikan*" (literally, the stagnant view of history), the dominant view of Korean history during late nineteenth and the first half of the twentieth century, in which they characterized Korea as lacking autonomy and originality (Hatada 1969, 209, 231–48). Bordering with China, Korea had received stronger pressure, as well as influence from China, than Japan, which was geographically separated from China by the sea. This pertains to why Korea came to be a "model tributary" (Kang 2010, 57) as opposed to Japan as "the liminal—or boundary—case" (9). However, contrasting the cases of Korea and Japan without considering these circumstances led to characterizing Korea as more subordinate to and Japan as more autonomous from Chinese influence. Since Japanese scholars dominated Korean history research during the Japanese colonial period (Hatada 1969, 180), the Japanese colonial scholars' view of Korea also influenced Western scholars (Kang 1997, 8–9).

THE GRAMMAR OF JAPANESE RACIALIZED DISCOURSE

Attending to those Western and Japanese historical relationships with and views of China and Korea with respect to Confucianism and Sinocentrism, I examined the discourse, representations of China/Chinese and Korea/

Koreans, and the style used in Gilbert's two books. The discourse primarily used in the two books is *racial differentiation* added to the element of hierarchy, which can be called *racial hierarchical differentiation.* The same grammar was used in the two 2014 bestsellers targeting Korea/Koreans (Murotani 2013; Lee 2014) that I analyzed elsewhere (Kawai 2018). In the following analysis, the 2017 bestseller book *Jukyō ni shihai sareta chūgokujin to kankokujin no higeki* (Tragedies of Chinese and South Koreans Controlled by Confucianism) is referred to as Book 1, and the 2018 sequel *Chūkashisō wo mōshinsuru chūgokujin to kankokujin no higeki* (Tragedies of Chinese and South Koreans Swallowing Sinocentrism) as Book 2.

Essentialization for Differentiation

Confucianism and Sinocentrism offer very useful means for differentiation through essentializing the Chinese and the Koreans. Since the two discursive entities have a long history, by stressing their relevance in contemporary China and Korea, they can turn into the "essence" shared by the Chinese and the Koreans. Gilbert's two books employ the two historical resources to depict the Chinese and the Koreans as completely different peoples from the Japanese. However, the Chinese, the primary players in establishing Confucianism and Sinocentrism, are essentialized slightly differently from the Koreans.

China/Chinese

Using Confucianism to differentiate the Chinese from the Japanese requires rhetorical tactics because Japanese culture has been influenced by Confucianism since ancient times and also because Confucianism was rejected in the twentieth-century China by both Chinese republicans and communists (Yao 2000, 263–64). Gilbert separates the Confucian values that the Chinese lost and those they kept. The author argues that while they discarded Confucian basic moral values—benevolence (仁), righteousness (義), ritual (礼), wisdom (智), and faithfulness (信)—due to the Cultural Revolution (Book 1, 24), they retained "a value that prioritizes family interests over public interests" (25). Supporting this argument, he cites a story from Book 13, Chapter 18 of the *Analects* (23). This is the only quote from the Five Classics and the Four Books[11] or the canon of Confucianism in Gilbert's 2017 book, whose main theme is Confucianism:

> The Governor of She in conversation with Confucius said, "In our village there is someone called 'True person.' When his father took a sheep on the sly, he reported him to the authorities." Confucius replied, "Those who are true in my village conduct themselves differently. A father covers for his son, and a son

covers for his father. And being true lies in this." (Ames and Rosemont 2010, 167)

The emphasis on family derives from a Confucian idea that "as the family is the basic unit of human community, harmonious family relationships are believed to be crucial for a harmonious society and a peaceful state" (Yao 2000, 181). Put simply, family is important for public interests in Confucian principle. However, interpreting this story as indicating Chinese tendency "to justify law infringement for the sake of private and family interests," Gilbert insists that "this value plays a significant role in exacerbating China's international isolation today" (Book 1, 25). In reference to a single section of the ancient Confucian book out of context as a central value of contemporary China, the author claims that this Confucian value influences China's international relations today, essentializing Chinese culture as static and unchangeable for thousands of years.

Using Sinocentrism to essentialize and thereby differentiate the Chinese is simpler because Sinocentrism is mostly a Chinese matter. That is probably why even in Book 1, whose main theme is supposed to be Confucianism, Gilbert gives Sinocentrism a significant role, claiming that it is inseparable from Confucianism (Book 2, 17). Sinocentrism is defined as the idea that "China is the center of not only the world but also the universe. Everything in the world belongs to the Chinese emperor. The places away from the center are barbaric, and people living there are equal to animals" (38). Although he initially suggests that Sinocentrism is particularly influential among Han Chinese elites (17), he later generalizes it as an essential Chinese value by claiming that Sinocentrism "penetrates deep into their [Chinese] DNA" (38). At the same time, Gilbert distances himself from "biological" racism in both Books 1 and 2, by stating that differences between the two Asian groups and the Japanese come from historical and cultural backgrounds, not from "hereditary factors such as the DNA" (6) or "from racial factors or the DNA" (Book 2, 4). This statement clearly exemplifies Étienne Balibar's (1991a) statement that "culture can also function like a nature" (22). The author treats Sinocentrism, a discursive entity, as if it were a biological feature of the Chinese that has remained the same and will do so in the future.

Korea/Koreans

Gilbert stresses Sinocentrism in both books to differentiate the Koreans from the Japanese. The author connects Confucianism with Sinocentrism by portraying the former as an inegalitarian ideology that upholds hierarchy as a core value and thereby provides rationale for the latter. For instance, in Book 1, Gilbert claims that "the Koreans had an absolute obedience to the Chinese emperor and accepted Confucianism and Sinocentrism entirely to have superiority over other neighboring countries" (64–65). Thus, the author argues, "the Koreans, calling themselves 'Little China,' came to be subservient to China, 'the older brother,' but developed a sense of superiority and arrogance to Japan, 'a younger brother'" (65). Following this statement, Gilbert contends that "the Koreans continue to have this mentality today" (65). Likewise, in Book 2, whose main theme is Sinocentrism, Gilbert condemns that the Koreans have a contemporary version of "Little Sinocentrism" (25–27). This reductive understanding of the relationship among the three East Asian countries to negatively essentialize Koreans is a "classical" Japanese far-right narrative circulated on the internet in the 2000s (e.g., Furuya 2017). However, this is not just a Japanese far-right discursive practice. The British China observer Martin Jacques ([2009] 2012) includes a similar depiction. In a chapter titled "China's own backyard" in which Jacques discusses China's tributary system, he states: "China was considered the big brother, Korea a middle brother, and Japan a younger brother" (345).

Little Sinocentrism or more appropriately, the idea of "Korea-as-central-kingdom" is Korean version of Sinocentrism. Already observable in earlier years of the Joseon dynasty (1392–1897), it intensified after the Manchu, who were regarded as "barbarians," the Qing's (1644–1912) overthrow of the Ming (1368–1644), a Han dynasty (Kang 1997, 11). Like the Japanese version of Sinocentrism, the Korean counterpart constructed its own world order in which Korea as the central kingdom is surrounded by "barbarians" such as the Japanese and the Manchu (Kang 1997, 66). After the fall of the Ming, Joseon intellectuals claimed that since a "barbarian" occupied the center, Korea, which had preserved the superior cultural traditions of the center, became "China" or the center of civilization. Therefore, Little Sinocentrism meant Korean intellectuals' subversion of China's Sinocentrism as in the case of the Japanese counterpart. Nevertheless, associating Korean version of Sinocentrism only with the Serving-the-Great-ism and ignoring Japan's Little Sinocentrism, Gilbert asserts that this idea entails Korea's continuing submission to the Sinocentric worldview. For example, after arguing that Little Sinocentrism exerts influence on contemporary Korean people's values, the author posits that "the Koreans have a strong inclination to be subservient to the powerful because of their age-long status as a vassal state" (25). This statement overlaps with the Japanese dominant view of Korean history that stressed Korea's lack of autonomy and originality.

Essentializing the Chinese and the Koreans by using Confucianism and Sinocentrism involves what can be called reductionistic historicism—characterizing one group simplistically with a couple of arbitrarily selected historical factors and events. Among numerous sections, one section of the *Analects*, an ancient book compiled more than 2000 years ago, is chosen and used as a determining value that characterizes people in China today. Likewise, while

Korea's complex historical relationship with Confucianism and Sinocentrism is ignored, its particular aspects are highlighted and generalized as a common value held by contemporary Korean people.

Hierarchization and Representations

Differentiating China/Chinese and Korea/Koreans from Japan/Japanese simultaneously involves hierarchization or inferiorization. The two groups are commonly represented as discriminatory and deceptive, and additionally, the former are also depicted as despotic.

China/Chinese

China/Chinese, who stand on the top of the Sinocentric world order, are depicted as hierarchical and thus discriminatory. This representation is often fused with another: China/Chinese as despotic. The conflation of the two representations is observable in Gilbert's reductionistic idea of Sinocentrism quoted above: China is the center of the world; everything in the world belongs to China; the rest are barbaric. Further simplifying this definition, the author repeatedly refers to Sinocentrism as the mentality that "yours is mine, and mine is mine" (e.g., Book 1, 18, 30; Book 2, 93, 121).

As a specific example, Sinocentrism, which Gilbert insists is intertwined with Confucianism, is held responsible for the territorial conflict involving the so-called "nine-dash line" (Book 2, 16–19; 89–93). This line was officially published on a map by Chiang Kai-shek's Nationalist government in 1947 on the grounds of historical rights and records dating back centuries (BBC 2016). China uses it to claim its sovereignty over a vast part of the South China Sea despite the 2016 United Nations-backed tribunal ruling that the line is invalid, which has caused conflicts with Southeast Asian countries such as the Philippines and Vietnam. Calling this line as "egoistically [*jibun katte*] drawn by China" and the constructions of artificial islands in the disputed area as "despotic [*ōbō*]" (Book 2, 17), Gilbert states as follows: "This is the essence [*honshitsu*] of Sinocentrism that they have embraced by tradition" (18). The Sinocentric tributary order had different modalities in different historical contexts (e.g., Brindley 2003). However, portraying Sinocentrism as a fixed and static entity that has been timelessly influential in China since ancient times, the author represents China/Chinese as inegalitarian and autocratic.

Sinocentrism is also held responsible for China's political conflicts with Tibet (Book 1, 28–29, 120–22) and for territorial disputes over the Senkaku/Diaoyu Islands (Book 1, 37–38; Book 2, 74–78) with Japan, which Gilbert calls "invasion [*sinryaku*]" by China (Book 2, chapter 2). Moreover, the author attributes China's historical and contemporary crackdowns on ethnic minority groups such as Uyghurs, Tibetans, and Mongolians to Confucianism and Sinocentrism (e.g., Book 1, 28–29, 120–22; Book 2, 43–44), and associates them with Nazi Germany (Book 1, 29) and fascism (Book 1, 120).

The representation of China/Chinese as discriminatory and despotic overlap with one of the dominant modes of contemporary representations of China in the West: China as a threat (e.g., Pan 2012). Gilbert portrays China/Chinese as despotic and thus threatening by claiming that China hopes to take control of Japan. In Book 1, citing a confidential document found in the 1970s, which is highly likely to be a fake (Yasuda 2018), Gilbert claims that the Chinese Communist Party has sought to bring Japan under control (176–80).[12] Then he provokes fear by introducing a fictional narrative: if Japan become part of China, Japanese people will be forced to speak in Chinese and discriminated against simply because they are Japanese (192). This is reminiscent of what Japan imposed on people in its colonies such as the Korean peninsula and Taiwan during its colonial rule. In Book 2, further developing this argument, the author contends that "China is serious about seizing Japan's territory" (86). To support this opinion, he claims that China has long held the belief that Okinawa is part of China (88) and warns that "the Chinese might become the majority in some municipalities" as more Chinese are living, buying up land and property there, and marrying Japanese (84–85).

When China/Chinese are depicted as discriminatory against Japan/Japanese, this representation is used to delegitimize China's demand that Japan acknowledge and reflect on its wartime atrocities committed against Chinese people. Insisting that Sinocentrism underlies the Chinese government's accusations against Japanese prime minister's visits to Yasukuni Shrine and Japan's downplaying of wartime aggressions, such as the Nanjing Massacre, Gilbert contends that "Chinese diplomacy is always arrogant to Japan in particular. Their demands to the Japanese government, such as 'Do not visit Yasukuni Shrine' and 'Look straight at history,' also come from the Sinocentric order" (Book 2, 19–20). Without mentioning the contexts behind these statements, the author insists that they show China's haughty and egoistic attitude. Here China, a victim of Japan's aggression, is made into the victimizer who subordinates Japan.

Moreover, Gilbert portrays the Chinese as deceptive by drawing on his opinion that Confucianism prioritizes private interests over those of the public based on the sole quote from the *Analects*. In Book 1, Gilbert writes that "the Chinese have lost moral values, so they do not hesitate to violate laws. They constantly tell lies but do not feel guilty at all" (41). In order to support this statement, the author mentions Chinese officials' corruption cases, such as the one involving former Chinese prime minister Wen Jiabao's relatives, who accumulated at least $2.7 billion, as reported in the *New York Times* (Barboza 2012) and refers to a report published by the Daiwa Institute of

Research (Kanamori 2012, 10) that states that bribery accounted for about 30 percent of China's GDP in 2008 (Book 1, 44). Then Gilbert contends that "Confucianism, which prioritizes private interests over public interests, plays the fundamental role in these dismal cases" (44).

The representation of China/Chinese as deceptive is also used to downplay and deny Japan's wartime violence. Gilbert asserts that the Chinese falsify the number of victims in the Nanjing Massacre and that of the Second Sino-Japanese War (1937–1945) because "they do not feel guilty for deceiving people" (Book 1, 47). Moreover, this representation is deployed in combination with the depiction of China/Chinese as discriminatory for this purpose. Gilbert contends that China internationally spreads propaganda that Japan is "a terrible country" by demanding apologies and compensation from Japan so as to "have people around the world including Americans distrust and hate Japan" (Book 2, 185). Here despite the actual position of China as a victim of Japan's military aggressions, China is portrayed as a victimizer that spreads false information about the violence caused by Japanese military forces and damages Japan's international reputation.

Korea/Koreans

While China/Chinese are represented hierarchical and thus discriminatory to everybody, Korea/Koreans are depicted as discriminatory against Japan/Japanese in particular. As mentioned in the previous section, Gilbert repeatedly insists that the Koreans diminish the Japanese because of their Confucian and Sinocentric values. For example, in Book 1, Gilbert contends that "it is an unbearable humiliation for the Koreans to see Japan doing better than Korea because according to Confucianism and Little Sinocentrism, Japan is inferior to Korea" (88). Likewise, in Book 2, the author writes that "the Koreans, under the control of the contemporary Little Sinocentrism, view Japan as inferior to them" (Book 2, 38).

The representation of the Koreans as discriminatory is tied to depicting them as *han-nichi* or anti-Japanese. Although Gilbert also depicts the Chinese as anti-Japanese, he maintains that "education has a great influence on the anti-Japanese atmosphere in China" (Book 2, 47) and attributes it mainly to a tactic used by Chinese Communist Party officials to divert people's discontent (e.g., Book 1, 47, 134–37; Book 2, 46–54). However, the Koreans are described as fundamentally anti-Japanese. The author claims that the successive presidents of South Korea made use of anti-Japanese policies to hide their inability and raise their reputation among the Koreans (Book 2, 54–62) because Korea is "a country founded on anti-Japanism" (Book 2, 57). Disregarding Japan's colonial violence and oppression, which is inseparable from Korea's critical attitude to Japan, the author insists that it is discrimination against the Japanese, for which Little Sinocentrism is responsible.

As in the case of China/Chinese, the representation of Korea/Koreans as deceptive is used to refute Korea's demand for Japan's sincere acknowledgment of its colonial exploitation of Korean people including "comfort women" and wartime laborers who were directly or indirectly forced to work in brothels, mines, or factories. Gilbert designates the "comfort women" issue as "fabricated [*netsuzō sareta*]" and "a false charge case [*enzai jiken*]" against Japan, denying the Japanese government and military's direct involvement in forcing them to provide sex against their will (Book 1, 200). The author describes the wartime laborer issue as "a scam [*ichamon*] to obtain apology and compensation from Japan" (Book 2, 138). Then he pejoratively calls these issues "victim's money-making business [*higaisha bijinesu*]" (139) in reference to the 1965 bilateral agreement on the settlement of issues concerning property and claims, which he insists has solved colonial and wartime compensation issues with South Korea.[13]

Article II of the 1965 agreement states that the problem concerning property, rights, and interests of the two countries including their nationals was "settled completely and finally." (Ministry of Foreign Affairs 1965). This phrase was included in exchange for grants and credit assistance from Japan, not for the Japanese government's sincere recognition of and apology for Japan's colonial rule (Ota 2015, chapter 4). While then South Korean president Park Chung-hee prioritized South Korea's economic development over rectifying social and personal damages suffered during Japan's colonization of the Korean peninsula, the Japanese government adhered to the view that the colonization contributed to the development of Korea (Takasaki 1996). The role played by the United States cannot be ignored: the U.S. government pushed South Korea and Japan to reach an agreement quickly in order to solidify cooperative ties among the two East Asian allies for the Vietnam War (e.g., Ota 2015, 224–35). In addition, regarding Japanese nationals' cases, such as atomic bomb victims, victims of crime committed by soldiers of the Allied Occupation forces, and prisoners of war detained by the Soviet Union, the Japanese government's long-standing position was: regardless of the San Francisco Peace Treaty that renounced the right to claim compensation for war-related damages, individuals retain the right to claim against a foreign government.[14] Neglecting these complicated historical contexts, Gilbert portrays the Koreans negatively as people who do not keep their own word: "Because of Little Sinocentrism, the Koreans look down on the Japanese completely. Consequently, they deceive Japan by breaking the bilateral agreement and feel no guilt about deceiving Japanese" (Book 2, 141).

Identification

Differentiating China/Chinese and Korea/Koreans from Japan/Japanese and depicting the two as discussed above concomitantly constructs a positive meaning of Japaneseness as *not* Chinese and Koreans. Gilbert's books do not just engage in identity construction but in what Goldberg (1993) calls identification or racist identity construction. Japanese identity is constructed not simply by differentiating the Japanese from the Chinese and the Koreans but also by inferioritizing or otherizing the latter. Moreover, through positively representing the Japanese, the author equates them with the Americans.

Japanese as not Chinese and Koreans

Gilbert turns to Bushido to create a positive Japanese identity as *not* Chinese and Korean—*not* discriminatory, deceptive, or despotic. Since Bushido accommodated Confucian values in the Edo and Meiji eras (e.g., Kanno 2004; Kasaya 2014), the author uses the same tactic of dividing Confucian influence in Chinese and Korean cultures and in Japanese culture. Claiming that the five virtues of Confucianism—benevolence, righteousness, ritual, wisdom, and faithfulness—were discarded by the Chinese and the Koreans but remained in Bushido (Book 1, 140–41), the author asserts that "the Japanese created their own unique culture through incorporating Confucian values selectively. Also assimilating Buddhist teachings, which are integrated into Shinto, they established a moral and ethical principle called Bushido in the Edo era" (140). In addition, the author attributes this Japanese "uniqueness" to *bansei ikkei* or the male-line continuity of the emperors (141) without referring to the samurais' antagonistic relationship with the imperial court that had lasted for centuries. While he depicts the Chinese and Korean ruling classes as oppressive and exploitative to common people because they abandoned the five Confucian virtues (140–41), he contends that the Japanese counterparts or the samurais, who followed Bushido, received "the common people's respect and admiration" (141). That is why, Gilbert contends, Bushido has impacted the Japanese in general, and thus the Japanese have "virtuous mind [*kōketsu na seishin*] that values the public, order, honor, courage, graciousness, and compassion" (140).

The notion of *wa* (和harmony) is another historical resource that Gilbert uses for a positive Japanese identity construction while denigrating the Chinese and the Koreans. Without mentioning the strong influences of Confucianism and Buddhism (e.g., Paramore 2016, 19–21; Gardner 2014, 4; Collcutt 1991, 115–16), the author asserts that the first article of the *Seventeen Article Constitution*, "harmony is to be valued," which scholars attribute to the *Analects* (e.g., Paramore 2016, 20; Collcutt 1991, 116), is an indigenous value on ground that the Japanese have been polytheists since ancient times (Book 1, 142–43). Due to the value of harmony, the author argues, the Japanese are "considerate of others," "tolerant," and "generous and flexible about receiving foreign ideas and religions" (143). For example, after insisting that Japan is the only country where customers apologize to cashiers when they have only a large bill for payment, Gilbert speculates that is because they "they subconsciously believe that the customer and the shop clerk are in not a hierarchical but an equal relationship. This exemplifies the Japanese value of harmony" (Book 1, 143). In contrast, the author contends that "people in China and Korea, Confucian states, always need to create hierarchy so that they cannot understand the idea that customers and shop clerks are equal" (144).

Japanese as Americans

Moreover, the Japanese are equated with the Americans, both of whom are depicted as fair, rational, and democratic as opposed to the Chinese and the Koreans who are not. For example, Gilbert asserts that "the Chinese and the Koreans live with values completely different from those held by the Japanese and the Americans" (Book 2, 4). In support of his opinion, the author posits that the Americans and the Japanese share similar moral values such as "telling a lie is not good" and "you must be fair," whereas the Chinese and the Koreans do not due to Confucian influences (4–5). As another example, Gilbert portrays the Americans and the Japanese as valuing freedom of speech, whereas the Chinese and the Koreans as not. After stating that "for the Americans, freedom of speech is extremely important," Gilbert claims that "there is no freedom of speech in China, a Communist state with a one-party dictatorship" (Book 2, 214), and that is also the case in South Korea because "you can never talk positively about Japan's colonial rule" (216). Incorporating Japan along with the United States into a group of countries that respect "freedom, democracy, the rule of law, and basic human rights," the author cheers the Japanese as follows: "I want Japanese people to fight for freedom as the leader of Asia" (217).

Furthermore, Gilbert uses an American historical experience to invalidate Korea's demand for Japan's more reflexive recognition of its colonial past by decontextualizing the meanings of colonization and independence for the Koreans and the Americans. Comparing the American independence war with Korean independence movements, the author claims that the Americans and the British teach the war differently at school but "do not distort historical facts completely or diminish each other," whereas the Koreans "treat Japan as an absolute villain and educate children so that they learn to denigrate Japan" (Book 2, 173). The author also contrasts Independence Hall in Philadelphia where the U.S. Declaration of Independence and the U.S. Constitution were discussed with the Independence Hall of Korea located in Cheonan where Korean history and their struggles against Japanese colonial oppression are exhibited. He contends that the former "celebrates independence based on historical facts," whereas the latter "based on fabricated history" (177).

This statement is problematic not only because Gilbert diminishes the Korean view of Japanese colonization and independence as distortion or fabrication but also because he compares the two cases by ignoring dissimilar colonizer-colonized relationships and parties involved there. The relationship between European settlers in North America and Europeans in Europe was certainly not equal. However, seen from Native American and African perspectives, the American independence war was fought between two groups of colonizers/enslavers: European settlers in North America and Europeans in Europe. This war thus meant independence for neither Native Americans, the colonized, nor liberation for Africans, the (largely) enslaved. In contrast, the Korean case had a clearer structure: the colonized (i.e., the Koreans) fought against the colonizer (i.e., the Japanese).

Style

The style used in Gilbert's book is the aversion, which was also employed in the 2014 bestseller "hate books" that targeted Korea/Koreans (Kawai 2018). This overlaps with what van Dijk (1992) calls, the denial of racism. Among the six forms of the denial identified by van Dijk, the style used in his books corresponds to *reversal* or "the strongest form of denial" in which the victimizer of racism makes the victim into the victimizer by claiming "*We* are not the racists, *they* are the *real* racists" (van Dijk 1992, 94; emphasis in original).[15] The denial of racism is necessary to compensate the element of hierarchy, which Goldberg (1993) argues has become obsolete and been replaced by differentiation.

Depicting China/Chinese and Korea/Koreans as discriminatory, deceptive, and/or despotic simultaneously represents Japan/Japanese as victims enduring oppression, contempt, deceit, or threat from the two groups. These representations function to deny, downplay, or dodge Japan's colonial and wartime violence and exploitation as "false accusation" or "fabrication" and thereby flip the victimizer and the victim of Japanese colonialism and racism. This style is indispensable for Gilbert's books because the element of hierarchy, which Goldberg argues is outdated and generally considered inappropriate, is explicitly deployed in his books.

That Gilbert, a white American man, was "chosen" to write these books also indicates the presence of the aversion style or the denial of racism. Nobody wants to be called a racist or associated with racism. The books written by this white American author are not only more persuasive for Japanese readers, as the publishing editor of his two books correctly assumed, but also more convenient because they can enjoy these books while dissociating themselves from the racist practice committed by an American. Gilbert's case has precedence: the author of a 2014 bestseller hate-Korea book *Chikanron* (Shameful South Korea) (Lee 2014) claims to be Korean; a 1993 bestseller *Minikui kankokujin* (Ugly South Koreans) (1993) was published under a Korean name, although it is widely accepted that its main author was a conservative Japanese writer (Shin 1996). By using a non-Japanese as a "spokesperson," Japanese racism, which often intersects with nationalism, becomes obscured and ceases being a Japanese problem that demands much more serious attention from the Japanese public.

CONCLUSION

The grammar of Japanese racialized discourse in Gilbert's books was primarily *racial hierarchical differentiation* or *racial differentiation* added with the element of hierarchy. For many centuries, Confucianism and Sinocentrism affected political, economic, and cultural relationships between China, Korea, and Japan. Although China's cultural authority was the norm for premodern Korean and Japanese ruling elites, they attempted to challenge it and were no less ethnocentric than those in China, developing their versions of Sinocentrism. Using Confucianism and Sinocentrism—two major topics for the Western understanding of China/Asia—and neglecting the complex and dynamic historical situations concerning the two, Gilbert's books portrayed China/Chinese and Korea/Koreans as essentially different from Japan/Japanese while depicting the two groups negatively as discriminatory and deceptive, and China/Chinese as despotic. Korea/Koreans were represented more pejoratively as subservient to China/Chinese and discriminatory especially to Japan/Japanese. These representations were crucial to invert the victim and the victimizer and avert the accusation of being a racist, colonizer, or invader. Following this discourse, the two books constructed a positive Japanese identity as *not* Chinese and Korean—not as discriminatory, deceptive, and despotic—or as fair, reasonable, trustable, flexible, egalitarian, or democratic as the Americans.

The more pejorative representations of Korea/Koreans indicate different positions of the two groups placed in the *minzoku* hierarchy. Historically, this difference overlaps with Japan's relationships with and views of China and Korea concerning Confucianism and Sinocentrism. Contemporarily, it is observable in the situation that people of Korean descent tend to be targeted more frequently and harshly than their Chinese counterparts in not only in "hate books" but also in far-right racist demonstrations and online comments. Japan's historical relationship with Korea was inseparable from the idea of China, which was tied to Confucianism and the Sinocentric tributary order. Until the nineteenth century, Japan's challenges to China's cultural authority simultaneously affected its relationship with Korea since both were deeply implicated in China's two bodies of thought. The colonization of Korea added another layer to Japanese memories and ideas of Korea/Koreans.

The discourse employed in Gilbert's books differs from the one used in *nihonjinron*, the popular literary genre for Japanese identity construction in the 1970s and 1980s, although both engage in constructing Japaneseness (Kawai 2018). Representing the Japanese as a depoliticized cultural group by embracing the Western Orientalist view of Japanese culture and people to differentiate themselves from the West (see chapter 1), *nihonjnron* writings primarily followed *racial differentiation*. Difference was stressed in constructing Japaneseness in relation to the West or *jinshu*-wise. However, hierarchy becomes significant when the meaning of the Japanese is created in relation to other Asians or *minzoku*-wise, while the Japanese are placed on the same side with the West or the white race (i.e., the Americans). The significance of *minzoku* is notable in Gilbert's frequent use of the term in referring to the Japanese (e.g., Book 1, 74, 142, 158, 205; Book 2, 185, 228, 236, 237), as well as in his reference to the male-line continuity of the emperors as an important source for Japanese cultural "uniqueness" (Book 1, 141). Although there are multiple reasons why "hate books" like those of Gilbert are far more problematic than *nihonjinron* books, one of them is undoubtedly the element of hierarchy.

In order to problematize "hate books" for the construction of a multiculturalist Japanese society, it is not enough to condemn their pejorative depictions of China/Chinese and Korea/Koreans; it is essential to interrogate how Japaneseness is constructed in relation to China/Chinese and Korea/Koreans *and* to the West, white America/Americans in particular, simultaneously. What it means to be Japanese must be scrutinized by looking into Japaneseness' discursive relationship with the West, including the invisibilization of the West as the "global" (see chapter 2) and its excessive identification with white America/Americans (see chapter 3), as well as a more complex and multifaceted understanding of both historical and contemporary trans-East Asian connections and disconnections.

NOTES

1. Nippan and Tohan are the two largest oligopolistic book distributors in Japan. *Bōkanron* (Murotani 2013) ranked third in the business category of Nippan's 2014 bestseller list and *Chikanron* (Lee 2014) ranked ninth in its paperback nonfiction category (Nippan 2014). The former ranked first and the latter seventh in the paperback nonfiction category of Tohan's 2014 bestseller list (Tohan 2014). *Bōkanron* was one of the twenty bestselling books of the year, ranking twentieth on Nippan's list and seventeenth on Tohan's.

2. The title of the law is "The Act on the Promotion of Efforts to Eliminate Unfair Discriminatory Speech and Behavior against Persons Originating from Outside Japan."

3. Sincere Lee, the author of *Chikanron*, published a praise-Japan book *Naze nihon no gohan wa oishii no ka* (Why Is Japanese Rice Delicious?) in 2016. Bunyu Ko, a naturalized citizen of Japan from Taiwan, published several hate books in 2014, targeting South Korea and China including *Hanchūkanron* (Criminal China and South Korea), *Hankanron* (Criminal South Korea), *Hankanron* (Grudging South Korea), and *Hikanron* (Miserable South Korea). Ko also wrote praise-Japan books, including *Sekai kara sukarete iru nihon* (The World Loves Japan) in 2016 and *Sekai wo kando saseta nihon seishin* (The Japanese Spirit Impressed the World) in 2017.

4. Although Gilbert refers to North Korea several times (e.g., Gilbert 2017, 76, 98, 198, 199; 2018, 7, 172, 216), the main target is South Korea.

5. The book ranked sixth in Nippan's list (2017) and fourth in Tohan's (2017).

6. This is a nationalist organization founded in 1997 by a group of right-wing academics and writers in response to the inclusion of the "comfort women" issue in high school textbooks.

7. See note 5 of Chapter 2 for the explanation of "comfort women."

8. These books include coauthored books. The data are collected by using the National Diet Library Search engine (http://iss.ndl.go.jp/).

9. According to Yasuda (2018), most of Gilbert's books are "written" from his spoken material: Publishers transcribe and edit his talks, which are checked by Gilbert and his assistants. As a reason for his books citing mostly far-right Japanese nationalist sources and very few English sources, Yasuda claims that his assistants choose necessary references and provide them to him.

10. For example, see Oizumi et al. (2015).

11. The Five Classics consist of *The Book of Changes*易経, *The Book of Documents*書経, *The Book of Songs*詩経, *Records of Rites*礼経, and *The Spring and Autumn Annals*春秋. The Four Books refer to *The Doctrine of the Mean*中庸, *Great Learning*大学, *Mencius*孟子, and *The Analects*論語.

12. Gilbert (2017) also confesses its authenticity is disputed (177).

13. The 1965 agreement titled "Agreement on the Settlement of Problems Concerning Property and Claims and on Economic Co-operation between Japan and the Republic of Korea" was signed along with the Treaty on Basic Relations that

normalized Japan's diplomatic relations with South Korea. Japan promised to provide South Korea with 500 million U.S. dollars in grants and credit assistance.

14. For example, in lawsuits filed by atomic bomb survivors in Hiroshima and Nagasaki in 1955, the Japanese government clarified that despite the San Francisco Peace Treaty, "an individual's rights to file a claim against the United States have yet to be renounced" (*Asahi Shimbun* 2018).

15. The six types of denial are: *defense*, *mitigation*, *justification*, *excuse*, *provocation and blaming the other*, and *reversal*. The first two types are "denial proper" (van Dijk 1992, 93), in which committing an action is denied, whereas in the rest four types, the actor admits that an action is committed but denies that it is negative.

Chapter 5

Entering the West and Encountering Asia

Trans-East Asian Friendships Made in the West

In the twenty-first century, Japan has become simultaneously more interconnected with and disconnected from its neighboring East Asian countries. South Korean popular culture has gone mainstream, and Japanese politicians and academics once actively discussed East Asian regionalism, such as creating the East Asian Community. At the same time, postcolonial and territorial disputes as well as the rise of their economies and the relative decline of Japan's have tainted Japanese perceptions of China and South Korea (hereafter Korea). In an annual governmental survey on Japanese people's attitudes toward countries that Japan has close relationships with, negative attitudes toward China and Korea has increased in the 2010s: from an average of 56 percent in the 2000s to 79 percent in the 2010s for China; from an average of 42 percent to 55 percent for Korea (Cabinet Public Relations Office 2019d).[1] It was recorded at an all-time high since the 1970s of 83.2 percent (China) and 71.5 percent (Korea) in 2015 and 2019, respectively. It stands in sharp contrast to the far less negative attitude toward the United States, whose average was 22 percent in the 2000s and 16 percent in the 2010s.

Many national governments and higher educational institutions, including those in Japan, are encouraging students to participate in study-abroad programs, responding to the demands and challenges arising from globalization. The Japanese government has supported a limited number of Japanese elites to study in American and European higher educational institutions since the mid-nineteenth century to gain "advanced" Western knowledge and technologies. However, in 2013, the Ministry of Education, Culture, Sports, Science and Technology (MEXT) launched the study-abroad promotional campaign called "*Tobitate* (Leap for Tomorrow) Japan" and began to offer study-abroad scholarships on a broader scale with financial contributions from major Japanese corporations such as Toyota, Softbank, and Mitsubishi Trading to double the number of Japanese people studying abroad by 2020 (MEXT n.d.). The background of this policy is the lack of "globally minded talent" pointed out by "roughly 70 percent of Japanese companies with operations outside of Japan" (MEXT n.d.). In particular, Japanese university students participating in short-term (from a few weeks to one year) study-abroad programs has increased from 40,158 in 2010 to 68,156 in 2013 and to 113,112 in 2018 (MEXT 2020).[2]

Western Anglophone countries such as the United States, Australia, Canada, and Britain are most popular destinations for Japanese university students. According to the latest data available, more than 40 percent of the 2018 study-abroad program participants went to these four countries, whereas approximately 19 percent went to China, Korea, and Taiwan (MEXT 2020). However, they come to interact closely with other Asian students in those Western countries, often for the first time in their life. Despite the tensions and negative perceptions toward China and Korea, I frequently hear Japanese students who have studied in a Western country say that they became most friendly with students from China, Korea, and Taiwan.

Meanwhile, the number of international students in Japan increased from 168,145 in 2014 to 312,214 in 2019 (MEXT 2020). More than 90 percent of them came from Asian countries and this percentage has been constant since 2000 (Japan Student Services Organization n.d.).[3] However, this increase does not necessarily lead to deepening Japanese students' relationships with them (e.g., Ohashi 2008). One problem is an inequitable communicational context. When their interactions occur in Japan, the Japanese language is usually the primary means of communication, which puts Japanese students in a privileged position. Another problem is Japanese people's less favorable attitudes toward people from non-Western countries. Asian international students in Japan tend to have more stress and experience difficulties in building relationships with Japanese students in comparison to Euro-American international students (e.g., Ohashi 2008). In Li's (2015) study on Chinese students' friendship in Japan, not only did Chinese interviewees complain about Japanese students' greater willingness to make friends with Euro-American students but all the Japanese interviewees admitted to the tendency as well (58–59).

Japanese students participate in a short-term study-abroad program in a Western country not only because they hope to improve their foreign language (mostly English) skills but also because they are often interested in Euro-American cultures. Then why do they become friends with other East Asian students in the West? One possible reason is the difficulty of making local Euro-American friends. Reviewing studies on East Asian international students in Anglophone countries, Gareis (2012) argues that East Asian students tend to have fewer host-nation friends in comparison with their European counterparts (313). The factors behind this tendency include negative Asian stereotypes in the West, as well as cultural, linguistic, and phenotypical distance between Asian international students and host Anglophone students (321–22). This suggests the relevance of Asia and the West in trans-East Asian friendships made in the West.

In this chapter, I examine the ideas of Asia and the West in friendships that Japanese students make with Asian students when they participate in a study-abroad program in the West. Both the West and Asia are multifaceted concepts. Referring to a wide range of entities such as a geographical area, the Judeo-Christian tradition, capitalist institutions, liberal democracy, and the white race, the West is "a patchwork, assembled quite arbitrarily, of entities that are sometimes called 'Western' and sometimes not" (Sakai 2005, 13–14). Likewise, Asia is "not only a political concept, but also a cultural concept; it is not only a geographical location, but also a measure of value judgement" (Sun 2000a, 13). Asia, "a shadow of the West" (Sakai 1997, 173), has been represented as what is not Western: Confucian values, non or semi-capitalism, totalitarianism, undemocratic, and the yellow race, among others.

Asia and the West as the significant discursive Others for Japaneseness since the late nineteenth century are particularly related to race and nation, and thus the two Japanese concepts of race, *jinshu* and *minzoku*. Against the backdrops of Western colonialism and imperialism in the nineteenth century, Western discourses at that time often depicted Asia—often represented by China—as opposite to the West: static versus dynamic, despotic versus democratic, and backward versus progressive (see chapter 4). Asia was a category that early modern Japanese elites and intellectuals wanted to simultaneously discard and keep as a source of cultural difference to construct Japanese identity as opposed to the West (Tanaka 1993). This desire pertaining to *jinshu*, which summarizes and inferioritizes peoples in Asia, eventually led to the idea of *minzoku*, which provided a means for the Japanese to differentiate themselves as the most superior group among Asians (see chapter 1). Contemporary Japanese people's less positive view of Asian countries and peoples in comparison to their view of the Western counterparts cannot be explained without considering the ideas of Asia and the West.

I begin this chapter with a historical discussion of Japan's ideas of Asia, which are necessarily intertwined with those of the West. Then analyzing interviews conducted with fourteen Japanese university students who participated in a short-term study-abroad program in a Western country between 2013 and 2018, I examine how Asia and the West—race and nation—are implicated in their trans-East Asian friendships and explore what problems and possibilities are embedded there.

ASIA AND THE WEST

Asia does not exist without the West (Takeuchi 2005, 53–81). As Said (1978) argues that Orientalism "has less to do with the Orient than it does with 'our' [Western] world" (12), Asia is a discursive means for the West to become the West. The notion of Asia (or Orient) originated in ancient Greece where the known world was divided between Europe and Asia, and the latter referred to the vast amorphous area that spread east beyond Europe (Frey and Spakowski 2016, 3). As discussed in chapter 4, in the late eighteenth and nineteenth centuries, Western industrial and civil revolutions, the development of capitalism, the intensification of Western colonialism and imperialism, and academic theories such as race theories and progressivism consolidated the idea of Asia as opposite and inferior to the West. The modern ideas of Asia and the West signified not simply difference but a hierarchical relationship between the two.

Although Asia is primarily a Western construction, people summarized as Asians have also invested in this idea. Asia became significant in Japan in the mid-nineteenth century and was initially connoted as "the area to be conquered by Europe" (Takeuchi 1993, 97). Sun (2000) argues that Japanese intellectuals' discussions about Asia since then can be divided into two camps. One sees Asia negatively and dissociates Japan from Asia; the other regards Asia positively and privileges Japan as the center of Asia. The two views are represented by the idea of "Leaving Asia" attributed to Fukuzawa Yukichi and Kakuzo Okakura's thesis of "Asia is one," respectively (Sun 2000, 15). However, the two views are similar in essentializing and counter-posing Asia against the West (21–22).

In the well-known "Leaving Asia" essay published in 1885 as an editorial in the newspaper established by Fukuzawa (who served as the chief editor), Asia was represented by China and Korea and was associated with "ancient ways and old customs," "ignorance" (Fukuzawa 1997, 352), "foolishness, lawless-ness, atrocity, and heartlessness," as well as depicted as "autocratic" and "unscientific" (353). In contrast, the West was characterized as opposite of Asia: as civilized, modern, progressive, enlightened and democratic. Differentiating the Japanese from the Chinese and the Koreans, the editorial claimed that Japan "has already moved away from the old conventions of Asia to the Western civilization" and thus "it may be that we [Chinese, Koreans, and Japanese] are different races [*jinshu*] of people, or it may be due to the differences in our heredity or education; significant differences mark these peoples" (Fukuzawa 1997, 35; 1933, 41). Sun (2000) points out that this essay shows commitment to "'the Survival of the Fittest' way of thinking" (17). Asia in this editorial was tied to the idea of *jinshu*, especially Western "biological" race theories under the strong influence of Social Darwinism at that time (see chapter 1). Regarding peoples categorized as Asians or the yellow race and their cultures as inferior to those in the West, the editorial called for "leav[ing] the ranks of Asian nations and cast[ing] our lot with civilized nations of the West" (Fukuzawa 1997, 353).

About twenty years later, Okakura (1920 [1903]) proposed that "Asia is one" in his English book titled *The Ideals of the East* (1). Sun (2000) posits that while the attention of Fukuzawa's editorial was on "how Japan could survive in the predatory modern world," Okakura was concerned about "how Japan could offer the modern world values for a new understanding of civilization" (20). For Okakura, peoples in the Middle East, Central Asia, South Asia, Southeast Asia, and East Asia "form[ed] a single web" (3). Asia as having "love for the Ultimate and the Universal" was contrasted to peoples in the West, who "love to dwell on the Particular, and search out the means, not the end of life" (1). Put differently, in Okakura's view, Asians care for fundamental and essential issues, whereas Westerners are preoccupied with technical and practical matters. Then Okakura elevated Japanese culture from other Asian cultures, describing it as "the real depository of the trust of Asiatic thought and culture" (5) and "a museum of Asiatic civilization" (7). In other words, Japanese culture represented the best of Asian culture, which was superior to Western culture. Okakura's Asia was tied to both *jinshu* and *minzoku* in the sense that while summarizing various cultures in Asia as one and asserting their Asianness, Okakura placed Japanese culture on top of them.

Asianism symbolized by Okakura's thesis "Asia is one" started in the nineteenth century as "a popularly based and relatively egalitarian vision of solidarity with Asia" (Morris-Suzuki 2016, 157) in the Japanese context, but later shifted to a ultranationalist Great Asianism in the 1930s and 1940s. Asianism often characterized Asia in terms of geography (e.g., the East), cultural unity (e.g., Confucianism), historical interconnectedness (e.g., the Sinocentric tribute order), racial kinship (e.g., the yellow race), and a common destiny (e.g., subordination by the West) (Saaler and Szpilman 2011, 34). Asianism involved transnationalism with its emphasis on Asia's commonality and was also compatible with Japanese nationalism when it advocated Japan's "superiority over Asia and leadership in Asia" (Saaler 2007, 3). That is why the idea of Asia itself was "at the same time colonialist and anti-colonialist, conservative and revolutionary, nationalist and internationalist" (Wang 2007, 27).

Asianism, primarily anti-Westernism (Saaler and Szpilman 2011, 34), was the antithesis of the pro-Western "Leaving Asia." The latter, the position adopted by the Japanese government until the 1920s, was later replaced with the former as exemplified by the state-founding proclamation of Manchukuo (Government of Manchukuo 1932) and the idea of the Greater East Asia Co-Prosperity Sphere—Japan's wartime propaganda to create a united political, economic, and military zone in cooperation with other Asian peoples.

As observable in Okakura's argument, Asianism entailed solidarity among Asian peoples as one *jinshu*, as well as Japan's superiority and leadership in line with the idea of *minzoku*. Considering the affinity between the two theses pointed out by Sun (2000), shifting from "Leaving Asia" to Asianism did not mean a complete change of Japan's ideological position.

The Japanese government came to embrace Asianism against the backdrops of the uplifting of Japan's power in the aftermath of World War I and the 1924 U.S. Immigration Act that barred Japanese immigration to the United States (Saaler and Szpilman 2011, 17–18). The accommodation of Asianism paralleled with the reevaluation of Confucianism, which also accelerated after World War I (see chapter 4). The bloodshed among European countries in World War I discredited the West's political and civilizational authority, which in turn mitigated the negative connotations of Asia described in Fukuzawa's editorial. The 1924 Immigration Act indicated that "leaving Asia" did not make Japanese people white. In the 1930s, Asianism was integrated into Japan's imperial and colonial policies as an ideology to legitimize its territorial expansion and control in Asia (Hotta 2007; Saaler and Szpilman 2011, 18–19).

After the end of World War II, discussions on Asianism disappeared from the dominant discourse. The press codes issued by the Supreme Commander for the Allied Powers (SCAP) banned terms and ideas associated with Asianism due to its connection with prewar Japanese nationalism (Miwa 2007, 31). However, Japanese left-wing intellectuals continued to engage in Asianism, referring to Asia as a point of reference to criticize Western modernity and the world dominated by the West in response to, for example, the 1949 Chinese Revolution, the Korean War, the Bandung Conference, anti-Vietnam War movements, and the activism of ethnic minorities, such as the Ainu, Okinawans, and Koreans (Oguma 2007). Yet, until the 1980s, the West played a far more visible role than Asia in constructing Japaneseness as shown in *nihonjinron* (see chapters 1 and 2). In short, Japan "left" Asia without confronting its prewar relationship with Asia.

It was after the mid-1980s, especially in the 1990s, that Asia reemerged in the mainstream discourse due to factors including the end of the Cold War, globalization, the rise of Asian economies, and intensifying Japan's economic and cultural interconnections with Asian countries (Avenell 2014, 619–20; Morris-Suzuki 1998, 5–9). The comeback of Asia is linked to the diversification of the Other for the construction of Japaneseness in the 1990s, decentering the West, the most significant Other in *nihonjinron*.

Analyzing Japan's "New Asianism" discourses in the 1990s and the early 2000s, Simon Avenell (2014) identified three positions: *Asia as Japan*, *Asia for Japan*, and *Japan in Asia*. The three positions shared "a recognition that regionalization and globalization are inevitable processes, which the Japanese must address through a renewed engagement with the Asian region" (620). Emphasizing Asian common values and identity, the *Asia as Japan* position used Asia as "a convenient substitute for Japan" (621) to handle economic competitions intensified under globalization while often taking Japan's leadership for granted. The *Asia for Japan* position was a "realist" version of the first position. This position stressed the inevitability and necessity of Asian regional integration for Japan's economic survival in a globalizing world. The third position, *Japan in Asia*, explored ways of creating transnational relationships with peoples in Asia by facing squarely and rectifying Japan's colonial and wartime injustices. This position overlaps with Asianism engaged by left-wing intellectuals in postwar Japan.

The first two positions use Asia as a "tool" for Japan to survive intensifying competitions under globalization. Thus they are constitutive of Japanese nationalism, and their Asia is similar to Asia in the governmental Asianism in the 1930s and 1940s. However, the two positions are different in their understanding of Asia. Following the primordialist and instrumentalist approaches of ethnicity theory, the former grasps Asia and Asianness as inherently existent, whereas the latter views it as a product of instrumental factors such as geographical proximity and tight economic interconnections among states in Asia. Moreover, the West in New Asianism differs from the West in the prewar Asianism. It is less visible in the latter not only because Westernization has been neutralized and was called globalization (see chapter 2) but also because the rise of Asian economies has made the West's economic and cultural power less dominant than before.

In the third position, the Other for Asia is not simply the West. Asia and the West in this position coincide with those in what Morris-Suzuki (2016) called "grassroots Asianism," which refers to "a widespread and loosely linked web of very small grassroots groups" that seek "in varied ways to deepen the integration of Japan and other parts of Asia" (157–58). Asia in grassroots Asianism is characterized not by a common culture or identity but "by the experience of exploitation and suffering" inflicted by the "First World," which is not limited to Europe and the United States but incorporates Japan (166). The exploitation and suffering of Asia include Western and Japanese imperialism and colonialism, transnational capitalism, and U.S. militarism. In short, Japan in this position is simultaneously Asia and the West.

TRANS-EAST ASIAN FRIENDSHIPS MADE IN THE WEST

I conducted interviews with fourteen Japanese university students (thirteen female and one male) who participated in a short-term study-abroad program (one or two semesters) between 2013 and 2018 in their sophomore and junior years (aged between nineteen and twenty-one).[4] I interviewed them between one semester and one year after their return, except for one interviewee, whose interview was held about two years later. Each interview lasted approximately one hour. Their destinations were Australia (1 interviewee), Britain (5), Canada (1), Spain (1), and the United States (7). One interviewee participated a study-abroad program twice in Britain and the United States. Each of them made multiple Asian friends, most of whom were from China, Korea, and Taiwan, and a few from Malaysia (a person of Chinese descent) and Vietnam. Seven out of the fourteen interviewees said that their closest friends were Korean. I asked them how and why they made friends with Asian students, what they talked about and did together, and how they have changed through the process. I analyze the interviews to examine how Asia and the West, thus race and nation, are implicated and explore problems and possibilities implicated in their relationships. In the following analysis, the interviewees are referred to using letters of the alphabet from A to N (e.g., Interviewee A) to preserve confidentiality, and the country in parenthesis indicates their destination.

The Centrality of Japanese Culture

Japanese culture played a key role in their trans-East Asian relationships, serving as an important factor for their friendship to develop. Before studying abroad, other than two interviewees (C and H) who had watched Korean TV drama regularly, the rest of the interviewees were unfamiliar with their friends' cultures, and none of them had visited the countries of their friends or learned another Asian language. However, their Asian friends often knew about Japan and Japanese culture by having interests in Japanese animation (anime) and comic books (manga), visiting Japan or learning the Japanese language.

Anime and Manga

As a common topic of conversation or factor that brought them closer with their Asian friends, six interviewees (B, C, F, G, I, K) mentioned anime and manga. For example, Interviewee F (Australia) stated that "I was living in a dorm and made many Chinese friends there. Almost all of them liked and knew about anime and manga. But I didn't know about them at all . . . I was really surprised and wondered why they knew so much." Her Chinese friends often asked her if she had watched or read a particular anime or manga series, assuming that she would know about it because she was Japanese. However, she could not say anything because she did not watch or read them much.

Realizing the gap between their knowledge about Japanese popular culture and her knowledge about theirs, she commented that "they were interested in Japanese culture, but I realized I didn't know much about their culture. Sometimes I felt sorry about that."

Likewise, Interviewee C's (Britain) Chinese friend was an anime and manga fan. Although anime and manga were their main topics of conversation, she would just listen to her friend, since she did not know much about them. However, she said, "We didn't talk much about China." In the case of Interviewee I (United States), she often talked about Japan with her Vietnamese roommate. Explaining her friend's interest in Japanese culture, she stated that "my friend told me that anime programs were often aired on TV in Vietnam, for example, Studio Ghibli films and *Doraemon*." Although her friend was not an anime fan, the friend developed her interest in Japanese culture by watching anime programs on TV. However, Interviewee I did not know much about Vietnam, to the point that she was not even certain whether Hanoi and Ho Chi Minh City were located in the north or the south of the country. Interviewee G (Canada) also said that "Taiwanese friends usually started talking to me by saying 'I know a lot about anime.'" She said, "*Detective Conan* was very popular among them. They also talked about *One Piece* and *Doraemon*. I have not watched all the episodes of *Doraemon*. I wasn't sure about the plot, but I learned it from them." Moreover, not knowing anything about Taiwanese popular culture then, Interviewee G started asking them about it.

Perhaps anime and manga are part of banal cultural consumption for the interviewees' Asian friends. Koichi Iwabuchi (2004) posits that "Japan's popular cultural presence no longer seems to be something spectacular or anomalous but, instead, seems to have become rather mundane in the urban landscape of East/Southeast Asia" (2). Japanese popular culture—initially animation and pop idols, and later others such as Japanese TV drama—has been available through both formal (e.g., cable television) and informal (e.g., pirated software and the internet) routes of distribution in East and Southeast Asia since the late 1970s (Iwabuchi 2004). The consumption of anime accelerated especially due to the rise of internet communities, which played an indispensable role in spreading Japanese animation in East Asia (Hernandez and Hirai 2015, 158).

The gap in their cultural knowledge implies that Japan's "superiority and leadership" rooted in prewar Asianism still looms over their friendships. The spread of anime and manga may be due to the lack of "cultural odor" or "the way in which the cultural presence of a country of origin and images or ideas of its way of life are positively associated with a particular product in the consumption process" (Iwabuchi 1998, 166). Their appeal to the global audience may be attributed to neutralized and depoliticized internationalization, such as racial and cultural mixing and blurring (Lu 2008). Despite these cultural politics, Japan is still credited as their place of origin. Referring to not specifically Asian friends but friends in general, Interviewee L (United States) stated that "since many students knew about anime, manga, and Japanese TV dramas, I was able to open a conversation and make friends by talking about them. Thanks to them, Japan has a positive image. I just happened to be born in Japan but got benefits from it."

However, Japanese popular cultural "leadership" does not privilege the interviewees completely. As seen in the cases of Interviewees C, F, and G, Japanese popular cultural "experts" are their Asian friends. As Interviewee L stated, they may gain some benefits from the prevalence of anime and manga. Yet being Japanese does not provide them with cultural "authority" because their friends are more knowledgeable about these than they are. Moreover, their Asian friends' expertise about anime and manga can make them aware of their ignorance of the friends' culture, which is observable in Interviewees F and G's comments.

Although Japanese youth's popular cultural consumption may not be as trans-East Asian as their counterparts in other Asian countries, there is one exception: Korean popular culture. For Interviewees C (Britain) and H (United States), who regularly watched Korean TV dramas in Japan, it was a common topic of conversation with their Korean and Chinese friends. Although Interviewee M (United States) mentioned that she was not particularly interested in Korean popular culture before making friends with Korean students in the United States, she was familiar with Korean popular music: "I often talked about Korean idol groups, for example, TWICE and Girls' Generation, with Korean and Chinese students. They are famous, and everyone knows about them. I talked about them even with American students."

Knowledge of Japan and the Japanese Language

Four interviewees' (D, E, K, M) close friends had travelled to Japan or lived in Japan. Interviewee D's (Britain) Chinese friend with a strong interest in Japanese fashion had worked in Tokyo for one year before coming to study in Britain. The friend approached D in an English course, knowing that D came from Japan. In the initial stage of their friendship, Japan was a main topic of their conversation. The friends of Interviewees E (Britain), K (Spain), and M (United States) were Korean. Japan is a travel destination far more accessible for Korean people than other Asian peoples because visiting Japan is less expensive due to Korea's geographical proximity to Japan, and the two countries have a visa waiver status, which is not available to, for example, the Chinese or Vietnamese. Interviewee E's Korean friend visited Japan several times before coming to study in Britain because he had a friend living in Tokyo. One of Interviewee K's Korean friends came to Japan many times because she was a fan of a Japanese idol group. Interviewee M's friends, who had been to Fukuoka, told her that they enjoyed their travel and liked Japan. She was pleasantly surprised that "young Koreans were interested in Japan, regardless of what happened between Korea and Japan in the past."

Statistics show the imbalanced flow of people between East Asian countries and Japan, which has been the case since a few years after the 2011 Great East Japan Earthquake. According to the latest available data, in 2018, 8,380,034 people from China, 7,538,952 from Korea, 4,757,258 from Taiwan, and 2,207,804 from Hong Kong visited Japan (Japan National Tourism Organization n.d.a.), whereas 2,689,662 Japanese travelled to China, 2,948,527 to Korea, 1,969,151 to Taiwan, and 852,192 to Hong Kong (Japan National Tourism Organization n.d.b.). The actual disparity will become even greater, considering that Korea's population is less than half, Taiwan's is one-fifth, Hong Kong's is merely 5 percent of Japan's population,[5] and China's Gross National Income (GNI) per capita is less than half of Japan's.[6]

Of course, these numbers alone do not prove Asian peoples' greater interest in Japanese culture. A decision to visit a particular overseas destination is influenced by multiple factors including travel cost, state tourism policies, media images, tourist attractions, and political and business relations among many others. People in developed countries often travel for leisure to a developing country because it is less costly to do so. For example, 389,005 people visited Japan from Vietnam, whereas 826,674 Japanese entered Vietnam in 2018 (Japan National Tourism Organization n.d.a., n.d.b.). Yet, this does not mean that Japanese people have more interests in and knowledge about Vietnam than the reverse. Moreover, there is no doubt that the increase of inbound visitors to Japan is largely attributable to the Japanese government's active involvement in promoting tourism, which started in 2003 under the Koizumi administration, as well as the rise of other Asian countries' economic prosperity and the relative decline of Japan's including its currency value.

However, young people would not consider travelling there if they did not have any interest in or connection with Japan. This is shown in the fact that twelve interviewees (A, C, D, E, F, G, H, I, K, L, M, N) started to become interested in travelling to or actually visited Asian countries after coming back to Japan. In addition, a short-term visit to a country would not guarantee enhancing mutual understanding between visitors and the people of the destination. Referring to personal contacts between Japanese citizens and people from other Asian countries, Morris-Suzuki (1998) states that "particularly where individuals meet on socially and economically unequal terms, the result may well be mutual disdain as much as mutual understanding or respect" (11). Yet, compared to the 1990s that Morris-Suzuki refers to, almost none or far fewer economic gaps exist between other East Asian countries and Japan. Although East Asian visitors to Japan will have not only positive but also negative experiences, at least they will become more familiar with and feel closer to this place.

Interests in Japanese popular culture and experiences of vising Japan are linked with learning the Japanese language (e.g., Northwood and Thomson 2012). The close friends of five interviewees (B, D, G, J, K) were able to speak Japanese or had some knowledge of the Japanese language due to their interest in or exposure to Japanese popular culture. Interviewee D's (Britain) Chinese friend who lived in Tokyo for one year was able to communicate in Japanese. Interviewee K's (Spain) two Korean friends, a Japanese idol group fan and a Japanese manga fan, had become fluent in Japanese by learning it on their own so that she communicated with them mostly in Japanese. Interviewee J's (Britain) Korean friend, a fan of a Japanese idol singer/actor, also understood the language.

Probably because Japanese culture is more available and visible in Taiwan, their Taiwanese friends were often familiar with the language even though they were not particularly interested in Japanese popular culture. Interviewee G (Canada) made friends with Taiwanese students. Many of them had some knowledge of the Japanese language, although they had not formally learned it. She said, "Probably they were familiar with it because they often watched Japanese animation. They knew how to write 'pretty (*kawaii*)' in Japanese or what certain Japanese words mean." Interviewee B's (United States) Taiwanese friend had taken a Japanese language course at her university in Taiwan. She heard her friend say that "Taiwanese people speak Taiwanese, Chinese, and a little bit of Japanese. The Taiwanese language is a little similar to Japanese. *Ringo* [apple] is also *ringo* in Taiwanese. So it was not difficult to study Japanese." Although it is dubious that Taiwanese people in general speak Japanese even "a little" today, Japanese words are undeniably visible in Taiwan. Due to Japan's half-a-century-long colonization of Taiwan, a good number of Japanese words have been incorporated into the Taiwanese language and are often used, for example, in product packages and restaurant signboards in Taiwan.

"Cultural Proximity"

Cultural proximity or similarity in values, behaviors, and backgrounds is an important factor in bringing people together into a friendship (e.g., Byrne 1971). The cultural proximity that prompted the interviewees' trans-East Asian friendships did not necessarily imply an essentialized notion of cultural similarity, for example, between Chinese and Japanese culture. It was rather made in the West. Similarity in food preference and English proficiency level played significant roles in their relationships.

Food

Eight interviewees (A, E, F, H, I, J, L, M) raised food as an important element for their trans-East Asian friendships. For instance, Interviewee E (Britain) described her experience when she cooked a soy sauce-based dish with potatoes and meat (*nikujaga*) and Japanese-style wheat noodles (*udon*) for other international students. While her Korean friend liked them very much, her British and Spanish friends did not: looking at the color of the soup, they asked her skeptically, "What is this? It is too brown." Likewise, recalling different reactions to Japanese food from other international students, Interviewee M (United States) said, "Asian students liked rice and instant noodles from Korea or Japan, but American and European students did not like them much. When I cooked Japanese rice for Korean students, they liked it. When I cooked it for European students, they complained it's too sticky."

Cooking smell is another significant issue. Interviewee I (United States) said, "I felt closer to Asian students because we liked similar food. Asian students often ate fish. My Vietnamese roommate cooked fish, but other students did not like fish very much." A European student told her friend, who often cooked fish in the dorm kitchen, that "it smells. Let me open the window." Interviewee H (United States) enjoyed cooking with her Chinese roommate. She said, "I cooked *mapo tofu* with a seasoning mix from Japan for her and she liked it. I didn't have to worry about food with her." Examples of her "worry about food" included cooking smells and choosing restaurants.

Food and identity are inseparable. Fischler (1988) posits that "food and cuisine are a quite central component of the sense of collective belonging" (290). Food smells and flavor are significant group "markers," which have been deployed in racial and ethnic identity construction (e.g., Slocum 2011, 305) as well as in racism and xenophobia (e.g., Wurgaft 2006, 57). In short, "food serves both to solidify group membership and to set groups apart" (Mintz and Du Bois 2002, 109). People away from their familiar environment, such as migrants, can place strong emotional attachment to their traditions of food, which are often invented or imagined (e.g., Parasecoli 2014). Human beings are omnivores (Fischler 1988, 277). The interviewees probably eat all kinds of food in Japan, preferring sandwiches to rice balls for lunch and consuming pasta, pizza, and hamburgers regularly. However, when they are in the West, non-Western dishes become more significant and emphasized as a similarity with their Asian friends.

This is reminiscent of Asianism that characterized Asia in terms of its cultural unity. As the ideas of Asia and the West are interwoven, stressing Asian culinary commonality is tied to being racially summarized as Asian in the West. Seven interviewees (A, C, E, J, H, I, K, L) mentioned their racialization experiences. For example, three of them (C, E, I) were often hailed with "*ni hao*" or "hello" in Chinese on the street or on campus. Interviewee L (United States) stated that her American classmates often mistook her for Chinese. She was often asked "What kind of place is Beijing?" or "What does this Chinese word mean?" by her classmates even after spending a few months in the same classroom. In the case of Interviewee K (Spain) described an incident that occurred in a film studies course in which twenty-six students were enrolled. After showing a documentary film about a murder case committed by a Japanese man, the instructor asked a student from Korea, "Did the Japanese spoken by the male character sound natural to you?" Interviewee K said, "The instructor couldn't tell us apart. I was shocked because it happened at the end of the semester." Through experiencing it and other incidents, she came to realize that there were often no clear distinctions among Chinese, Koreans, and Japanese in the West: "I had thought Japanese, Chinese, and Koreans are completely different . . . But I realized that was just a Japanese idea."

English Proficiency Level

Nine interviewees (A, B, D, G, H, I, J, M, N) mentioned similarity in English proficiency level as another significant factor for their friendships. Since all the interviewees learned English as a foreign language in Japan, it was not easy for them to communicate with local students who spoke English as their first or primary language. For example, Interviewee A (Britain and United States) explained his initial motivation to talk with Korean students as follows: "My English level wasn't high enough to communicate with local American students. At the beginning, I approached them to speak in English because their English was still better than mine . . . not because they were Korean." Interviewee I (United States) said that it was difficult to become close to American students because "I was able to talk about only superficial things with American students because of my English level. I could say only simple things in English so conversation with them didn't last." However, with her Vietnamese friend, she said, "I didn't care about making mistakes when I was talking with her because our English levels were similar."

English is intertwined with the white race, which is constitutive of the idea of the West. Interviewee J (Britain) made close friends with people from Korea and Taiwan. Although she had classmates from Western countries such as Spain and Switzerland in English language courses, she did not become close to them because "to be honest, English was the major issue . . . I felt lost because I couldn't keep up with conversation with them." However, her Taiwanese friend, who completed a graduate program in Britain, spoke fluent English, but she did not feel the same way with the friend. When I asked her why, she said, "I don't know. I just felt more comfortable with her.

I don't know why." Interviewee D (Britain) clarified the connection between English and the white race. Explaining why Asian students including herself often made friends among themselves, she raised "phenotype [*mitame*] and English" as two main reasons. Commenting that "facial and bodily features are different between Europeans and Asians. I felt so isolated among European students," she said, "when I saw European-looking students, I automatically thought they would speak English well." Whereas English spoken by European students "actually sounded better" to her, she felt closer to her Asian friends because their English "sounded a little strange," like her own English.

Naoki Sakai (2005) argues that "the identity 'West' confers a certain pride upon 'Westerners' who identify with the 'West.' Because identification with the West asserts one's superiority vis-à-vis 'non-Westerners,' the non-Westerners inevitably feel coerced or threatened by the Westerners who stress their own 'Western' identity" (16). European students might or might not have stressed their Western identity in front of the interviewees. However, the interviewees, at least, perceived that European students had confidence in English, a Western language, and/or in themselves. As a result, they felt "coerced or threatened" by the confidence. For example, Interviewee I (United States) stated that "I couldn't join European students because their appearance [*mitame*] was very different. They looked very confident to me. I felt an Asian could not join them." Describing the difference between Asian and European international students' attitudes to English, Interviewee M (United States) stated that "European students never said English is difficult. But both Japanese and Korean students often said English is difficult. That is probably why we came to develop a common identity and formed a group."

Problems and Possibilities

The interviewees' trans-East Asian friendships entailed both problems and possibilities. While Japan's colonial and wartime past, which still overshadows its relationships with other Asian countries, also hovered over their friendships, the interviewees experienced changes in their views and attitudes toward people and countries in Asia.

Not Talking about Historical and Political Issues

By making Asian friends, Japan's colonial and wartime past became more immediate for the interviewees. For instance, Interviewee E (Britain) thought that she had to be prepared for talking about historical issues between Asian countries and Japan before going to Britain. A senior student who had studied in Britain often said to her, "if you make Chinese and Korean friends, they will talk about history [between their countries and Japan]. Japanese students often don't know much about it so they [Chinese and Korean students] would say, 'Oh, you don't know that?'"

Ten interviewees (A, B, C, E, F, G, I, K, L, M) confessed that they hesitated or avoided discussing Japan's historical and political relationships with the countries of their friends. As a reason, seven (A, C, E, F, G, L, M) of the ten mentioned their fear that talking about these issues would negatively impact their friendships. Their hesitation was expressed, for instance, as that would "damage our friendship" (A), "make them feel uncomfortable" (C), and "make our relationship awkward" (E) and also as these topics were "very sensitive" (L) and "taboo" (M). Two interviewees (B, I) were afraid of hearing from their friends' adverse feelings about Japan and the Japanese. Interviewee B (United States) stated that "Japan colonized Taiwan so at first I was afraid my friend would have negative feelings about Japan." Interviewee I (United States) also commented that "I was afraid if we talked about these issues, they would start accusing Japan." For Interviewee K (Spain), she wanted to avert such a topic because she was "not in a position to say anything about it."

Six interviewees (A, G, J, K, L, N) were drawn into a situation in which they had to discuss historical and political issues with their friends or in class. For example, Interviewee L (United States) described her experience in an English language course. Two English teachers in their fifties from China, who visited the university as part of their professional training, were participating in the course. One of them was from Changchun where Xinjing, the capital of Manchukuo, was located. She knew about Manchukuo but did not know that Changchun was the capital. When she told the classmate that she was not sure where it is, the classmate said to her, "I'm sure you know it. You're Japanese, aren't you?" and told her about Japan's invasion and control of Manchuria. Recalling this episode, she said, "I realized I had not learned enough. I learned about historical events in Manchuria, but I didn't know at all about what Japan actually did there and how local people there feel about it now."

Understanding the link between the past and the present is a crucial matter in such an experience. Interviewee G's (Canada) Taiwanese asked her what she thought about "comfort women" when they were chatting after class. Although she was not confident about expressing her idea about this topic in English, she said to her friend, "I think it is important for the Japanese to know this history as the victimizer. But the situation does not go anywhere if we continue to be held responsible and criticized." Her friend stopped talking. Interviewee G said, "at that moment, I realized I should have said it in a different way because this is a delicate issue." She was shocked because her friend, a smiling and talkative person, suddenly became silent. Her friend did not bring up this topic after that.

Interviewee J's (Britain) Korean friend referred to Toyotomi Hideyoshi, who attacked Korea twice in the late sixteenth century, as "the most terrible person" jokingly while travelling with other friends in France. Since it was said in a casual conversation over a meal, this topic did not develop further. Although she learned about Hideyoshi's invasions of Korea in history class, she had not given much thought to it. Recalling this incident, she said, "my Korean friend said she likes Japan and was friendly to me. But I realized she has held the idea that Japan did terrible things to Korea." She also commented that "we should be able to say openly, 'that's a thing of the past.' I don't understand why we always have to feel apologetic whenever they say, 'Japan did a terrible thing.'"

Contemporary Japanese people's postwar responsibility was actively discussed in the late 1990s in response to the rise of historical revisionism, which intensified after Kim Hak-sun, a Korean former "comfort woman," made her silenced experience public in 1991. One major question in the debate was how this responsibility could be endorsed without reinforcing the essentialist national narrative. Literary critic Kato Norihiro (2015 [1995]) contended that Japanese people cannot offer a sincere apology for twenty million Asian war victims without fully becoming a national subject through mourning for three million Japanese who died during the Pacific War (95). Criticizing Kato's argument, philosopher Takahashi Tetsuya (2005 [1999]) claimed that prioritizing consolidating Japanese identity over mourning for the Asian victims is problematic (214–16). Yet not completely discarding the idea of Japanese identity, Takahashi argued that Japanese people today have responsibility to respond to voices of the Asian victims because they are the sovereigns of the Japanese nation—a political group (53). Opposing both Kato and Takahashi, gender studies scholar Ueno Chizuko (2012 [1998]) maintained that the mourning should be promoted in a way other than urging Japanese individuals to identify themselves with the nation-state Japan; she did not elaborate what such a way would look like (190–96). Clarifying Ueno's unanswered concern, Sakai Naoki (2006) posited that although contemporary Japanese people cannot avoid being identified by Asian peoples as Japanese, they can take that responsibility not by identifying themselves with Japan, but by failing to do so, or more specifically, by criticizing and pushing the Japanese government to rectify its negligence in squarely facing Japan's state crimes (176–85).

What is necessary is becoming Japanese and other than Japanese simultaneously in a similar situation experienced by Interviewees G, J and L, which Takahashi (2005 [1999]), Ueno (2012 [1998]), and Sakai (2006) suggested in different manners. For this purpose, one's identity needs to be understood as intersected with multiple categories, including nation, race, ethnicity, gender, class, sexuality, and many others. When their Asian friends identified the interviewees as Japanese by referring to Manchukuo, "comfort women," and Hideyoshi, they did not refuse to be identified as Japanese. However, two of them (G and J) were reluctant to be held responsible for Japan's ugly past, while Interviewee L was not. Their reactions are different but similar in the sense that they were caught up in the nation-state framework, or in other words, they identified themselves *only* as Japanese in that context. Interviewees G and J's reactions might have differed if they had thought about the "comfort women" issue not only as Japanese but also as women, who are often sexually exploited in wars and colonization, or Hideyoshi's invasions of Korea as ordinary people, who are usually victimized against their will by a foreign military invasion and see their houses destroyed and family members killed. Although Interviewee L's attitude is admirable, it can potentially resonate with and reinforce the nationalist narrative as Ueno pointed out. By viewing one's multiple belongings, it may become possible to see a connection and build solidarity across national differences.

Transformation

All interviewees went through various forms of transformation through getting to know their friends. As I mentioned earlier, twelve out of the fourteen interviewees came to develop an interest in visiting the countries of their friends, and two of them (Interviewees A, G) actually went there to see their friends. Their previous lack of interest was often tied to negative perceptions about these countries and peoples. Six interviewees (C, D, E, H, I, M) modified or overcame such ideas and started to think about travelling to their friends' countries. Interviewee H (United States), who became closest with a Chinese roommate, said, "I really want to go to China. I want to go there this year . . . I haven't thought about going to China before because my parents and friends don't have good images of China. They say, 'Hong Kong is okay, but not [mainland] China.'" For Interviewee C (Britain), China and Chinese people were associated with negative images that she heard from a friend who used to live in China, such as "polluted" and "dangerous" and those typically circulated in Japan's mainstream media, such as "mimicry" and "binge shoppers [*bakugai*]." However, after getting to know some Chinese students, she said, "I was able to communicate with them and felt connected. Now I think going there is not a bad idea." In the case of Interviewee E (Britain), before making friends with a Korean student, she had not thought about visiting Korea because of Japan's thorny relationship with Korea. She said, "I realized people are different, and I started to feel like going to Korea and knowing more about Korea."

After making Asian friends, all interviewees became more interested in or enhanced their understanding of friends' cultures and countries in general, and some of them took actions to learn more about their friends' cultures.

Three interviewees (A, G, M) took a course to learn Chinese (G) and Korean (A, M), and two interviewees (A, N), who made close friends with students from Korea, started to enjoy Korean popular culture. For example, Interviewee M (United States) stated that "I had thought I would never enjoy Korean food and understand the Korean language before knowing them." However, after making friends with a group of Korean students, her thought changed as follows: "I began to feel like learning Korean. I thought it would be great to be able to communicate with them in Korean." When she told her Korean friends on social media that she was learning Korean, she felt happy about the friends' very positive reactions. Interviewee A (Britain and United States), who became an avid viewer of Korean TV drama, confessed that "I had looked down on Korean TV dramas and their middle-aged female drama fans before . . . I started watching them and now I am hooked on them."

Referring to Takeuchi Yoshimi's criticism that Japanese intellectuals have discussed Asia primarily to utilize it for the sake of Japan rather than to deepen the understanding of it since the late nineteenth century, Sun (2000) points out that "the ignorance of the intellectuals and the ordinary folk in Japan about their Asian neighbors, not to mention the whole of the rest of Asia, is a blind spot not to be overlooked in the Japanese views of Asia" (37). This is detectable in the *Asia as Japan* and the *Asia for Japan* positions (Avenell 2014) in which Asia is mainly discussed for the advancement of Japan. Although initially the interviewees were "ignorant" about their Asian friends' cultures, through making friends with other Asian young people, they started trying to learn more about their friends' social and cultural backgrounds.

Daily interactions with Asian students made some interviewees think more about Japan's historical and political issues involving Asian countries and peoples. Recalling an experience of talking with Korean friends about far-right groups' racist demonstrations often targeting people of Korean descent (see chapter 1), Interviewee N (United States) said, "I thought hate speech was bad before, but it was somebody else's problem. After making Korean friends, I have started to think it more seriously. My friends are part of the target. I don't like it." Through hearing from her close Chinese friend about social issues in contemporary China, such as economic disparities, Interviewee D (Britain) became interested in knowing more about China. In addition, she said, "I want to know see her again, so I don't want Japan's relationship with China to get worse. I want to know more about what is happening in China. I've started to pay more attention to news reports about China." Interviewee L (United States), who experienced discussing Japan's control of Manchuria with a Chinese classmate, came to develop a perspective similar to the *Japan in Asia* position (Avenell 2014): "I became more interested in thinking about Japan's wartime relationship with Asian countries and what we should do about it from now on."

CONCLUSION

The ideas of Asia and the West were interwoven in the interviewees' trans-East Asian friendships. Historically, Asia was imagined as either inferior or superior to the West, was associated with Japan's "superiority and leadership," and signified solidarity with Asian peoples in opposition to the West. Although not explicitly manifested, the Asia-West and the Asia-Japan hierarchies were still relevant in forming their relationships as observable in their initial knowledge gap about each other and in the "cultural proximity" constructed in the West against the backdrop of racialization. While Japan's colonial and wartime past cast a shadow, friendships with Asian students encouraged the interviewees to revise their views of peoples in Asia and know more about them, which can potentially modify the knowledge gap and rectify Japan's cultural "superiority and leadership."

Elaborating Takeuchi Yoshimi's notion of "Asia as method" (2004), Kuan-Hsing Chen (2010) suggests that "using the idea of Asia as an imaginary anchoring point, societies in Asia can become each other's points of reference, so that the understanding of the self may be transformed, and subjectivity rebuilt" (212). Making Asian friends in the West can be a way for Japanese students to use Asia as a method to change their understanding of peoples and countries in Asia. It also leads to a different understanding of the self and making a different self through becoming more conscious about Japan's colonial and wartime past—if not directly discussing it with their friends—and developing their interests in Asian peoples and their cultures.

More trans-East Asian friendships need to be made in Asia. Its importance and difficulty are pointed out by Interviewee H (United States) as follows: "I think it's not so meaningful for Asians to stick together because there is prejudice against us. We should become friends in Japan as well, but I pay more attention to our differences when I'm in Japan." The West provides a context that is easier for Japanese students to make friends with Asian students. A more challenging issue is to do so outside the West, for which, firstly, unlearning the idea of the West is necessary. Interviewee F (Australia) stated that "I was more interested in the West before because in Japan the West is often viewed as superior." Studying abroad and interacting with Western students, she said, "I realized they are not different from us . . . They also oversleep and make mistakes. As human beings, we are not different at all. I now feel the tendency to admire the West is strange." By heterogenizing and demystifying the West, the idea of Asia could be also transformed without being essentialized.

Confronting Japan's colonial and wartime relationships with Asian neighbors is indispensable to further develop trans-East Asian friendships. Knowing historical facts is certainly important, but it is not enough. What is also needed is understanding those facts critically and transnationally by attending to power relations, being sensitive to differences in historical memories as well as their impact on identities, and going beyond national borders. Although the interviewees' study-abroad experiences were short, most of them keep in touch with their Asian friends through social media. Their friendships made in the West can continue to develop further in Asia, providing them with more chances to engage in trans-East Asian dialogues.

NOTES

1. No data is available for North Korea.

2. Approximately 60 percent of them participated in a study-abroad program for less than one month. The number of participants who studied abroad for more than one year was 1,713 in 2013 and 2,034 in 2018 (MEXT 2020).

3. In 2019, the largest group was Chinese (124,436; 40 percent), followed by Vietnamese (73,389; 24 percent), Nepalese (26,308; 8 percent), Koreans (18,338; 6 percent), and Taiwanese (9584; 3 percent) (MEXT 2020). These numbers include Japanese language school students. Before the Japan Student Services Organization (JASSO) started to include their numbers in 2014, Chinese, Korean, and Taiwanese students were the three largest groups until 2012 (Japan Student Services Organization n.d.).

4. I recruited the interviewees by explaining my research purpose and asking for voluntary participation from students who enrolled in several of my courses between 2015 and 2018.

5. As of 2018, China's population is approximately 1.38 billion; Korea's is 51.4 million; Taiwan's is 23.5 million; Hong Kong's is 7.21 million; and Japan's is 126 million (Central Intelligence Agency 2018).

6. As of 2018, China's GNI per capita was $18,170, Hong Kong's was $67,810, Korea's was $40,090, and Japan's was $44,380 (World Bank 2019). The World Bank's data for Taiwan is not available.

Conclusion

The Japanese concepts of race, *jinshu* and *minzoku*, were created by intertwining with the Western notions of race, nation, *Volk*, and ethnicity (chapter 1). The two concepts are inseparable from Japaneseness as well as tied to the ideas of Asia and the West. Pertaining to the West-Asia hierarchy and the Japan-Asia hierarchy, respectively, *jinshu* and *minzoku* have been ingrained in the meaning of Japaneseseness even after the two words fell out of use in self-reference to the Japanese. In prewar modern Japan, both Asia and the West were significant discursive Others in constructing Japaneseness, which was observable in the pro-Western "Leaving Asia" and the anti-Western "Asia is one" positions. In postwar pre-globalization Japan, the West played the most significant role in constructing Japaneseness, while Asia withdrew to the background. At that time, *nihonjinron* writers represented the Japanese as a depoliticized cultural group in contrast to what they believed Western cultural characteristics. However, in Japan under globalization, the West has become less visible than before, turning into the "global" (chapter 2), and Asia has made a comeback as a significant discursive Other for Japaneseness.

The discursive practices that I analyzed in this book indicate two notable points for Japaneseness, which are simultaneously issues that need to be tackled for a multiculturalist Japanese society. First, the West is not always on the opposite side of Japan. The shift of the West's role itself is not bad. The problem is that this shift is not due to scrutinizing the ideas of Asia and the West but neutralizing the West and reacting to the return of Asia. The 2000 governmental report "The Frontier Within" encouraged Japanese people to shed what *nihonjinron* writers called Japanese "unique" characteristics, such as collectivism and indirect or high contextual communication, and to become English speakers and more "global" by acquiring the characteristics that used to be defined as Western (chapter 2). The two television drama series about Japanese immigration to Brazil and the United States stressed identification and continuity between Japanese Americans and the Japanese as a group recognized by white Americans (chapter 3). In the "hate books" written by a white American male, Japan/Japanese were positively equated with white America/Americans, while degrading and differentiating China/Chinese and Korea/Koreans from Japan/Japanese (chapter 4). However, Japanese interviewees placed themselves on the side of Asia, confronting racialization experiences in the West. Their trans-East Asian friendships, which were very meaningful and entailed transformative aspects, were not disconnected from both the West-Asia (i.e., *jinshu*) and the Japan-Asia (i.e., *minzoku*) hierarchies (chapter 5).

Second, the myth of *tan'itsu minzoku* or Japan as a single race/ethnic nation is still intact although the three unities of language, culture, and nation, which have underpinned this myth, may not be as rigid as before. The 2000 governmental report proposed that English be an official language of Japan, and migrants be invited as long as they are "flexible tools" to diversify and thus vitalize Japan's competitiveness under neoliberal globalization, while pressuring Japanese women to be fully engaged in both reproduction and production labor (chapter 2). The drama series represented Japanese Brazilians as loyal to the emperor and patriarchal, and thus more Japanese than the Japanese in Japan, while celebrating Japanese Americans as more American than other Americans and equating them with the Japanese in Japan (chapter 3). As discussed in chapter 1, the emperor system was interdependent with the three unities in prewar Japanese nationalist ideology with the emperor serving as the patriarch of the Japanese, a people "tied in blood." Gilbert's books examined in chapter 4, in which *minzoku* was both conceptually and nominally present, constructed Japaneseness attached to the emperor system, while identifying Japan/Japanese with white America/Americans. In these communicational practices of constructing Japaneseness, the prewar meaning of the Japanese is called back while the "globalness" (i.e., "Western-ness") of the Japanese is stressed. The difficulty of maintaining the three unities in a globalizing world strengthens the force of maintaining the three unities.

More discursive practices and diverse Others have to be examined to provide an overall picture of the construction of Japaneseness in the era of globalization. One important Other is Okinawa/Okinawans—another notable target of far-right nationalists due to their tenacious anti-U.S. military base movements. Another is "*hafu*" or "mixed blood" Japanese, who have become more visibly present especially in entertainment and sports, and have been used as the national Self and the Other in the construction of Japaneseness as in the case of Japanese Americans and Japanese Brazilians.

Yet, one thing is certain: Asia has fully returned, and thus the role of the West has become different. Due to this change, in theory, Japaneseness can be constructed by identifying sometimes with the West (i.e., "Leaving Asia") and at other times with Asia (i.e., "Asia is one"). In the 1990s, when the "Asia" in the return of Asia largely excluded China and Korea (e.g., Morris-Suzuki 1998), taking the "Asia is one" position was perhaps not difficult. However, in the twenty-first century, when China and Korea have come back, it has been more difficult to do so because of their stronger economies that threaten the *minzoku* hierarchy and of the Japanese government's reluctance to wholeheartedly reflect its colonial and wartime past that inflicted larger-scale damage on people in both areas. In contrast, adopting the pro-Western "Leaving Asia" position is easier because the West has been neutralized as the "global" and less overwhelming than before. Nevertheless, a gap exists between this discursive desire expressed in texts and personal actions. When Japanese individuals actually enter the West, "leaving Asia" does not seem to be easy because in the West they are often summarized and racialized as Asian, and the "old" idea of the West is still relevant (chapter 5).

Although the discursive comeback of Asia has produced negative consequences, these are simultaneously opportunities to transform Asia as a discursive Other for Japaneseness. Rendering more visible the idea of *minzoku* and politicizing Japaneseness again, the return of Asia is tied to the rise of historical revisionism, rampant racist demonstrations, and the popularity of "hate books" targeting Korea/Koreans and China/Chinese. At the same time, Asia's return brings to the fore Japan's imperial and colonial past, reversing "a hollowing-out of *minzoku* from Japanese identity" (Yoon 1994, 6). It is certainly problematic that current far-right discursive practices are much more vocal than those based on the *Japan in Asia* position (Avenell 2014) or grassroots Asianists (Morris-Suzuki 2016). However, now that Asia is present, it is easier to identify and attack exclusionist practices, such as their "grammar," epistemological rules that govern these practices. The presence of Asia provides Japanese people with more opportunities to reflect and rectify the Japan-Asia hierarchy embedded in the notion of *minzoku*, an "absent presence," in the postwar Japaneseness.

Japanese people today have many more occasions to think about Asia than they did before the 1990s. They are daily more exposed to stories about Asia, especially Korea and China, in the media. These stories are often negative, but at least they are there. Moreover, they have more opportunities to directly form relationships with other Asian peoples both inside and outside Japan. As discussed in chapter 5, trans-East Asian relationships can change interviewees' negative perceptions about East Asian neighbors and could potentially dismantle the Japan-Asia hierarchy and thereby challenge the ideas of Asia and the West. If Asia, which entails this hierarchy, is shaken, the West, which makes Asia possible (Takeuchi 2005 [1948], 53–81), cannot avoid being affected. Interrogating the ideas of Asia and the West is indispensable in transforming Japaneseness, not only because the two have been significant discursive Others for Japaneseness but also because Japaneseness has been tied to the notion of hierarchy ingrained in the two interdependent notions.

Transnational critique offers a useful perspective to reimagine Japanese nationhood for a multiculturalist Japan. Attending to the interrelatedness of seemingly conflicting and separated entities, such as the past and the present, the discursive and the material, the self and the other, and the local and the global, transnational critique challenges neoliberal worldview, illuminates the role played by discursive Others to construct Japaneseness, and thereby denaturalizes the meaning of the Japanese. However, in order to make transnational critique more approachable to a wider range of people and usable in everyday life, instead of highlighting the ontological and epistemological principles of transnational critique, such as anti-positivism, the dialectical view of society, and immanent transcendence, the notion of "implicature" will be necessary and appropriate.

Implicature is an ontological and epistemological principle for realizing a just intercultural communication proposed by Karen Dace and Mark Lawrence McPhail (2001). Challenging the independent and atomistic view of humans, Dace and McPhail define implicature as the idea that "human beings are linguistically, materially, psychologically, and spiritually interrelated and interdependent, or 'implicated' in each other" (345–46). If human beings are implicated in each other, human actions and consequences of their actions are necessarily implicated in each other. That is why no culture or society has been completely separated from other cultures and societies but always interrelated.

Overlapping with the ontological and epistemological principles of transnational critique, implicature presents these principles in a more positive and simpler manner, which is important to inspire more people to pursue a multiculturalist Japan. On the one hand, the dialectical view of society sheds light on the opposite-ness of, for example, the self and the other or the local and the global. On the other hand, implicature focuses on the interdependence and interconnection of these seemingly opposite entities. Because the self is implicated in the other, or the local is implicated in the global, immanent transcendence is possible. In addition, stressing the interrelatedness and interdependence of humans, implicature offers a means to challenge neoliberal values, such as decontextualization, the neutralization of power relations, and the atomization of human beings, which bolster neoconservative practices exemplified by far-rightists' decontextualizing and thereby arbitrarily rehistoricizing Japan's relations with Asian neighbors in search for a more positive Japanese identity.

Transnational critique elucidates that Japaneseness is constructed in relation to and often at the expense of various discursive Other; Japaneseness communicated at present is inseparable from historical narratives; and these discursive entities—Japaneseness and discursive Others—have material or actual consequences. By viewing seemingly discrete people, ideas, events, and things as interconnected, it becomes possible to clarify specific processes of creating the meaning of the Japanese. Looking into everyday communication where the construction of Japaneseness occurs with transnational critique is one way of intervening and reimaging what it means to be Japanese.

References

99 nen no ai [*99 Years of Love*]. 2011. DVD. Tokyo: TC Entertainment.

Abbott, H. Porter. 2008. *The Cambridge Introduction to Narrative*, 2nd ed. Cambridge: Cambridge University Press.

Abrams, Lynn. 2010. *Oral History Theory*. London and New York: Routledge.

Allen, Chizuko T. 2003. "Empress Jingū: A Shamaness Ruler in Early Japan." *Japan Forum* 15(1): 81–98.

Ames, Roger T., and Henry Rosemont, Jr., trans. 2010. *The Analects of Confucius: A Philosophical Translation*. New York: Ballantine Books.

Anderson, Benedict. 1991. *Imagined Communities: Reflections on the Origin and Spread of Nationalism*. London: Verso.

———. 1992. *Long-Distance Nationalism: World Capitalism and the Rise of Identity Politics*. Amsterdam: Center for Asian Studies Amsterdam.

Ang, Ien. 2001. *On Not Speaking Chinese: Living Between Asia and the West*. London: Routledge.

Anthias, Floya. 1998. "Evaluating "Diaspora": Beyond Ethnicity?" *Sociology* 32(3): 557–580.

Aoki, Tamotsu. 1991. *Nihonbunkaron no henyō: Sengo nihon no bunka to aidentiti* [Transformation of the Studies of Japanese Culture: Postwar Japanese Culture and Identity]. Tokyo: Chūō Kōron Sha.

Arudou, Debito. 2015. *Embedded Racism*. Lanham, MD: Lexington Books.

Asahi Shimbun. 2005a. "Ka'kkyō no i'ppō kakusa kakudai" [Booming Economy and Widening Income Gap]. September 8, 2005.

———. 2005b. "Shushō 'kokueki sokonezu' yasukuni sanpai keizoku" ['Visiting Yasukuni Shrine Does Not Damage Japan's Interests': Prime Minister Continues to Visit the Shrine]. April 20, 2005.

———. 2018. "Court Rules That Wartime Korean Laborers Claims Have Not Expired." November 30, 2018. http://www.asahi.com/ajw/articles/AJ201811300061.html.

Assmann, Jan. 2011. *Cultural Memory and Early Civilization: Writing, Remembrance, and Political Imagination.* Cambridge: Cambridge University Press.

Aston William G., trans. 1956a. *Nihongi: Chronicles of Japan from the Earliest Times to A.D. 697* (volume 1). London: George Allen & Unwin.

———. 1956b. *Nihongi: Chronicles of Japan from the Earliest Times to A.D. 697* (volume 2). London: George Allen & Unwin.

Avenell, Simon. 2014. "Japanese Debates on Asia and Asianism: A Conceptual Framework." *History Compass* 12(8): 619–631.

Azuma, Eiichiro. 2005. *Between Two Empires: Race, History, and Transnationalism in Japanese America.* Oxford: Oxford University Press.

Back, Les, and John Solomos. 2009. "Introduction." In *Theories of Race and Racism: A Reader*, 2nd ed., edited by Les Back and John Solomos, 1–30. New York: Routledge.

Balibar, Etienne. 1991a. "Is There a 'Neo-Racism'?" In *Race, Nation, Class*, edited by Etienne Balibar and Immanuel Wallerstein, 17–28. London: Verso.

———. 1991b. "Racism and Nationalism." In *Race, Nation, Class*, edited by Etienne Balibar and Immanuel Wallerstein, 37–67. London: Verso.

———. 1991c. "The Nation Form: History and Ideology." In *Race, Nation, Class*, edited by Étienne Balibar and Immanuel Wallerstein, 86–106. London: Verso.

Banton, Michael. 1983. *Racial and Ethnic Competition.* Cambridge: Cambridge University Press.

Barboza, David. 2012. "Billions in Hidden Riches for Family of Chinese Leader." *New York Times*, October 25, 2012. https://www.nytimes.com/2012/10/26/business/global/family-of-wen-jiabao-holds-a-hidden-fortune-in-china.html?_r=1.

Barker, Chris. 2010. "Structuralism, Poststructuralism, and Cultural Studies." In *The Encyclopedia of Literary and Cultural Theory*, edited by Michael Ryan. Hoboken, NJ: John Wiley & Sons. DOI: 10.1002/9781444337839.wbelctv3s010.

Barker, Michael. 1981. *The New Racism.* London: Junction Books.

Bauböck, Rainer, and Thomas Faist, eds. 2010. *Diaspora and Transnationalism.* Amsterdam: University of Amsterdam Press.

BBC. 2016. "Why Is the South China Sea Contentious?" July 12, 2016. https://www.bbc.com/news/world-asia-pacific-13748349.

Befu, Harumi. 1993. "Nationalism and *Nihonjinron.*" In *Cultural Nationalism in East Asia: Representation and Identity*, edited by Harumi Befu, 107–135. Berkeley, CA: Institute of East Asian Studies, University of California at Berkeley.

———. 2001. *Hegemony of Homogeneity: An Anthropological Analysis of "Nihonjinron".* Melbourne: Trans Pacific Press.

Belasco, Warren. 2008. *Food: The Key Concepts.* Berg: Oxford.

Benedict, Ruth. 1946/1989. *The Chrysanthemum and the Sword: Patterns of Japanese Culture.* Boston: Houghton Mufflin.

Bhabha, Homi. K. 1990. "DissemiNation: Time, Narrative, and the Margins of the Modern Nation." In *Nation and Narration*, edited by Homi K. Bhabha, 291–322. London: Routledge.

Bignell, Jonathan. 2013. *An Introduction to Television Studies*, 3rd ed. London and New York: Routledge.

Billig, Michael. 1995. *Banal Nationalism*. Los Angeles: SAGE.

Blumenbach, Johann Friedrich. 2000. "On the Natural Variety of Mankind." In *The Idea of Race*, edited by Robert Bernasconi and Tommy Lee Lott, 27–37. Indianapolis, IN: Hackett Publishing.

Bonilla-Silva, Eduardo. 2010. *Racism Without Racists*, 3rd ed. Lanham, MD: Rowman & Littlefield.

Bonnett, Alastair. 2000. *Anti-Racism*. London: Routledge.

Bowles, Paul. 2013. "Globalization and Neoliberalism: A Taxonomy with Implications for 'Anti-Globalization.'" In *Development in an Era of Neoliberal Globalization*, edited by Henry Veltmeyer, 98–121. London and New York: Routledge.

Brindley, Erica. 2003. "Barbarians or Not? Ethnicity and Changing Conceptions of the Ancient Yue (Viet) Peoples, ca. 400–50 BC." *Asia Major* 16(1): 1–32.

Bronner, Stephen Eric. 2011. *Critical Theory: A Very Short Introduction*. Oxford: Oxford University Press.

Brown, Wendy. 2015. *Undoing the Demos*. New York: Zone Books.

Brubaker, Rogers. 2005. "The 'Diaspora' Diaspora." *Ethnic and Racial Studies* 28(1): 1–19.

Byrne, Donn Erwin. 1971. *The Attraction Paradigm*. New York: Academic Press.

Cabinet Office. 2019a. "Reiwa gannen ban shoshika shakai taisaku hakusho" [White Paper on the Decline of Birthrate 2019]. https://www8.cao.go.jp/shoushi/shoushika/whitepaper/measures/w-2019/r01pdfhonpen/r01honpen.html.

———. 2019b. "Reiwa·gannen ban kourei shakai hakusho" [White Paper on Aging Society 2019]. https://www8.cao.go.jp/kourei/whitepaper/w-2019/zenbun/01pdf_index.html.

———. 2019c. "Reiwa gannen ban danjyo kyōdō sankaku hakusho" [White Paper on Gender Equality 2019]. http://www.gender.go.jp/about_danjo/whitepaper/r01/zentai/index.html.

Cabinet Public Relations Office. 2019d. *Gaikō ni kansuru yoron chōsa* [Public Opinion Survey on Diplomatic Relationships]. https://survey.gov-online.go.jp/r01/r01-gaiko/index.html.

Cahill, Damien, and Martijn Konings. 2017. *Neoliberalism*. Cambridge: Polity.

Calhoun, Craig. 1997. *Nationalism*. Buckingham: Open University Press.

Cameron, Deborah. 2002. "Globalization and the Teaching of 'Communication Skills.'" In *Globalization and Language Teaching*, edited by David Block and Deborah Cameron, 67–82. London: Routledge.

Cantle, Ted. 2016. "The Case for Interculturalism, Plural Identities and Cohesion." In *Multiculturalism and Interculturalism: Debating the Dividing Lines*, edited by Naser Meer, Tariq Modood, and Ricard Zapata-Barrero, 133–157. Edinburgh, UK: Edinburgh University Press.

Cash, John. 2014. "Ideology and Social and Cultural Theory." In *Routledge Handbook of Social and Cultural Theory*, edited by Anthony Elliott, 113–136. London and New York: Routledge.

Central Intelligence Agency. 2018. "The World Factbook." https://www.cia.gov/library/publications/the-world-factbook/wfbExt/region_eas.html.

Chapman, Malcolm. 1993. "Social and Biological Aspects of Ethnicity." In *Social and Biological Aspects of Ethnicity*, edited by Malcolm Chapman, 1–46. Oxford: Oxford University Press.

Chen, Frederick Tse-shyang. 1991. "The Confucian View of World Order." *Indiana International and Comparative Law Review* 1: 45–69.

Chen, Kuan-Hsing. 2010. *Asia as Method: Toward Deimperialization*. Durham, NC: Duke University Press.

Clarke, Simon. 2005. "The Neoliberal Theory of Society." In *Neoliberalism: A Critical Reader*, edited by Alfredo Saad-Filho and Deborah Johnston, 50–59. London: Pluto.

Clifford, James. 1997. *Routes: Travel and Translation in the Late Twentieth Century*. Cambridge, MA: Harvard University Press.

Cohen, Paul A. 2010. *Discovering History in China: American Historical Writing on the Recent Chinese Past*. New York: Columbia University Press.

Collcutt, Martin. 1991. "The Legacy of Confucianism in Japan." In *The East Asian Region: Confucian Heritage and Its Modern Adaptation*, edited by Gilbert Rozman, 111–154. Princeton, NJ: Princeton University Press.

Collins, Donald E. 2001. "Loyalty Questions." In *Encyclopedia of Japanese American History*, edited by Brian Niiya, 260–262. New York: Checkmark Books.

Comaroff, Jean, and John L. Comaroff. 2001. "Millennial Capitalism." In *Millennial Capitalism and the Culture of Neoliberalism*, edited by Jean Comaroff and John. L. Comaroff, 1–56. Durham: Duke University Press.

Commission on Japan's Goals in the Twenty-First Century (CJGTC). 2000a. "Sōron" [Overview]. Accessed May 11, 2003. http://www.kantei.go.jp/jp/21century/houkokusyo/1s.pdf.

———. 2000b. "Overview." http://www.kantei.go.jp/jp/21century/report/pdfs/3chap1.pdf.

———. 2000c. "Sekai ni ikiru nihon" [Japan's Place in the World]. http://www.kantei.go.jp/jp/21century/houkokusyo/6s.pdf.

———. 2000d. "Japan's Place in the World." http://www.kantei.go.jp/jp/21century/report/pdfs/8chap6.pdf.

———. 2000e. *"Hajimeni/Mokuji"* [Preface and Contents]. http://www.kantei.go.jp/jp/21century/houkokusyo/0s.pdf.

———. 2000f. "Preface." http://www.kantei.go.jp/jp/21century/report/pdfs/1preface.pdf.

———. 2000g. "Yutakasa to katsuryoku" [Prosperity and Dynamism]. http://www.kantei.go.jp/jp/21century/houkokusyo/2s.pdf.

———. 2000h. "Prosperity and Dynamism." http://www.kantei.go.jp/jp/21century/report/pdfs/4chap2.pdf.

———. 2000i. "Anshin to uruoi no seikatsu" [Achieving a Contended and Enriching Life]. http://www.kantei.go.jp/jp/21century/houkokusyo/3s.pdf.

———. 2000j. "Achieving a Contended and Enriching Life." http://www.kantei.go.jp/jp/21century/report/pdfs/5chap3.pdf.

Conway, David. 1995. *Classical Liberalism: The Unvanquished Ideal*. London: Macmillan.

Council of Europe. 2008. "White Paper on Intercultural Dialogue: Living Together as Equals in Dignity." https://www.coe.int/t/dg4/intercultural/source/white%20 paper_final_revised_en.pdf.

Council on Economic and Fiscal Policy. 2006. "Gurōbaru senryaku" [Strategies for Globalization]. https://www5.cao.go.jp/keizai-shimon/cabinet/2006/global/item1 .pdf.

Dace, Karen L., and Mark Lawrence McPhail. 2001. "Crossing the Color Line: From Empathy to Implicature in Intercultural Communication." In *Readings in Intercultural Communication*, 2nd ed., edited by Judith N. Martin, Thomas K. Nakayama, and Lisa A. Flores, 344–351. New York: McGraw Hill.

Dale, Peter N. 1986. *The Myth of Japanese Uniqueness*. London: Routledge.

Danjo, Hiroshi. 2012. *Eirakutei: Kai chitsujyo no kansei* [Emperor Yongle: The Establishment of the Sinocentric Order]. Tokyo: Kōdansha. Kindle.

Darder, Antonia, Marta P. Baltodano, and Rodolfo D. Torres, eds. 2009. *The Critical Pedagogy Reader*, 2nd ed. London and New York: Routledge.

Dardot, Pierre, and Christian Laval. 2014. *The New Way of the World*. New York: Verso.

Davis, Angela. 1997. "Gender, Class, and Multiculturalism." In *Mapping Multiculturalism*, edited by Avery F. Gordon and Christopher Newfield, 40–48. Minneapolis, MN: University of Minnesota Press.

De Groot, Jerome. 2016. *Consuming History: Historians and Heritage in Contemporary Popular Culture*. London and New York: Routledge.

Degler, Carl N. 1991. *In Search of Human Nature*. Oxford: Oxford University Press.

Delanty, Gerard. 2012. "The Idea of Critical Cosmopolitanism." In *Routledge Handbook of Cosmopolitanism Studies*, edited by Gerard Delanty, 38–46. London and New York: Routledge.

Doak, Kevin M. 1997. "What Is a Nation and Who Belongs? National Narratives and the Ethnic Imagination in Twentieth-Century Japan." *American Historical Review* 102(2): 283–309.

———. 2007. *A History of Nationalism in Modern Japan*. Leiden: Brill.

Doi, Takeo. 1971. *Amae no kōzō* [The Anatomy of dependence]. Tokyo: Kōbundō.

Dower, John W. 1993. "Peace and Democracy in Two Systems." In *Postwar Japan as History*, edited by Andrew Gordon, 3–33. Berkeley: University of California Press.

———. 1999. *Embracing Defeat: Japan in the Wake of World War II*. New York: Norton and the New Press.

Dyer, Richard. 1996. *White*. New York: Routledge.

Elisonas, Jurgis. 1991. "The Inseparable Trinity: Japan's Relations with China and Korea." In *The Cambridge History of Japan. Vol. 4, Early Modern Japan*, edited by John Whitney Hall, 235–300. Cambridge: Cambridge University Press.

Endoh, Toake. 2009. *Exporting Japan: Politics of Emigration Toward Latin America*. Urbana and Chicago: University of Illinois Press.

Eriksen, Thomas Hylland. 2010. *Ethnicity and Nationalism*, 3rd ed. New York: Pluto Press.

Erll, Astrid. 2011. *Memory in Culture*. New York: Palgrave Macmillan.

Fackler, Martin. 2013. "Japanese Court Fines Rightist Group Over Protests at a School in Kyoto." *New York Times*, October 7, 2013. http://www.nytimes.com/2013/10/08/world/asia/japanese-court-fines-rightist-group-in-elementary-school-protest.html.

Fairbank, John K. 1968. "A Preliminary Framework." In *The Chinese World Order*, edited by John K. Fairbank, 1–19. Oxford: Oxford University Press.

Fairclough, Norman. 1995. *Critical Discourse Analysis: The Critical Study of Language*. London and New York: Longman.

Feng, Zhang. 2009. "Rethinking the 'Tribute System': Broadening the Conceptual Horizon of Historical East Asian Politics." *The Chinese Journal of International Politics* 2(4): 597–626.

Fenton, Steve. 2010. *Ethnicity*. Cambridge: Polity.

Fischler, Claude. 1988. "Food, Self and Identity." *Social Science Information* 27(2): 275–292.

Foss, Sonja K., and Karen A. Foss. 2003. *Inviting Transformation: Presentational Speaking for a Changing World*, 2nd ed. Prospect Heights, IL: Waveland.

Foucault, Michel. 1972. *The Archaeology of Knowledge*. New York: Pantheon Books.

———. 2008. *The Birth of Biopolitics*. New York: Picador.

Fox, Dennis, and Isaac Prilleltensky, eds. 1997. *Critical Psychology: An Introduction*. London: SAGE.

Frey, Marc, and Nicola Spakowski. 2016. "Introduction." In *Asianism*, edited by Marc Frey and Nicola Spakowski, 1–18. Singapore: NUS Press.

Fujimoto, Etsuko. 2001. "Japanese-ness, Whiteness, and the "Other" in Japan's Internationalization." In *Transforming Communication About Culture: Critical New Directions*, edited by Mary Jane Collier, 1–24. Thousand Oaks, CA: SAGE.

Fujitani, Takashi. 2011. *Race for Empire: Koreans as Japanese and Japanese as Americans During World War II*. Berkley and Los Angeles: University of California Press.

Fukuzawa, Yukichi. 1933. *Zoku Fukuzawa zenshū dai 2 kan* [Fukuzawa Complete Works 2, Vol. 2]. Tokyo: Iwanami Shoten. http://dl.ndl.go.jp/info:ndljp/pid/1078022.

———. 1959. *Fukuzawa Yukichi zenshū dai 2 kan* [Fukuzawa Yukichi Complete Works, Vol. 2]. Tokyo: Iwanami Shoten.

———. (1885) 1997. "Good-by Asia (Datus-a), 1885." In *Japan: A Documentary History Volume II*, edited by David John Lu, 351–353. Armonk, NY: M. E. Sharpe.

Füredi, Frank. 1998. *The Silent War: Imperialism and the Changing Perception of Race*. New Brunswick, NJ: Rutgers University Press.

Furuya, Tsunehira. 2017. "Kattewa ikenai 'jukyō bon' osomatsuna nakami" [Don't Buy the Lousy Confucianism Book]. *President Online*. https://president.jp/articles/-/22895.

Galton, Francis. (1869) 1999. "Hereditary Genius." In *Documents of American Prejudice*, edited by Sunand T. Joshi, 157–163. New York: Basic Books.

———. (1909) 2000. "Eugenics: Its Definition, Scope and Aims." In *The Idea of Race*, edited by Robert Bernasconi and Tommy Lee Lott, 79–83. Indianapolis, IN: Hackett Publishing.

Gardner, Daniel K. 2014. *Confucianism: A Very Short Introduction*. Oxford: Oxford University Press.

Gareis, Elisabeth. 2012. "Intercultural Friendship: Effects of Home and Host Region." *Journal of International and Intercultural Communication* 5(4): 309–328.

Garner, Steve. 2009. *Racisms*. London: SAGE.

Giddens, Anthony. 1994. *Beyond Left and Right: The Future of Radical Politics*. Cambridge: Polity.

Gilbert, Kent. 2017. *Jukyō ni shihai sareta chūgokujin to kankokujin no higeki* [Tragedies of the Chinese and the Koreans Under the Control of Confucianism]. Tokyo: Kōdansha.

———. 2018. *Chūkashisō ni sihai sareta chūgokujin to kankokujin no higeki* [Tragedies of Chinese and South Koreans Swallowing Sinocentrism]. Tokyo: Kōdansha.

Giroux, Henry A. 2004. *The Terror of Neoliberalism: Authoritarianism and the Eclipse of Democracy*. Boulder, CO: Paradigm.

Goebel, Rolf J. 1995. "China as an Embalmed Mummy: Herder's Orientalist Poetics." *South Atlantic Review* 60(1): 111–129.

Goldberg, David Theo. 1990. "The Social Formation of Racist Discourse." In *Anatomy of Racism*, edited by David Theo Goldberg, 295–318. Minneapolis, MN: University of Minnesota Press.

———. 1993. *Racist Culture*. Malden, MA: Blackwell.

———. 1994. "Introduction: Multicultural Conditions." In *Multiculturalism: A Critical Reader*, edited by David Theo Goldberg, 1–41. Cambridge, MA: Blackwell.

———. 2002. *The Racial State*. Malden, MA: Blackwell.

Goldberg, David Theo, and John Solomos. 2002. "General Introduction." In *A Companion to Racial and Ethnic Studies*, edited by David Theo Goldberg and John Solomos, 1–12. Malden, MA: Blackwell.

Government of Manchukuo. 1932. "Manshūkoku kenkoku sengen" [The Proclamation of the state of Manchukuo]. https://www.jacar.archives.go.jp/aj/meta/MetSearch.cgi (Reference Number: B02030709100).

Graburn, Nelson H. H., John Ertl, and R. Kenji Tierney, eds. 2008. *Multiculturalism in the New Japan: Crossing the Boundaries Within*. New York and Oxford: Berghahn Books.

Gramsci, Antonio. 2000. "Some Aspects of the Southern Question." In *The Antonio Gramsci Reader: Selected Writings 1916–1935*, edited by David Forgacs, 171–185. New York: New York University Press.

Grossberg, Lawrence, Ellen Wartella, and D. Charles Whitney. 1998. *Media Making: Mass Media in a Popular Culture*. Thousand Oaks, CA: SAGE.

Guardian. 2012. "London 2012: Greece Expel Triple Jumper Over Racist Twitter Remark." July 25, 2012. http://www.guardian.co.uk/sport/2012/jul/25/london-2012-greece-racist-twitter.

Guibernau, Montserrat, and John Rex. 2010. "Introduction." In *The Ethnicity Reader*, edited by Montserrat Guibernau and John Rex, 1–9. Cambridge: Polity.

Guimarães, António Sérgio Alfredo. 1999. "Racism and Anti-Racism in Brazil: A Postmodern Perspective." In *Racism*, edited by Leonard Harris, 314–330. Amherst, NY: Humanity Books.

Halbwachs, Maurice. 1992. *On Collective Memory*. Chicago: University of Chicago Press.

Hall, Stuart. 1988. "The Rediscovery of 'Ideology': Return of the Repressed in Media Studies." In *Culture, Society, and the Media*, edited by Michael Gurevitch, Tony Bennett, James Curran, and Janet Woollacott, 56–90. London and New York: Routledge.

———. 1990. "Cultural Identity and Diaspora." In *Identity: Community, Culture, Difference*, edited by Jonathan Rutherford, 222–237. London: Lawrence & Wishart.

———. 1992. "The West and the Rest: Discourse and Power." In *Formations of Modernity*, edited by Stuart Hall and Bram Gieben, 275–320. Cambridge: Polity Press.

———. 1996. "The Question of Cultural Identity." In *Modernity: An Introduction to Modern Sciences*, edited by Stuart Hall, David Held, Don Hubert, and Kenneth Thompson, 596–634. Malden, MA: Blackwell.

———. 1997. "The Work of Representation." In *Representation: Cultural Representations and Signifying Practices*, edited by Stuart Hall, 13–64. London: SAGE.

———. 2013. "The Work of Representation." In *Representation*, 2nd ed., edited by Stuart Hall, Jessica Evans, and Sean Nixon, 1–47. London: SAGE.

Hamashita, Takeshi. 2008. *China, East Asia and the Global Economy: Regional and Historical Perspectives*. London and New York: Routledge.

Han, Sam. 2014. "Structuralism and Post-structuralism." In *Routledge Handbook of Social and Cultural Theory*, edited by Anthony Elliott, 39–55. London and New York: Routledge.

Hannaford, Ivan. 1996. *Race: The History of an Idea in the West*. Baltimore, MD: Johns Hopkins University Press.

Hara, Hideshige. 2006. *Nihonkoku kenpō seitei no keifu 3* [The Origins of the Japanese Constitution, Vol. 3]. Tokyo: Nihon Hyōronsha.

Haru to Natsu [Haru and Natsu]. 2006. DVD. Tokyo: NHK Enterprise.

Harvey, David. 1990. *The Condition of Postmodernity*. Cambridge, MA: Blackwell.

———. 2005. *A Brief History of Neoliberalism*. Oxford: Oxford University Press.

Hatada, Takashi. 1969. *Nihonjin no chōsen kan* [Japanese Views of Korea]. Tokyo: Keisō shobō.

Hayek, Friedrich August. (1945) 2014. *The Road to Serfdom: Text and Documents: The Definitive Edition Volume 2*. London and New York: Routledge.

Herman, David. 2009. *Basic Elements of Narrative*. Chichester, UK: Wily-Blackwell.

Hernandez, Alvaro David, and Taiki Hirai. 2015. "The Reception of Japanese Animation and Its Determinants in Taiwan, South Korea and China." *Animation* 10(2): 154–169.

Higuchi, Naoto. 2014. *Nihongata haigaishugi* [Japanese Xenophobia]. Nagoya, Japan: Nagoya Daigaku Shuppankai.

Hiroshima City. n.d. "*Genbaku to fukkō*" [Atomic Bomb and Hiroshima's Reconstruction]. Accessed April 17, 2017. http://www.city.hiroshima.lg.jp/www/genre/1001000002091/index.html.

Hofstadter, Richard. 1944. *Social Darwinism in American Thought*. Boston: Beacon Press.

Horkheimer, Max. 2002. *Critical Theory: Selected Essays*. New York: Continuum.

Hotta, Eri. 2007. *Pan-Asianism and Japan's War 1931–1945*. New York: Palgrave Macmillan.

Hozumi, Yatsuka. (1897) 1910. *Kokumin kyōiku: aikokushin* [National Education: Patriotism]. Tokyo: Yūhikaku. http://dl.ndl.go.jp/info:ndljp/pid/754599.

Hu, Shaohua. 1997. "Confucianism and Western Democracy." *Journal of Contemporary China* 6(15): 347–363.

Huntington, Samuel P. 1993. "The Clash of Civilizations?" *Foreign Affairs* 72(3): 22–49.

Hutton, Christopher M. 2005. *Race and the Third Reich*. Cambridge: Polity.

Hyakuta, Naoki. 2017. *Imakoso kankoku ni ayamarō* [Now Is the Time to Apologize Korea]. Tokyo: Asukashinsha.

Ichioka, Yuji. 1988. *The Issei*. New York: Free Press.

———. 2006. *Before Internment: Essays in Prewar Japanese American History*. Stanford, CA: Stanford University Press.

Iesaka, Kazushi. 1986. *Nihonjin no jinshukan* [Japanese Views of Race]. Tokyo: Kōbundō.

Iino, Masako. 2000. *Mō hitotsu no nichibei kankeishi* [Another Japan-US Relation]. Tokyo: Yūhikaku.

Immigration Bureau. 2007. *Heisei 18 nendo matsu ni okeru gaikokujin tōrokusha tōkei ni tsuite* [Foreign Populations in Japan for Fiscal Year 2006]. http://www.moj.go.jp/PRESS/070516-1.pdf.

Inoue, Mitsumasa. 2017. "Abe Promises No More Wars but Lacks Remorse in Aug. 15 Speech." *The Asahi Shimbun*, August 15, 2017. http://www.asahi.com/ajw/articles/AJ201708150044.html.

Ishibashi, Hideaki. 2013. "Anti-Korean Protests Trigger Counter-Protests Against Hatemongers." *Asahi Shimbun*, March 26, 2013. http://ajw.asahi.com/article/behind_news/social_affairs/AJ201303260097.

Ishihara, Shintaro. 2001. "Nihon yo uchinaru bōei wo" [Japan, Defend Yourself from Inner Foes]. *Sankei Shimbun*, May 8, 2001, p. 1.

Iwabuchi, Koichi. 1998. "Marketing 'Japan': Japanese Cultural Presence Under a Global Gaze." *Japanese Studies* 18(2): 165–180.

———. 2004. "Introduction: Cultural Globalization and Asian Media Connections." In *Feeling Asian Modernities: Transnational Consumption of Japanese TV Dramas*, edited by Koichi Iwabuchi, 1–22. Hong Kong: Hong Kong University Press.

———. 2007. *Bunka no taiwaryoku* [The Power of Cultural Dialogue]. Tokyo: Nihon Keizai Shuppansha.

———. 2015. *Resilient Borders and Cultural Diversity*. Lanham, MD: Lexington Books.

Jackson, John P., and Nadine M. Weidman. 2004. *Race, Racism, and Science*. New Brunswick, NJ: Rutgers University Press.

Jacques, Martin. (2009) 2012. *When China Rules the World*, 2nd ed. Penguin UK.

Japan National Tourism Organization. n.d.a. "Visit Japan jigyō kaishi ikō no hōnichi kyaku sū no suii (2003 nen-2018 nen)" [International Tourists to Japan After the Launch of the Visit Japan Campaign (Between 2003 and 2018)]. Accessed April 25, 2020. https://www.jnto.go.jp/jpn/statistics/marketingdata_tourists_after_vj.pdf.

———. n.d.b. "Kakkoku chiikibetsu nihonjin hōmonsha sū (2013 nen-2018 nen)" [Japanese Visitors to Foreign Countries (Between 2013 and 2018)]. Accessed April 25, 2020. https://www.jnto.go.jp/jpn/statistics/20200318_3.pdf.

Japan Student Services Organization (JASSO). n.d. "Gaikokujin ryūgakusei zaiseki chōsa" [Reports on International Students]. Accessed June 28, 2019. https://www.jasso.go.jp/about/statistics/intl_student_e/index.html.

Japan Times. 2006. "Testing Japanese Democracy." *LexisNexis Academic*, April 13, 2006.

———. 2013. "Nippon Ishin Expels Right Winger Nishimura Over Prostitute Remark." May 21, 2013. http://www.japantimes.co.jp/news/2013/05/21/national/nippon-ishin-expels-rightwinger-nishimura-over-prostitute-remark/#.Ubufw-WCjIU.

———. 2015. "Don't Duck War Responsibility." January 7, 2015. https://www.japantimes.co.jp/opinion/2015/01/07/editorials/dont-duck-war-responsibility/#.Wsqfg7kUnIU.

Japanese Communist Party. 1946. "Nihon kyōsantō no nihon jinmin kyōwakoku kenpō sōan" [Japanese Communist Party's Draft Constitution for the People's Republic of Japan]. http://www.ndl.go.jp/constitution/shiryo/02/119/119tx.html.

Jenkins, Richard. 2008. *Rethinking Ethnicity*, 2nd ed. London: SAGE.

Jones, David Martin. 2001. *The Image of China in Western Social and Political Thought*. New York: Palgrave Macmillan.

Kakihana, Masahiro. 2020. "Aso Apologizes If 'Single-Race Nation' Remark Misunderstood." *Asahi Shimbun*, January 14, 2020. http://www.asahi.com/ajw/articles/AJ202001140019.html.

Kanamori, Toshiki. 2012. "Chūgoku keizai: keizai taikoku ga kakaeru hinkon to shotoku kakusa" [Chinese Economy: An Economic Superpower's Poverty and Income Gap]. Daiwa Institute of Research Group, August 1, 2012. https://www.dir.co.jp/report/research/economics/china/12080101china.pdf.

Kanbe, Takenori. 2007. *Saraba mongoroido* [Good Bye, Mongoloid]. Tokyo: Seikatsu Shoin.

Kang, David C. 2010. *East Asia Before the West: Five Centuries of Trade and Tribute*. New York: Columbia University Press.

Kang, Etsuko Hae-Jin. 1997. *Diplomacy and Ideology in Japanese-Korean Relations: From the Fifteenth Century to the Eighteenth Century*. London: Macmillan.

Kang, Jae Eun. 2012. *Chōsen jukyō no nisen nen* [Two Thousand Years of Confucianism in Korea]. Tokyo: Kōdansha. Kindle.

Kanno, Kakumyo. 2004. *Bushidō no gyakushū* [A Counter Attack of Bushido]. Tokyo: Kōdansha.

Kasaya, Kazuhiko. 2014. *Bushidō* [Bushido]. Tokyo: NTT Shuppan.

Kashiwazaki, Chikako. 2010. "Nihon no toransunashonarizumu no isō: tabunka kyōsei gensetu saikō" [The Phase of Japanese Transnationalism: Rethinking Multicultural Co-Living Discourses]. In *Taminzokukashakai nihon* [Multiethnic Japan], edited by Ichiro Watado and Yasuki Izawa, 237–255. Tokyo: Akashi Shoten.

Kato, Norihiro. (1997) 2015. *Haisengoron* [On Postwar Japan]. Tokyo: Chikuma Shobō.

Kawai, Yuko. 2007. "Japanese Nationalism and the Global Spread of English: An Analysis of Japanese Governmental and Public Discourses on English." *Language and Intercultural Communication* 7: 37–55.

———. 2008. "Communicating Globalization." In *Intercultural Communication in a Transnational World: International and Intercultural Communication Annual*, Vol. 31, edited by Lisa A. Flores, Mark P. Orbe, and Brenda J. Allen, 119–149. Washington, DC: National Communication Association.

———. 2015. "Japanese as Both a 'Race' and a 'Non-Race': The Politics of *Jinshu* and *Minzoku* and the Depoliticization of Japaneseness." In *Race and Racism in Modern East Asia (Vol. 2): Interactions, Nationalism, Gender and Lineage*, edited by Rotem Kowner and Walter Demel, 368–388. Leiden: Brill.

———. 2016a. "Intersecting Japanese Nationalism and Racism as Everyday Practices: Toward a Multiculturalist Japanese Society." In *Multiculturalism in East Asia: A Transnational Exploration of Japan, South Korea and Taiwan*, edited by Koichi Iwabuchi, Hyun Mee Kim, and Hsiao-Chuan Hsia, 103–123. London and New York: Rowman & Littlefield.

———. 2016b. "Using Diaspora: Orientalism, Japanese Nationalism, and the Japanese Brazilian Diaspora." In *Intercultural Masquerade: New Orientalism, New Occidentalism, Old Exoticism*, edited by Regis Machart, Fred Dervin, and Minghui Gao, 97–117. Berlin, Heidelberg: Springer.

———. 2018. "The Grammar of Japanese Racialized Discourse in Hate-Korea Books." *Asia Review* 8(1): 289–313.

Kawata, Junzo. 1999. "Minzoku gainen ni tsuite no memo" [On the Concept of *minzoku*]. *Minzokugaku kenkyū / Japanese Journal of Ethnology* 63: 451–461.

———. 2009. "Minzoku." In *Bunka jinruigaku jiten* [Encyclopaedia of Cultural Anthropology], edited by Nihon bunka jinruigakkai [The Japanese Society of Cultural Anthropology], 136–141. Tokyo: Maruzen.

Kenpō kenkyūkai. 1945. "*Kenpō sōan yōkō*" [Constitutional Draft Outline]. http://www.ndl.go.jp/constitution/shiryo/02/052/052tx.html.

Kidd, Jenny. 2016. *Representation*. London and New York: Routledge.

Ko, Mika. 2010. *Japanese Cinema and Otherness: Nationalism, Multiculturalism, and the Problem of Japaneseness*. London and New York: Routledge.

Kojima, Tsuyoshi. 2018. *Tennō to jukyōshisō* [The Emperor and Confucianism]. Tokyo: Kōbunsha.

Kondo, Dorinne K. 1990. *Crafting Selves: Power, Gender, and Discourses of Identity in a Japanese Workplace*. Chicago: University of Chicago Press.

Korean Residents Union in Japan. n.d. "*Tōkei*" [Statistics]. Accessed January 6, 2008. http://mindan.org/toukei.php.

Koshiro, Yukiko. 1999. *Trans-Pacific Racisms and the U.S. Occupation of Japan*. New York: Columbia University Press.

Koyasu, Nobukuni. 2006. "Nihon minzoku gainen no arukeorogī" [Archaeology of the Japanese *Minzoku*]. *Asoshie/Associé* 17: 8–19.

Kubota, Ryoko. 2002. "The Impact of Globalization on Language Teaching in Japan." In *Globalization and Language Teaching*, edited by David Block and Deborah Cameron, 13–28. London: Routledge.

———. 2011. "Questioning Linguistic Instrumentalism: English, Neoliberalism, and Language Tests in Japan." *Linguistics and Education* 22: 248–260.

———. 2016. "Neoliberal Paradoxes of Language Learning: Xenophobia and International Communication." *Journal of Multilingual and Multicultural Development* 37(5): 467–480.

Kurokawa, Midori. 2004. "Buraku sabetsu ni okeru jinshushugi" [Racism in Discrimination Against *Buraku* People]. In *Ajia no mibunsei to sabetsu* [The Social Class System and Discrimination in Asia], edited by Kazuteru Okiura, Nobuaki Teramoto, and Kenzō Tomonaga, 241–261. Kaihō Shuppansha.

Kurozumi, Makoto. 2003. *Kinsei nihon syakai to jukyō* [Early Modern Japanese Society and Confucianism]. Tokyo: Perikansha.

Kymlicka, Will. 2016. "Defending Diversity in an Era of Populism: Multiculturalism and Interculturalism Compared." In *Multiculturalism and Interculturalism: Debating the Dividing Lines*, edited by Naser Meer, Tariq Modood, and Ricard Zapata-Barrero, 158–177. Edinburgh, UK: Edinburgh University Press.

Lee, Sincere. 2014. *Chikan ron* [Shameful South Korea]. Tokyo: Fusōsha.

———. 2016. *Nihon no gohan wa naze oishii no ka* [Why Is Japanese Rice Delicious?]. Tokyo: Fusōsha.

Lentin, Alana. 2011. *Racism and Ethnic Discrimination*. New York: Rosen Publishing.

Lesser, Jeffery. 2003. "Japanese, Brazilians, Nikkei: A Short History of Identity Building and Homemaking." In *Searching for Home Abroad: Japanese Brazilians and Transnationalism*, edited by Jeffery Lesser, 5–19. Durham, NC: Duke University Press.

———. 2007. *A Discontented Diaspora*. Durham, NC: Duke University Press.

Li, Wen. 2015. "*Chūgokujin ryūgakusei no yūjin ne'towāku*" [The Friendship Network of Chinese International Students in Japan]. *Doshisha Review of Sociology* 19: 47–63.

Lie, John. 2001. *Multi-Ethnic Japan*. Cambridge, MA: Harvard University Press.

Lu, Amy Shirong. 2008. "The Many Faces of Internationalization in Japanese Anime." *Animation* 3(2): 169–187.

Mackerras, Colin. 1989. *Western Images of China*. Oxford: Oxford University Press.

Maeyama, Takashi. 1979. "Ethnicity, Secret Societies, and Associations: The Japanese in Brazil." *Comparative Studies in Society and History* 21: 589–610.

Maia, Alexandre Gori, Arthur Sakamoto, and Sharron Xuanren Wang. 2015. "Socioeconomic Attainments of Japanese Brazilians and Japanese Americans." *Sociology of Race and Ethnicity* 1(4): 547–563.

Mainichi Shimbun. 2012. "Tsuittā de jinshu sabetsu hatsugen" [A Racist Comment Via Twitter]. July 26, 2012. http://sportsspecial.mainichi.jp/news/20120726ddm041050109000c.html.

———. 2016. "Hundreds of Hate Speech Rallies Held Across Japan Annually: Justice Ministry Report." March 31, 2016. https://mainichi.jp/english/articles/20160331/p2a/00m/0na/003000c.

Malik, Kenan. 1996. *The Meaning of Race*. New York: New York University Press.

Martin, Judith N., and Thomas K. Nakayama. 2013. *Intercultural Communication in Contexts*, 6th ed. New York: McGraw Hill.

Masterson, Daniel. M. 2004. *The Japanese in Latin America*. Urbana and Chicago, IL: University of Illinois Press.

McClintock, Anne. 1996. "'No Longer in a Future Heaven': Nationalism, Gender, and Race." In *Becoming National: A Reader*, edited by Geoff Eley and Ronald Grigor Suny, 260–285. Oxford: Oxford University Press.

McLaren, Peter. 1994. "White Terror and Oppositional Agency: Towards a Critical Multiculturalism." In *Multiculturalism: A Critical Reader*, edited by David Theo Goldberg, 45–74. Cambridge, MA: Blackwell.

McNally, Mark Thomas. 2016. *Like No Other: Exceptionalism and Nativism in Early Modern Japan*. Honolulu, HI: University of Hawai'i Press.

Meer, Nasar, and Tariq Modood. 2016. "Interculturalism, Multiculturalism and Citizenship." In *Multiculturalism and Interculturalism: Debating the Dividing Lines*, edited by Naser Meer, Tariq Modood, and Ricard Zapata-Barrero, 27–52. Edinburgh, UK: Edinburgh University Press.

Meiji Shrine. n.d. "Divine Virtues." Accessed May 3, 2014. http://www.meijijingu.or.jp/english/about/6.html.

Miles, Robert. 1989. *Racism*. London: Routledge.

Ministry of Defense. 2019. "*Zainichi beigun shisetsu kuiki no jyōkyō*" [U.S. Military Facilities and Areas]. Last Modified January 1, 2019. http://www.mod.go.jp/j/approach/zaibeigun/us_sisetsu/.

Ministry of Education. 1943. *Shotōka kokushi: jyō* [Elementary National History: Volume 1]. http://dl.ndl.go.jp/info:ndljp/pid/1277108.

Ministry of Education, Culture, Sports, Science, and Technology (MEXT). 2003a. "Action Plan to Cultivate 'Japanese with English Abilities.'" http://www.mext.go.jp/b_menu/houdou/15/03/03033101/001.pdf.

———. 2003b. "Eigo ga tsukaeru nihonjin no ikusei no tame no kōdō keikaku" [Action Plan to Cultivate 'Japanese with English Abilities]. http://www.mext.go.jp/b_menu/houdou/15/03/03033102.pdf.

———. 2013a. "Kyōkasho kaikaku jikkō puran" [Action Plans for School Textbook Reform]. http://www.mext.go.jp/b_menu/houdou/25/11/__icsFiles/afieldfile/2013/11/15/1341515_01.pdf.

———. 2013b. "Grōbaruka ni taiōshita eigo kyōiku kaikaku ji'shi keikaku" [Action Plans for English Language Education Reforms to Cope with Globalization]. http://www.mext.go.jp/b_menu/houdou/25/12/__icsFiles/afieldfile/2013/12/17/1342458_01_1.pdf.

———. 2020. "Gaikokujin ryūgakusei zaiseki chōsa oyobi nihonjin no kaigai ryūgakusya sū ni tsuite" [The Number of International Students in Japan and the Number of Japanese Students Studying Abroad]. https://www.mext.go.jp/content/20200421-mxt_gakushi02-100001342_1.pdf.

———. n.d. "About Tobitate! (Leap for Tomorrow) Study Abroad Initiative." Accessed December 28, 2016. http://www.tobitate.mext.go.jp/about/english.html.

Ministry of Foreign Affairs. 1919. "1919 nen Pari kōwa kaigi no keika ni kansuru chōsho sono 3" [Reports on the 1919 Paris Peace Conference Vol. 3]. *Nihon gaikō bunsho dejitaru ākaibu* [Digital Archive for Japanese Diplomatic Documents]. http://www.mofa.go.jp/mofaj/annai/honsho/shiryo/archives/tt-1.html.

———. 1965. "Agreement on the Settlement of Problems Concerning Property and Claims and on Economic Co-operation between Japan and the Republic of Korea." *The World and Japan Database*. http://worldjpn.grips.ac.jp/documents/texts/JPKR/19650622.T9E.html.

———. 1995. "Statement by Prime Minister Tomiichi Murayama: On the Occasion of the 50th Anniversary of the War's End." http://www.mofa.go.jp/announce/press/pm/murayama/9508.html.

———. 2000. "Comments of the Japanese Government on the Concluding Observations Adopted by the Committee on the Elimination of Racial Discrimination on March 20, 2000, Regarding Initial and Second Periodic Report of the Japanese Government." http://www.mofa.go.jp/policy/human/comment0110.html.

———. 2013. "Seventh, Eighth, and Ninth Combined Periodic Report by the Government of Japan Under Article 9 of the International Convention on Elimination of All Forms of Racial Discrimination." http://www.mofa.go.jp/policy/human/pdfs/report_789_1.pdf.

Ministry of Health, Labour and Welfare. 2012. "Hiseiki koyō no genjō" [The Present State of Non-Regular Employment]. https://www.mhlw.go.jp/stf/shingi/2r9852000002k8ag-att/2r9852000002k8f7.pdf.

Ministry of Internal Affairs. 2006. "Chiiki ni okeru tabunka kyōsei suishin puran" [Multicultural Co-living Promotion Plan in Municipalities]. http://www.soumu.go.jp/main_content/000400764.pdf.

Ministry of Justice. 2001. "Heisei 12nen matsu ni okeru gaikokujin tōrokusha tōkei ni tsuite" [The Number of Registered Foreigners in 2000]. http://www.moj.go.jp/nyuukokukanri/kouhou/press_010613-1_010613-1-6.html.

———. 2020. "Reiwa gannen matsu ni okeru zairyū gaikokjin su ni tsuite" [The Number of Foreign Residents in 2019]. http://www.moj.go.jp/nyuukokukanri/kouhou/nyuukokukanri04_00003.html.

———. n.d. "Zairyū gaikokujin tōkei" [Statistics on Foreign Residents in Japan]. Accessed August 8, 2019. http://www.moj.go.jp/housei/toukei/toukei_ichiran_touroku.html.

Mintz, Sidney W., and Christine M. Du Bois. 2002. "The Anthropology of Food and Eating." *Annual Review of Anthropology* 31(1): 99–119.

Miwa, Kimitada. 2007. "Pan-Asianism in Modern Japan: Nationalism, Regionalism and Universalism." In *Pan-Asianism in Modern Japanese History*, edited by Sven Saaler and J. Victor Koschmann, 21–33. London and New York: Routledge.

Modood, Tariq. 2016. "Multiculturalism, Interculturalisms and the Majority." In *Multiculturalism and Interculturalism: Debating the Dividing Lines*, edited by Naser Meer, Tariq Modood, and Ricard Zapata-Barrero, 246–265. Edinburgh, UK: Edinburgh University Press.

Morris-Suzuki, Tessa. 1998. *Re-inventing Japan: Time, Space, Nation*. Armonk, NY: M.E. Sharpe.

———. 2002. *Hihanteki sōzōryoku no tameni: gurōbaruka jidai no nihon* [In Search of Critical Imagination: Japan in an Age of Globalization]. Tokyo: Heibonsha.

———. 2016. "Asianisms from Below: Japanese Civil Society and Visions of Asian Integration from the Late 20th to the 21st Century." In *Asianisms: Regionalist Interactions and Asian Integration*, edited by Frey Marc and Spakowski Nicola, 156–180. Singapore: NUS Press. http://www.jstor.org/stable/j.ctv1nthd7.11.

Mosse, George L. 1964. *The Crisis of German Ideology*. New York: Howard Fertig.

Mouer, Ross, and Yoshio Sugimoto. 1986. *Images of Japanese Society*. London: Kegan Paul International.

Murotani, Katsumi. 2013. *Bōkan ron* [Stupid South Korea]. Tokyo: Sankei Shimbun Shuppan.

Muta, Kazue. 2016. "The 'Comfort Women' Issue and the Embedded Culture of Sexual Violence in Japan." *Current Sociology Monograph* 64(4): 620–636.

Nakai, Kate Wildman. 1980. "The Naturalization of Confucianism in Tokugawa Japan: The Problem of Sinocentrism." *Harvard Journal of Asian Studies* 40: 157–199.

Nakamura, Yuka. 2005. "The Samurai Sword Cuts both Ways: A Transnational Analysis of Japanese and US Media Representation of Ichiro." *International Review for the Sociology of Sport* 40(4): 467–480.

Nakane, Chie. 1967. *Tateshakai no ningen kankei* [Japanese Society]. Tokyo: Kōdansha.

Nakayama, Thomas K., and Rona Tamiko Halualani, eds. 2010. *The Handbook of Critical Intercultural Communication*. Malden, MA: Wiley-Blackwell.

Nihonshoki: Kokushi taikei dai 1 kan [The *Nihonshoki*: A Compendium of Japanese History Volume 1]. 1901. Tokyo: Keizaiza' shisha. http://dl.ndl.go.jp/info:ndljp/pid/991091.

Niiya, Brian, ed. 2001. *Encyclopedia of Japanese American History*. New York: Checkmark Books.

Nikkan SPA. 2017. "Heito bon wa dōshite umareta no ka" [Why Have Hate Books Been Written?]." September 16, 2017. https://nikkan-spa.jp/1394897.

Nippan. 2014. "*2014 nen nenkan besuto serā*" [Bestselling books of 2014]. http://www.nippan.co.jp/wp-content/uploads/2014/11/annual_20141128.pdf.

———. 2017. "*2017 nen nenkan besuto serā*" [Bestselling Books of 2017]. http://www.nippan.co.jp/wp-content/uploads/2017/11/annual_20171201.pdf.

Nojima, Toshihiko. 1989. "*Susumetai nikkeijin no tokubetsu ukeire*" [Special Acceptance of People of Japanese Descent as Guest Workers Should Be Promoted]. *Gekkan jiyū minshu* [Monthly Liberal Democracy] 440: 92–99.

Nora, Pierre. 1989. "Between Memory and History: Les Lieux de Mémoire." *Representations* 26: 7–24.

Northwood, Barbara, and Chihiro Kinoshita Thomson. 2012. "What Keeps Them Going? Investigating Ongoing Learners of Japanese in Australian Universities." *Japanese Studies* 32(3): 335–355.

Nosco, Peter. 2014. "Kokugaku Critiques of Confucianism and Chinese Culture." In *Dao Companion to Japanese Confucian Philosophy*, edited by Chun-chieh Huang and John Allen Tucker, 233–256. Dordrecht: Springer.

Obara, Jun. 2011. *Foruku to teikoku sōsetsu* [Volk and Empire Building]. Tokyo: Sairyūsha.

Oguma, Eiji. 1995. *Tan'itsu minzoku shinwa no kigen* [The Origin of the Myth of Ethnic Homogeneity]. Tokyo: Shin'yōsha.

———. 1998. *Nihonjin no kyōkai* [The Boundaries of the Japanese]. Tokyo: Shin'yōsha.

———. 2002. *Minshu to aikoku* [Democracy and Patriots]. Tokyo: Shin'yōsha.

———. (1995) 2002. *A Genealogy of Japanese Self-Images*. Translated by David Askew. Malborne: Trans Pacific Press.

———. 2007. "The Postwar Intellectuals' Views of 'Asia.'" In *Pan-Asianism in Modern Japanese History*, edited by Sven Saaler and J. Victor Koschmann, 200–212. London and New York: Routledge.

———. (1998) 2014. *The Boundaries of the Japanese Volume 1: Okinawa 1818–1972*. Translated by Leonie R. Stickland. Malborne: Trans Pacific Press.

———. (1998) 2017. *The Boundaries of the Japanese Volume 2: Korea, Taiwan and the Ainu 1868–1945*. Translated by Leonie R. Stickland. Malborne: Trans Pacific Press.

Oguni, Ayako. 2015. "Ken-kan ken-chū sinogu ikioi?: Nihon raisan bon ga būmu no wake" [More Popular Than Hhte-Korea and Hate-China Books?: Why Are Books Glorifying Japan Popular?]. *The Mainichi Shimbun*, Evening Edition, February 25, 2015.

Oh, Bonnie B. 1980. "Sino-Japanese Rivalry in Korea, 1876–1885." In *The Chinese and the Japanese: Essays in Political and Cultural Interactions*, edited by Akira Iriye, 37–57. Princeton, NJ: Princeton University Press.

Ohashi, Toshiko. 2008. *Gaikokujin ryūgakusei no mental herusu to kiki kainyū* [International Students' Mental Health and Crisis Intervention]. Kyoto: Kyoto University Press.

Oizumi, Mitsunari, Naoki Kato, and Yukihiko Kimura. 2015. *Saraba, heito bon!* [Good-Bye, Hate Books!]. Tokyo: Korokara.

Okakura, Kakuzo. (1903) 1920. *The Ideals of the East: With Special Reference to the Art of Japan*. London: J. Murray.

Okamoto, Masataka. 2011. "Nihonjin naibu no minzoku ishiki to gainen no konran" [Ethnic Identities Among Japanese Nationals]. *Fukuoka kenritsu daigaku ningen kagakubu kiyō* 19(2): 77–98.

Okamoto, Takashi. 2008. *Sekai no naka no nisshinkan kankeishi* [A History of Relationships Among Japan, Qing China, and Korea]. Tokyo: Kōdansha.

Okihiro, Gary Y., ed. 2013. *Encyclopedia of Japanese American Internment*. Santa Barbara, CA: Greenwood.

Okinawa Prefectural Peace Memorial Museum. n.d. "*Okinawa sen Q&A*" [The Battle of Okinawa Q&A]. Accessed April 20, 2018. http://www.peace-museum.pref.okinawa.jp/heiwagakusyu/kyozai/qa/q2.html.

Omi, Michel, and Howard Winant. 2015. *Racial Formation in the United States*, 3rd ed. London and New York: Routledge.

Oricon. 2010. "Kusanagi Nakama w-shuen dorama 99 nen no ai saishūya no heikin shichōritsu 19.1% saiko shunkan 23.1%" [The Last Episode of the Drama "99 Years of Love" Starring Tsuyoshi Kusanagi and Yukie Nakama Attracted an Average Audience Rating of 19.1% and Recorded 23.1% at Its Highest]. November 8, 2010. http://www.oricon.co.jp/news/81838/full/.

Osher, David. 2000. "Race Relations and War." In *The Oxford Companion to American Military History*, edited by John Whiteclay Chambers II, 584–586. Oxford: Oxford University Press.

Ota, Osamu. 2015. *Nikkan kōshō shinsō shinban* [Japan-South Korea Diplomatic Negotiations, revised ed.]. Tokyo: Crane.

Pan, Chengxin. 2012. *Knowledge, Desire, and Power in Global Politics: Western Representations of China's Rise*. Cheltenham, UK: Edward Elgar.

Paramore, Kiri. 2016. *Japanese Confucianism: A Cultural History*. Cambridge: Cambridge University Press.

Parasecoli, Fabio. 2014. "Food, Identity, and Cultural Reproduction in Immigrant Communities." *Social Research: An International Quarterly* 81(2): 415–439.

Parekh, Bhikhu. 2006. *Rethinking Multiculturalism*, 2nd ed. New York: Palgrave Macmillan.

———. 2016. "Afterword: Multiculturalism and Interculturalism—A Critical Dialogue." In *Multiculturalism and Interculturalism: Debating the Dividing Lines*, edited by Naser Meer, Tariq Modood, and Ricard Zapata-Barrero, 266–279. Edinburgh, UK: Edinburgh University Press.

Park, Tae Heok. 1993. *Minikui kankokujin* [Ugly Koreans]. Tokyo: Kōbunsha.

Pecora, Vincent P. 2001. "Introduction." In *Nations and Identities: Classic Readings*, edited by Vincent P. Pecora, 1–42. Malden, MA: Blackwell.

Phillipson, Robert. 2003. *English-Only Europe?: Challenging Language Policy*. London and New York: Routledge.

Pickering, Michael. 2001. *Stereotyping: The Politics of Representation*. London: Palgrave.

Popular Memory Group. 2011. "Popular Memory: Theory, Politics, Method." In *The Collective Memory Reader*, edited by Jeffery K. Olick, Vered Vinitzky-Seroussi, and Daniel Levy, 254–260. Oxford: Oxford University Press.

Rattansi, Ali. 2007. *Racism*. Oxford: Oxford University Press.

———. 2011. *Multiculturalism: A Very Short Introduction*. Oxford: Oxford University Press.

Renan, Ernest. (1882) 2011. "What Is a Nation?" In *The Collective Memory Reader*, edited by Jeffrey K. Olick, Vered Vinitzky-Seroussi, and Daniel Levy, 80–83. Oxford: Oxford University Press.

Riessman, Catherine Kohler. 2008. *Narrative Methods for the Human Sciences*. Thousand Oaks, CA: SAGE.

Rigney, Ann. 2016. "Cultural Memory Studies." In *Routledge International Handbook of Memory Studies*, edited by Anna Lisa Tota and Trever Hagen, 65–76. London and New York: Routledge.

Rogers, Katie, and Nicholas Fandos. 2019. "Trump Tells Congresswomen to 'Go Back' to the Countries They Came From." *New York Times*, July 14, 2019. https://www.nytimes.com/2019/07/14/us/politics/trump-twitter-squad-congress.html.

Roth, Joshua Hotaka. 2002. *Brokered Homeland*. Ithaca, NY: Cornell University Press.

Rottenberg, Catherine. 2014. "The Rise of Neoliberal Feminism." *Cultural Studies* 28(3): 418–437.

Saad-Filho, Alfredo, and Deborah Johnston. 2005. "Introduction." In *Neoliberalism: A Critical Reader*, edited by Alfredo Saad-Filho and Deborah Johnston, 1–6. London: Pluto Press.

Saaler, Sven. 2007. "Pan-Asianism in Modern Japanese History." In *Pan-Asianism in Modern Japanese History*, edited by Sven Saaler and J. Victor Koschmann, 1–18. London and New York: Routledge.

Saaler, Sven, and Christopher W. A. Szpilman. 2011. "Introduction: The Emergence of Pan-Asianism as an Ideal of Asian Identity and Solidarity, 1850–2008." In *Pan Asianism: A Documentary History*, Vol. 1, edited by Sven Saaler and Christopher W. A. Szpilman, 1–41. Lanham, MD: Rowman & Littlefield.

Said, Edward W. 1978. *Orientalism*. New York: Vintage Books.

Sakai, Naoki. 1996. *Shizan sareru nihongo nihonjin* [The Stillborn of the Japanese as Language and as Ethnos]. Tokyo: Shin'yōsha.

———. 1997. *Translation and Subjectivity: On "Japan" and Cultural Nationalism*. Minneapolis, MN: University of Minnesota Press.

———. 2005. "Introduction: Nationality and the Politics of the 'Mother Tongue'." In *Deconstructing Nationality*, edited by Naoki Sakai, Brett de Bary, and Toshio Iyotani, 1–38. Ithaca, NY: Cornel University Press.

———. 2006. "Nihonshi to kokuminteki sekinin" [Japanese History and Japanese National Responsibility]. In *Nashonaru hisutorī wo manabi suteru* [Unlearning National History], edited by Naoki Sakai, 161–190. Tokyo: Tokyo daigaku shuppan kai.

———. 2008. *Kibō to kenpō* [Hope and the Constitution]. Tokyo: Ibunsha.

Sakano, Toru. 2005. "Jinshu, minzoku, nihonjin" [*Jinshu, minzoku*, the Japanese]. In *Jinshu no fuhensei o tou* [Is Race a Universal Idea?], edited by Yasuko Takezawa, 229–254. Kyoto: Jinbun Shoin.

———. 2009. "Konketsu to tekiō nōryoku" [Mixed Blood and Adaptability]. In *Jinshu no hyōshō to shakaiteki riaritii* [Racial Representations and Social Realities], edited by Yasuko Takezawa, 188–215. Tokyo: Iwanami Shoten.

Saussure, Ferdinand de. 1983. *Course in General Linguistics*. Chicago: Open Court.

Schmid, Andre. 2000. "Colonialism and the 'Korea Problem' in the Histography of Modern Japan: A Review Article." *Journal of Asian Studies* 59(4): 951–976.

Sedgwick, Peter. 1999. "Structuralism." In *Key Concepts in Cultural Theory*, edited by Andrew Edger and Peter Sedgwick, 381–384. London and New York: Routledge.

Shibuya, Nozomu. 2003. *Tamashii no rōdō: Neoriberarizumu no ken'ryoku-ron* [Spiritual Labor: On Neoliberalism and Power]. Tokyo: Seidosha.

Shiga, Shigetaka. (1888)1980. "Nihonjin ga kaihō suru tokoro no shigi wo kokuhaku su" [The Principles of the Japanese]. In *Meiji bungaku zenshū 37 kan: Seikyōsha bungaku shū* [The Collection of Literature in the Meiji Period, Volume 37: Seikyōsha], edited by Sannosuke Matsumoto, 99–102. Tokyo: Chikuma Shoten.

Shimazu, Naoko. 1998. *Japan, Race and Equality*. London: Routledge.

Shin, Tonghun. 1996. "Minikui kankokujin no chosha ronsō ni kanzen ke'chaku" [Settling the Dispute of the Book "Ugly Koreans" Authorship]. *Shūkan kinyōbi* 4(37): 31–33, October 4, 1996.

Shirona, Masakazu, and Teiichi Ikeda. 2016. "Terebi de hon de: Nihon sugoi bumu no iku saki wa" [Ubiquitous on Television and in Books: Where Does the 'Japan-is-great' Boom Go from Here?]. *The Tokyo Shimbun*, Morning Edition, December 23, 2016, pp. 28–29.

Slocum, Rachel. 2011. "Race in the Study of Food." *Progress in Human Geography* 35(3): 303–327.

Sollors, Werner. 2002. "Ethnicity and Race." In *A Companion to Racial and Ethnic Studies*, edited by David Theo Goldberg and John Solomos, 97–104. Malden, MA: Blackwell.

Soysal, Yasemin Nuhoglu. 2000. "Citizenship and Identity: Living in Diasporas in Post-War Europe?" *Ethnic and Racial Studies* 23(1): 1–15.

Spencer, Stephen. 2006. *Race and Ethnicity*. London: Routledge.

Spickard, Paul. R. 2009. *Japanese Americans: The Formation and Transformations of an Ethnic Group*. New Brunswick, NJ: Rutgers University Press.

Stewart, Henry. 2002. *Minzoku gensō ron* [The Illusion of *minzoku*]. Osaka: Kaihō Shuppansha.

Stierstorfer, Klaus, and Janet Wilson. 2018. "General Introduction." In *The Routledge Diaspora Studies Reader*, edited by Klaus Stierstorfer and Janet Wilson, xiii–xxv. London and New York: Routledge.

Sturrock, John. 2003. *Structuralism*, 2nd ed. Malden, MA: Blackwell.

Sugimoto, Yoshio, and Ross Mouer. 1995. *Nihonjinron no hōteishiki* [The Equation of *nihonjinron*]. Tokyo: Chikuma Shobo.

Sun, Ge. 2000. "How Does Asia Mean? (Part I)." *Inter-Asia Cultural Studies* 1(1): 13–47.

Supreme Commander for the Allied Powers. 1946. "Constitution of Japan." http://www.ndl.go.jp/constitution/shiryo/03/076a_e/076a_etx.html.

Suzuki, Zenji. 1993. *Nihon no yūseigaku* [Eugenics in Japan]. Tokyo: Sankyō Shuppan.

Tachibanaki, Toshiaki. 2006. *Kakusa shakai* [An Unequal Society]. Tokyo: Iwanami Shoten.

Taguieff, Pierre-André. 1999. "National Identity Framed in the Logics of Racialization." In *Racism: Key Concepts in Critical Theory*, edited by Leonard Harris, 297–313. New York: Humanity Books.

Tai, Eika. 1999. *Tabunkashugi to diasupora* [Multiculturalism and Diaspora]. Tokyo: Akashi Shoten.

———. 2003. "Tabuka kyōsei to sono kanōsei" [Multicultural Co-living and Its Potential in Japan]. *Jinken mondai kenkyū* [The Journal of Human Rights] 3: 41–52.

Takaguchi, Kota. 2018. "Girubāto no dokusha wa dare ka" [What the Data Reveals]. *Newsweek*, October 30, 2018, pp. 26–28.

Takahashi, Jere. 1997. *Nisei/Sansei*. Philadelphia, PA: Temple University Press.

Takahashi, Tetsuya. (1999) 2005. *Sengo sekinin ron* [Postwar Responsibility]. Tokyo: Kōdansha.

Takahashi, Yoshio. (1884) 2001. "Nihon jinshu kairyō ron" [A Treaties on Improvement of the Japanese *jinshu*]. In *Nihon no yūseigaku shiryō senshū 1 kan* [A Collection of Eugenic Studies in Japan, Volume 1], edited by Zenji Suzuki, 515–605. Tokyo: Kress Shuppan.

Takaku, Jun, and Emi Tadama. 2018. "Kento girubāto shi no chūkanbon ureru riyū wa" [Why Do Kent Gilbert's Book on China and Korea Sell Well?]. *The Asahi Shimbun*, Morning Edition, March 6, 2018, p. 37.

Takasaki, Soji. 1996. *Kenshō nikkan kaidan* [Examining Japan-South Korea Diplomatic Normalization Talks]. Tokyo: Iwanami Shoten.

Takeuchi, Yoshimi. 1993. *Nihon to ajia* [Japan and Asia]. Tokyo: Chikuma shobō.

———. 2005. *What Is Modernity?* New York: Columbia University Press.

Takezawa, Yasuko. 2005. "Jinshu gainen no hōkatsuteki rikai ni mukete" [Toward a Comprehensive Understanding of the Concept of Race]. In *Jinshu no fuhensei o tou* [Is Race a Universal Idea?], edited by Yasuko Takezawa, 9–109. Kyoto: Jinbun Shoin.

Tanaka, Stefan. 1993. *Japan's Orient*. Berkeley, CA: University of California Press.

Taylor, Charles. 2012. "Interculturalism or Multiculturalism?" *Philosophy and Social Criticism* 38(4–5): 413–423.

Thomas, Bronwen. 2016. *Narrative*. London and New York: Routledge.

Thompson, John. B. 1990. *Ideology and Modern Culture*. Stanford, CA: Stanford University Press.

Thornham, Sue, and Tony Purvis. 2005. *Television Drama*. New York: Palgrave Macmillan.

Tipps, Dean C. 1973. "Modernization Theory and the Comparative Study of National Societies: A Critical Perspective." *Comparative Studies in Society and History* 15(2): 199–226.

Toby, Ronald P. 1991. *State and Diplomacy in Early Modern Japan: Asia in the Development of the Tokugawa Bakufu*. Stanford, CA: Stanford University Press.

Todo, Akiyasu, Akira Takeda, and Terukuni Kageyama, trans. and eds. (2010). *Wakokuden* [Accounts of *Wa*]. Tokyo: Kōdansya.

Tohan. 2014. "2014 nenkan besuto serā" [Bestselling Books of 2014]. http://www.tohan.jp/bestsellers/upload_pdf_past/141201bestseller_2014y.pdf.

———. 2017. "2017 nenkan besuto serā" [Bestselling Books of 2017]. http://www.tohan.jp/bestsellers/upload_pdf_past/171201bestseller_2017y.pdf.

Tokyo Shimbun. 2017. "Heito supīchi taisakuhō wa ima taisaku hō ichi nen" [One Year After the Enactment of the Hate Speech Act]. September 16, 2017. http://www.tokyo-np.co.jp/article/culture/hiroba/CK2017091602000215.html.

Tomiyama, Iichiro. 1994. "Kokumin no tanjō to nihon jinshu" [The Birth of the Nation and the Japanese *jinshu*]. *Shisō* 845: 37–56.

Tomlinson, John. 2003. "Globalization and Cultural Identity." In *The Global Transformations Reader*, 2nd ed., edited by David Held and Anthony McGrew, 269–277. Cambridge: Polity.

———. 2007. "Globalization and Cultural Analysis." In *Globalization Theory*, edited by David Held and Anthony McGrew, 148–168. Cambridge: Polity.

Toyosaki, Satoshi, and Shinsuke Eguchi. 2017. *Intercultural Communication in Japan*. London and New York: Routledge.

Tsuda, Takeyuki. 2003. *Strangers in the Ethnic Homeland*. New York: Columbia University Press.

———. 2009a. "Introduction." In *Diasporic Homecomings: Ethnic Return Migration in Comparative Perspective*, edited by Takeyuki Tsuda, 1–20. Stanford, CA: Stanford University Press.

———. 2009b. "Global Inequalities and Diasporic Return: Japanese American and Brazilian Encounters with the Ethic Homeland." In *Diasporic Homecomings: Ethnic Return Migration in Comparative Perspective*, edited by Takeyuki Tsuda, 227–269. Stanford, CA: Stanford University Press.

———. 2016. *Japanese American Ethnicity*. New York: NYU Press.

Tsujimura, Akira. 1987. "Some Characteristics of the Japanese Way of Communication." In *Communication Theory: Eastern and Western Perspectives*, edited by D. Lawrence Kincaid, 115–126. San Diego: Academic Press.

Turner, Bryan S., and Robert J. Holton. 2016. "Theories of Globalization: Issues and Origins." In *The Routledge International Handbook of Globalization Studies*, 2nd ed., edited by Bryan S. Turner and Robert J. Holton, 3–23. London and New York: Routledge.

Ueda, Kazutoshi. (1894)1968. "Kokugo to kokka to" [The National Language and the State]. In *Meiji bungaku zenshū 44 kan: Ochiai Naobumi, Ueda Kazutoshi, Haga Yaichi, and Fujioka Sakutarō shū* [The Collection of Literature in the Meiji Period, Volume 44], edited by Sen'ichi Hisamatsu, 108–113. Tokyo: Chikuma Shobō.

Ueno, Chizuko. (1998) 2012. *Nashonarizumu to jendā* [Nationalism and Gender]. Tokyo: Iwanami shoten.

UNESCO. 1969. *Four Statements on the Race Question*. Paris: UNESCO. http://unesdoc.unesco.org/images/0012/001229/122962eo.pdf.

———. 2009. "Investing in Cultural Diversity and Intercultural Dialogue." https://unesdoc.unesco.org/ark:/48223/pf0000184755.

Unno, Kotoku. 1911. *Nihon jinshu kaizō ron* [Remodeling the Japanese *jinshu*], rev. ed. Tokyo: Toyamabō.

———. (1910) 2010. "Nihon jinshu kaizō ron" [Remodeling the Japanese *jinshu*]. In *Nihon no yūseigaku shiryō senshū 5 kan* [A Collection of Eugenic Studies in Japan, Volume 5], edited by Zenji Suzuki, 1–109. Tokyo: Kress Shuppan.

Urciuoli, Bonnie. 2008. "Skills and Selves in the New Workplace." *American Ethnologist* 35(29): 211–228.

van Dijk, Teun A. 1992. "Discourse and the Denial of Racism." *Discourse and Society* 3(1): 87–118.

Vertovec, Steven, 2007. "Super Diversity and Its Implications." *Ethnic and Racial Studies* 30(6): 1024–1054.

Video Research Ltd. (n.d.a). "Shumokubetsu kō setai sichōritsu bangumi 10: 2005.10.3–10.9" [Ten Programs with High Audience Ratings by Genre Between October 3 and October 9, 2005]. Accessed February 2, 2006. http://www.videor.co.jp/data/ratedata/backnum/2005/vol.41.htm.

———. (n.d.b). "NHK asa no renzoku terebi shōsetsu" [NHK Serialized Morning Television Drama]. Accessed March 25, 2017. http://www.videor.co.jp/data/ratedata/program/02asa.htm.

Vogel, Ezra F. 1979. *Japan as Number One*. Cambridge, MA: Harvard University Press.

Vološinov, V. N. 1973. *Marxism and the Philosophy of Language*. Cambridge, MA: Harvard University Press.

Vora, Neha. 2018. "Diaspora." In *The International Encyclopedia of Anthropology Volume III*, edited by Hilary Callan, 1577–1580. Hoboken, NJ: Wiley Blackwell.

Wang, Hui. 2007. "The Politics of Imagining Asia: A Genealogical Analysis." *Inter-Asia Cultural Studies* 8(1): 1–33.

Wang, Yuan-kang. 2013. "Explaining the Tribute System: Power, Confucianism, and War in Medieval East Asia." *Journal of East Asian Studies* 13: 207–232.

Watanabe, Osamu. 2001. *Nihon no taikoku ka to neo nashonarizumu no keisei: Tennōsei nashonarizumu no mosaku to airo* [Japan's Desire of Becoming a Superpower and Neonationalism: Nationalism Based on the Emperor System and Its Difficulties]. Tokyo: Sakurai Shoten.

———. 2007a. "Characteristics of Neoliberalism in Japan: Late Start and Different Modality." *Japonesia Review* 3: 8–18.

———. 2007b. "Nihon no sinjiyūshugi" [Japanese Neoliberalism]. In *Sinjiyushugi* [Neoliberalism], authored by David Harvey and translated by Osamu Watanabe et al., 289–329. Tokyo: Sakuhinsha.

Webb, Jen. 2009. *Understanding Representation*. London: SAGE.

Weiner, Michael, ed. 2009. *Japan's Minorities: The Illusion of Homogeneity*, 2nd ed. London and New York: Routledge.

White, Paul. 2003. "The Japanese in Latin America: On the Uses of Diaspora." *International Journal of Population Geography* 9(4): 309–322.

Willis, David Blake, and Stephen Murphy-Shigematsu, eds. 2008. *Transcultural Japan: At the Borderlands of Race, Gender, and Identity*. London and New York: Routledge.

Wilson, Julie, A. 2018. *Neoliberalism*. London and New York: Routledge.

World Bank. 2019. "GNI Per Capita, PPP (Current International $)." http://data.worldbank.org/indicator/NY.GNP.PCAP.PP.CD.

World Economic Forum. 2020. "The Global Gender Gap Report 2020." http://www3.weforum.org/docs/WEF_GGGR_2020.pdf.

Wurgaft, Benjamin Aldes. 2006. "Incensed: Food Smells and Ethnic Tension." *Gastronomica* 6(2): 57–60.

Yamamuro, Shin'ichi. 2000. *Shisō kadai to shite no Ajia* [Asia as a Conceptual Issue]. Tokyo: Iwanami Shoten.

Yamashiro, Jane. H. 2011. "Racialized National Identity Construction in the Ancestral Homeland." *Ethnic and Racial Studies* 34(9): 1502–1521.
Yao, Xinzhong. 2000. *An Introduction to Confucianism.* Cambridge: Cambridge University Press.
Yasuda, Hiroshi. 1992. "Kindai nihon ni okeru minzoku kannen no keisei" [Construction of the Concept of *minzoku* in Modern Japan]. *Shisō to gendai* 31: 61–72.
Yasuda, Minetoshi. 2018. "Shuppankai wo sekken suru kento girubāto genshō" [The Kent Gilbert Phenomenon]. *Newsweek*, October 30, 2018, pp. 19–23.
Yoneyama, Lisa. 2003. *Bōryoku, sensō, ridoresu* [Violence, War, and Redress]. Tokyo: Iwanami Shoten.
Yoon, Keun Cha. 1994. *Minzoku gensō no satetsu* [The Failure of the Illusion of *minzoku*]. Tokyo: Iwanami Shoten.
Yoshimi, Shunya. 2007. *Shinbei to hanbei* [Pro-American and Anti-American]. Tokyo: Iwanami Shoten.
Yoshino, Kosaku. 1992. *Cultural Nationalism in Contemporary Japan: A Sociological Enquiry*. London and New York: Routledge.
Yoshitake, Yu. 2006. "Koizumi Blames China, S. Korea for Stalemate." *International Herald Tribune/The Asahi Shimbun*, January 5.
Yuval-Davis, Nira. 1997. *Gender & Nation*. London: SAGE.
Zapata-Barrero, Ricard. 2016. "Theorising Intercultural Citizenship." In *Multiculturalism and Interculturalism: Debating the Dividing Lines*, edited by Naser Meer, Tariq Modood, and Ricard Zapata-Barrero, 53–76. Edinburgh, UK: Edinburgh University Press.
Zhang, Longxi. 1988. "The Myth of the Other: China in the Eyes of the West." *Critical Inquiry* 15(1): 108–131.

Index

About the Author

Yuko Kawai is professor of Communication in the College of Intercultural Communication at Rikkyo University located in Tokyo. Her research interests lie in nationalism, racism, and multiculturalism in Japan. She is particularly interested in critically examining and transforming the dominant idea of Japaneseness.

www.ingramcontent.com/pod-product-compliance
Lightning Source LLC
Chambersburg PA
CBHW022319280326
41932CB00010B/1160

9781498599023